HEART OF THIS FAMILY

LESSONS IN DOWN SYNDROME AND LOVE

LINDA MORROW

Embrace Diversity!

Linda

HEART OF THIS FAMILY

LESSONS IN DOWN SYNDROME AND LOVE

LINDA MORROW

Sidekick Press

Sidekick Press
Bellingham, Washington
United States of America

Published 2020
Printed in the United States of America
ISBN: 978-1-7344945-0-1
LCCN: 2020934724

Sidekick Press
2950 Newmarket Street
Suite 101-329
Bellingham, WA 98226
www.sidekickpress.com

Linda Morrow 1940-
Heart of This Family: Lessons in Down Syndrome and Love

Cover design by: spokendesigns.com
Illustration by: John Doerper

To Family ~ Always

Roger

Steve, Mike, Josh

And especially Sue

Family Meeting, 2015

Salty rivulets of sweat track down the back of my neck, slither under my bra, and gather in a pool at the base of my spine. This is not a hot flash. At seventy-five I've long ceased dealing with that issue. Nor is my excessive perspiration due to the hot August sun pouring through the west-facing window of the conference room. My frayed nerves are solely responsible for my overheated condition.

At my request, my family has scheduled a session with two facilitators from the local dispute resolution center in Bellingham, Washington. With me are my wife, Sue, two of my three adult sons, Mike and Josh, and Mike's wife, Pamela. We're not embroiled in a fractious argument, but the decision before us feels monumental. I want to use the professional skills of trained mediators to ensure everyone's voices are heard.

The five of us are about to deliberate the future of the one family member not in attendance—my oldest son, Steve, born with Down syndrome almost forty-nine years ago. He is 3,000 miles away in Burlington, Vermont, where he's lived for the past twenty years, supported by the Howard Center, the area's designated provider of services for individuals with developmental disabilities.

For most of those years Sue and I lived less than a two-hour drive from Steve in a rural area of the state. But in 2013 we sold our house and moved to Bellingham where Mike, Pamela, and their daughter, Piper, live. While we've embraced our new surroundings, the decision to make this cross-country relocation was difficult. When we left Vermont, we invited Steve to move with us. Steve, however, chose to stay in his Burlington condo and keep the part-time job he'd held for many years. "I sad you and Sue move far away. But I stay here," he told me.

Now, Steve, like many middle-aged adults with Down syndrome, is beginning to show signs of premature aging. His brothers feel he should move to Bellingham, closer to family. Sue and I are less certain this is the best solution. As we settle into our seats, I glance around the table and take stock of those present.

Sue and I have both retired from long careers in public school education. We married five years earlier but have been a couple for over a quarter century. Though years have lined our faces and turned our hair gray, we are living proof of the philosophy "opposites attract." Sue is caring, calm, and patient. She believes collaboration leads to good decisions. I'm powered by the ever-present adrenaline coursing through me. My mood swings mirror my fast-twitch reactions, which seek quick solutions to every problem.

At our Vermont home the two-cord wood rack that stood on the back porch served as a visual metaphor for how we approach life. Under Sue's watch the rack slowly emptied until down to its last few logs. With me, as soon as two rows burned in our stove, I'd trudge up the path to the wood pile and lug back more wood to top off the rack—heedless of raging storms or below-zero temperatures. Over time we've learned to merge our vastly dissimilar dispositions, aided by shared values including fairness, justice, and integrity, framed within an ardent feminist bent. Together we are a strong and effective team.

Mike is a few months shy of forty-eight. He wears his wavy auburn hair cropped close and tinges of gray show at his temples. With his measured personality, I've long seen him as the rock of our family—responsible in the stereotypical way of a first child, even though chronologically he is my middle son. He and Pamela met when they were students at college and have been married for nineteen years. Pamela's blond hair hints at her Norwegian ancestry. Kind, with a sly sense of humor, her eyes look weary. Birthing a child at thirty-nine and working full time comes with its challenges and a perpetual state of exhaustion.

Josh, my youngest son, has flown from Bozeman, Montana, his off-and-on home since he finished high school in 1988 and headed west to pursue his love of downhill skiing. At forty-five he's lost much of his tightly curled brown hair and his shaved skull glistens in the sunlight. Josh's emotions are always close to the surface and he gives much of himself to others—sometimes too much.

The mediator explains that the meeting will begin with opening statements from each of us. She adds, "Linda, let's hear from you first." My palms are sweaty, and my throat tightens as I look around the table.

"Sue and I share your concerns about Steve's premature aging. Right now, the couple who are Steve's live-in caregivers are doing a fantastic job. However, they'll be leaving in a year. So, I'll need to begin looking for new caregivers very soon."

Stating this reality out loud causes my stomach to tighten. My eyes fill and I struggle for composure. Finding a live-in caregiver has always been stressful for me. Over the years I'd made good choices. Face-to-face interviews allowed me to trust my reliable intuition. But the two caregivers prior to the current couple had been terrible. I'd interviewed them via Skype after our move across the country to Bellingham. I'd missed some critical clues and put my son at risk. The possibility that this might happen a third time fills me with dread now.

One of the mediators prods gently. "What else are you worried about?"

"Everything. Everyone," I say. Beside me, Sue nods. She's seen up close what it's taken to keep Steve safe and happy.

I direct my next comments to my sons and Pamela. "I'm not sure any of you can truly understand how moving Steve to Bellingham will impact all of our lives. Sue and I have been orchestrating Steve's care for a long time. The network we've established in Burlington over twenty years is priceless. Moving Steve to Bellingham will mean re-creating that support system. I'm seventy-five. Sue is seventy-one. I don't know if we have the energy or emotional resources to start over again." Sue reaches for my hand and I continue.

"I don't know what to do," I admit. "Over the years I've always felt so sure of what path to take, how to support not only Steve, but...," I pause and look at Mike and Josh, "both of you, too. But now I'm so uncertain. Besides, we all know Steve doesn't want to move. Burlington is his community. What is his role in this decision? Does he get to have a say?"

This is my family. The people I care about deeply. I want everyone to be happy, but I can feel a weight settling on my shoulders that I haven't felt in years.

PART ONE
CHILDHOOD
1966-1987

ONE

Doctor's Orders, 1966

On a November morning I glanced out the living-room windows of our five-room apartment, located in a Boston suburb, at a gun-metal sky muddied by snow clouds. I settled into a maple rocking chair with my first-born child. Steve, ten weeks old, gazed at me as I brought the bottle of warmed formula to his lips. On the schedule for today was his first well-baby checkup. While Steve began his vigorous and noisy sucking, I sighed and allowed myself to drift into thoughts buried deep in the basement of my soul, a place I didn't visit often.

Yes, I adored the infant snuggled in my arms, but why this haunted feeling of something missing? Hadn't I fulfilled all of society's expectations for women? Here I was, twenty-six, married for three years, and now the mother of a sweet little boy. But the past two months had also been sleep-deprived, lonely, and almost completely devoid of adult conversation and stimulation. Frequently I'd caught myself longing for the person I no longer was—a sixth grade teacher in an inner-city school in Syracuse, New York.

I met Roger Cohen in the fall of 1961, my senior year at Syracuse University, and, while I hadn't fallen madly in love, I liked him. He was smart, liberal-thinking—a graduate student far more mature than the undergraduates I'd dated. He stood just under six feet tall, and wore his tightly curled, dark brown hair in a crew cut. One spring night, as we drove to Cornell University to hear a young singer named Joan Baez, Roger proposed to me. I said yes. With that single word, I took the first step down the prescribed path many women my age were only too happy to follow. Our wedding took place on July 13, 1963, in

Marshfield, Massachusetts, a seashore town thirty miles south of Boston where I'd spent my childhood. After a brief honeymoon we returned to Syracuse to begin our life as husband and wife.

Our friends included several young married couples who'd already begun their families. They lived in the semi-squalor that was married students' housing and pinched every penny. Roger and I wanted to avoid the stress these folks faced and agreed on something different. He had his heart set on earning his doctorate in sociology. I would work and we'd delay having children until Roger completed his studies. Birth control pills were brand new. I was delighted at how easy they made our decision.

I taught at an elementary school located in The Ward, a Black neighborhood packed with sagging three-story wooden tenements. I survived a rocky rookie year, found my groove, and settled in. I loved working with underserved children and gained confidence in my ability to educate and, more importantly, connect to the kids and their families. Since my early teens, I'd harbored a dream of working with at-risk children. My work both challenged and fulfilled me. This job felt important, the right response to JFK's stirring call in his inaugural address: "Ask not what your country can do for you—ask what you can do for your country." I knew I'd discovered my calling.

As Roger closed in on the completion of his PhD dissertation, we followed our plan. I stopped taking my birth control pills and within two months I was pregnant. I congratulated myself on having ticked off another accomplishment on my expected path. Our baby was due in late September. At the end of spring term, I told my principal I wouldn't be returning the following year.

Roger accepted a position as a research sociologist at a community health center on the outskirts of Boston. His new job meant returning to the area where I'd grown up. Roger made the traffic-choked, ten-mile commute to work in our only car, while I kept myself busy unpacking and setting up our apartment. On sunny days I walked a block to a nearby beach. There I ensconced my bulging body in a lounge chair turning the pages of my already well-worn copy of Dr. Spock's book *Baby and Child Care*. Steve arrived on September 27, 1966.

The slam of a car door and the sound of footsteps on the enclosed porch signaled Roger's arrival and brought a sudden halt to my reverie. When leaving for work that morning, Roger said he didn't want me taking the bus alone to the doctor's appointment and would be coming with me. I knew I was capable of safely getting Steve and myself to the doctor's office, but also happy my husband wanted to join us.

I'd been looking forward to this day with increasing anticipation. Steve had changed so much since his birth. He'd gained weight, started sleeping six hours between feedings at night, and recently begun entertaining us with smiles and the occasional hint of a laugh.

Roger entered the living room and mumbled a distracted hello before saying, "Put Steve in something warm, it's pretty cold outside."

I bundled up Steve, headed for the car, and lowered him into the small, soft-sided bassinette which was already resting on the rear bench seat. During the fifteen-minute drive to the pediatrician's office I tried, without success, to engage Roger in conversation. He responded to me with curt replies and seemed fidgety and anxious. *Fine, be that way*, I thought. *But I won't let your moodiness curtail my excitement.* I couldn't wait to show Steve off to the doctor. I just knew he'd be impressed.

We pulled into the parking lot a few minutes early and as I carried Steve inside, sooty clouds released the first snowflakes of the approaching winter. Perky mothers and children of varying ages filled the waiting room. Steve, the only infant present, drew everyone's attention.

"What an adorable baby!"

"Must be a boy, dressed in that Curious George outfit."

"What's his name? How old is he?"

"His name is Steven Jeffery Cohen," I announced proudly. "But we call him Steve."

One mother noticed Roger, the only male in the room. "And you must be the proud daddy! Is he your first?"

My husband nodded and gave a weak smile.

Soon a nurse called Steve's name and we followed her to an examining room. Her crisp demeanor matched her starched whites. She pointed to the exam table. "Take everything off the baby. Doctor should be in shortly," she said before leaving.

When Dr. Tarbox strode in, his authoritative presence filled the room. A stethoscope hung from his neck, and a bristle of pens peeked from the breast pocket of a knee-length lab coat. Black, horn-rimmed glasses sat on an aquiline nose and flecks of gray showed at the edges of the dark brown spikes of his crew-cut. He nodded in our direction and immediately started checking Steve over from head to toe. Roger and I looked on as the doctor listened to Steve's heart, palpated his stomach, rotated his arms and legs, and measured the circumference of his skull. Next the doctor lifted Steve's naked body and placed him on the baby scale. I smiled to myself when the reading showed Steve had gained several pounds from his 6 lb., 7 oz. birth weight. Steve's liquid brown eyes followed this stranger standing over him but otherwise he seemed indifferent. A transparent bubble formed on his pursed lips. Dr. Tarbox didn't seem to notice.

Finally, the doctor grunted and turned to us. "I can still hear the heart murmur I told you about at the hospital. But it's really not a concern at the moment. Get him dressed and meet me in my office. We'll talk there."

I diapered Steve, snapped him back into his onesie and picked him up, but Roger stepped in front of me and took him from my arms. "Let me hold him."

"OK," I shrugged.

Dr. Tarbox sat at his mahogany desk shuffling papers. Paintings in gilded frames hung on paneled walls. Various certificates proclaimed his competence. A worn oriental rug covered the polished wooden floor. He looked up and waved me toward the armchair facing his desk. Roger and Steve sat behind me on a deacon's bench. I settled in and smiled at the doctor, who cleared his throat, peered over his glasses, and looked directly at me.

"I am sorry to have to tell you this. Your baby is a mongoloid idiot."

My head jerked. My stomach dropped. My heart plummeted to my toes. I stared at the doctor. There had to be a mistake. "Huh? What do you mean? How do you know?"

The doctor's voice took on a resigned tone. "He has all the soft signs: the deep crease extending fully across each palm, the slant of his eyes, the flat nose and abnormal configuration of his ears, the way his skull flattens in the back, the poor muscle tone and excessive flexibility..."

I twisted in my chair and shot a frantic look at Roger and the bundle in his arms. Abject sorrow flooded his face and he lowered his eyes.

Dr. Tarbox's voice droned on. "Your husband knows all about this. I explained everything to him when we met two weeks after the baby's arrival. I advised him not to tell you. I felt you still needed time to recover after giving birth."

What?! A runaway train of questions roared through my head. Roger had kept this to himself? How could he not tell me? How could he follow the advice of a stranger?

Puzzle pieces began falling into place. Now I knew why, several weeks earlier, Roger had traveled alone to Syracuse for the defense of his PhD dissertation. I had begged to go with him. I wanted to be there to acknowledge his hard-won accomplishment and show off our new son. Roger refused, stating Steve was too young and he didn't want him exposed to any germs.

Now I knew why Roger had insisted switching channels on our black and white TV last night when I'd turned it on to watch a show I'd read about in the *Boston Globe*—something about the horrible conditions at Bridgewater State Hospital where "mental defectives" of all ages were warehoused. "No, I don't want to watch that," Roger had grumbled, and changed to a mindless game show.

Now I knew why he'd insisted on coming with me to this appointment and why he took Steve from me as we headed for the doctor's office.

Now I knew everything. And nothing.

Dimly I became aware of the doctor's voice. "...I've arranged an appointment at Boston Children's Floating Hospital. Specialists in their birth defects clinic will check the child's heart and draw blood for a chromosomal analysis, to confirm my diagnosis."

His name is Steve, I screamed silently. *Call him by his name.* Then I remembered the words he'd uttered seconds before—horrible, hurtful words. I turned back toward the doctor and fixed my blazing eyes on this supposedly well-educated man. "Wait! Wait! What did you call my son?"

Dr. Tarbox's face flushed crimson. "Well, some people call this affliction Down syndrome," he stammered. "My advice to you is, take him home and do what you can for him. Or you may want to consider institutional placement. But I must tell you, children like this seldom outlive their teens."

My pulse pounded. Beads of sweat formed on my pressed lips. Every fiber of my being longed to escape that room. How could he sit there so calmly and utter these outrageous statements about my baby boy?

I stood up so suddenly I nearly tipped over the chair and turned to face Roger. "We need to leave right now," I said forcefully and headed for the door. *You're being rude* said a voice inside me. *Yeah, and I couldn't care less*, I muttered silently.

Roger scrambled to his feet and followed me, his eyes welling with tears. For a moment I felt sorry for him and the burden he had shouldered alone. As we moved toward the door my arms reached out for our son.

Approaching our car, I climbed into the passenger side of the front seat and wrapped my arms around Steve, holding him protectively to my chest. I couldn't put him in his bassinette, alone in the back seat. "It's OK, buddy," I whispered in his ear. "It's OK, Steve. Everything will be OK. We'll figure this out. You'll be fine."

An oppressive silence permeated every atom of our car's interior. I imagined the doors bulging outward. I was a piece of driftwood, bobbing on a vast sea, not knowing where I was headed, or what unknown shore would claim me.

When Roger pulled into our driveway and shut off the ignition, I flung open the passenger door and, clutching Steve, raced up the porch steps and inside. He'd fallen asleep, his clenched fist resting against his lips. After settling him in his crib in the corner of our bedroom, I plodded into the living room and collapsed onto our couch. Roger, collar unbuttoned and tie askew, sat mute and slumped in the rocking chair facing me. I glanced at my watch; it read 2:15 p.m. Only two hours had passed since we'd left for the appointment. I gazed vacantly around the room. *Everything looks the same,* I whispered to myself. *But everything feels different.*

Angry words exploded from me. "Why didn't you tell me?! I'm your wife! How could you keep this to yourself?! How will I ever trust you again?" Tears poured from my eyes and tracked down my face.

Roger looked up at me and wiped his eyes. "Dr. Tarbox told me not to tell you. He told me you wouldn't be able to handle the news. He said you were too weak, that you needed time to recover after giving birth." His voice shook with emotion. "I was just following his orders."

"Following his orders? Bullshit! He knows nothing about me!" My face flushed. The tendons in my neck pulsed. My vision clouded. My ears pounded. "He met me for the first and only time in the hospital! You've known me for four years!"

The cries of an unhappy baby drifted from our bedroom. We moved as one toward our son whose eyes were squeezed shut, his face crimson from the effort of his summons. Roger got to the crib first and picked Steve up.

"Phew! He needs a fresh diaper!" Roger smiled through his tears.

"OK." I sniffled and grabbed a tissue to wipe the tears from my face. "Are you hungry, Steve? I'll go warm up a bottle while Daddy changes you." Steve's needs superseded our argument.

Roger and I spent the rest of that afternoon in a fog of confusion and despair.

"Have you ever even seen anyone with Down syndrome?" I asked Roger.

"No," he admitted. "Have you?"

"I don't think so."

"That's probably because everyone with Down syndrome is in an institution," muttered Roger.

"That's not going to happen to Steve!" I looked wildly at my husband.

"You're right," Roger responded fiercely. "Steve stays with us. We are his parents and we will raise him."

Whew! I knew we had just arrived at a critical juncture; the worst was over. We moved toward each other and embraced. "Together we can do this," I said, my voice muffled against Roger's shoulder. I didn't exactly forgive him for keeping Steve's diagnosis from me. But we needed each other.

Sleep took a long time coming that night. As I listened to Roger's rhythmic breathing, I allowed myself some time to wallow in self-pity. Why me? Why us? What's next? Maybe I will wake up in the morning and this will all be a dream. Ha, fat chance of that!

Eventually I felt a subtle shift in my thinking. OK. I know nothing about this Down syndrome thing. But I can handle it. I'd always wanted to work with at-risk kids. I'd always felt compassion for the underdog. Sure as hell, Steve now fit that description. Perhaps I had a new mission. Maybe I'd still be a teacher and an educator, just not the kind I'd envisioned. I vowed no one would ever take advantage of Steve or disrespect him.

But I couldn't shut out the most ominous words I'd heard from Dr. Tarbox: "Children like this seldom outlive their teens." Yes, I had much to learn about what Steve's diagnosis meant. But I knew far too much about the pain and grief parents experience when a child dies. Two years earlier my twenty-one-year-old sister, and only sibling, had died of kidney failure due to lupus. I'd watched her passing consume my mother and father and threaten the foundation of their marriage. My mother struggled with continuing depression and my father's tears flowed whenever he spoke Carol's name.

My eyelids began to flutter. Down syndrome didn't scare me. But I didn't want to lose my baby, my precious son. I didn't think I could survive that. I rolled over onto my side, wrapped both of my arms around myself, and sank into a dreamless sleep.

Broken Heart, 1966

When Steve's cries woke me at 4:00 a.m. the following morning, I staggered from bed, plucked him from his crib, and headed for the kitchen to warm his formula. As the saucepan holding his bottle began to steam, I held Steve in the crook of one arm and studied him closely. I gently turned his hand and compared our palms. I saw a distinctive crease, so different from the faint one which faded out halfway across my hand. I ran my fingers across the back of his head, over his nose and ears. I pulled him close and felt his heart beating. Steve looked up at me and a smile transformed his face.

Streetlights bathed the living room in a soft glow as I settled in the rocking chair.

Ker-eek...ker-eek. My feet pumped the rocker slowly back and forth and Steve's soulful eyes stared up at me as I cradled him in my arms. "Uh, uh, uh." Warmth coursed through me. I loved the cute, earnest sounds Steve made as he sucked at the bottle's nipple. You are just a baby. My baby.

While Steve fed, I thought back to the days in the hospital just after his birth, when I'd tried so hard to nurse him. But none of the nurses gave me any encouragement. "He's just a sleepy baby," they'd told me. "He'll do better with a bottle."

For the next two weeks I became a ghost of a person, encased in a large empty bubble, floating aimlessly through our apartment on the first floor of a two-family house. Unable to concentrate, I didn't know what to do with myself. Our small home required little cleaning. Cooking gourmet meals or baking fancy desserts held no interest for me. I didn't sew or knit.

The neighborhood we'd moved into consisted mostly of folks in their fifties with grown children. The Harrisons, who had two elementary-school-aged boys and a baby on the way proved the notable exception. Gail and I had met at the nearby beach. Our protruding bellies acted as magnets drawing us together as we sat in our chairs, feet in the water, enjoying the cooling ocean breezes. Gail's daughter, Amy, arrived just a few weeks before Steve, and I'd looked forward to the mornings we spent pushing our baby carriages, chatting about our newborns and comparing notes. For me, with no other friends or family nearby, those walks were often the only break in an endless stretch of long and lonely days.

But since Steve's diagnosis, being with Gail and her perfect baby had become too painful. Likewise, I'd kept phone calls from my mom and dad brief, claiming Steve needed me to change a diaper or feed him. On weekends when I left Roger with the baby to go grocery shopping, I'd been grateful for the anonymity our new surroundings afforded me. The community I thought I belonged to—young mothers with healthy, typical babies—vanished.

What I really wanted and needed was information on Down syndrome. Unless I educated myself, I wouldn't know how to help my son. I hoped our visit to the birth defects clinic, arranged by Dr. Tarbox, would be the first step in that process.

On the appointed December day, we entered the drab, overheated, and crowded waiting room of the birth defects clinic at Boston Children's Floating Hospital—a room devoid of stimulation: no pictures on the dull grey walls; no books, no toys. Nothing. Evidently children with birth defects weren't expected to play or be read to. *God, this is really grim*, I thought. Parents huddled, faces blank. No one made eye contact or looked up as we entered. Swaddled babies held close to chests made it impossible to see most of their faces. From one bundle came a weak cry—an almost mewling kitten-like sound. In a corner a child, three or four years old, sprawled on her mother's lap, unable to sit unassisted. Her tongue spilled from her mouth and she stared straight ahead through vacant eyes. A sense of confusion, despair, and even shame hung in the air like an ominous and stifling cloud. Sudden fear, mingled with shock, rose in my chest.

But just then Steve looked at me and grinned. I returned the smile and bent down to nuzzle the soft folds of his neck. "You're going to be fine, buddy. Back home you've got plenty of toys and books." I reached into the blue-print quilted diaper bag hanging from Roger's shoulder and pulled out a set of plastic keys. "Look, Steve," I whispered. "Your noisy keys!" His face came alive.

A gray-haired RN called Steve's name. "Good morning," she said and smiled. "I've been told to start you out in the blood lab."

A young technician nodded as we entered and instructed me to sit in a chair along with Steve. Roger stood to one side trying to stay out of the way. The tech unsnapped Steve's blue cotton onesie and extracted his left leg.

"I'm going to be drawing some blood for a chromosomal analysis, called a karyotype. We will be looking for any abnormalities, especially in the twenty-first pair, where I expect there will be an additional chromosome. That's known as trisomy-21 and is found in over ninety-five percent of babies with Down syndrome."

"OK," I said. The medical jargon overwhelmed me. I felt idiotic and ill-prepared for all the unfamiliar words he bandied about and applied to my child without explanation. "Is there anything you have on hand you could give me to read? I'm having trouble finding any information on Down syndrome."

The tech shook his head as he readied a needle. "Sorry, I don't have anything."

He swabbed Steve's heel with alcohol and jabbed a needle into a thin blue vein. Steve howled in protest. I held my baby closer, protectively. "Easy, little guy, this won't take long." With practiced expertise, the tech attached a tube to the needle, and watched it fill with blood. Then he removed the needle, placed a gauze pad over the puncture site, and asked me to apply pressure. I did, silently apologizing to Steve for the indignity we were putting him through.

The tech straightened up and gently cupped his hand on Steve's head. "This little guy's a real cutie," he commented. I appreciated both his tender gesture and his words. "OK, I'm finished here. Your next stop will be with a pediatric cardiologist. I'll take you there." We followed him down another hallway.

"Mr. and Mrs. Cohen?" inquired the man who was waiting for us in the small examining room. We nodded and he continued. "I am Dr. Reedy. I've been reviewing your son's records. I'd like a few minutes to examine your baby and then we'll talk."

Steve's face was still flushed from his experience in the lab, but as I placed him on the table and began to remove his onesie, I put my mouth close to his ear and began to croon "A Bushel and a Peck" by Frank Loesser. I'd grown up in the fifties listening to Doris Day sing this song, and now the tune had become our song—Steve's and mine. We locked eyes and Steve relaxed.

Dr. Reedy's salt-and-pepper hair and lined face exuded confidence and knowledge. For the next several minutes the only sound heard was an occasional "hmmm" as he intently moved his stethoscope up and down Steve's naked torso. I held my breath, glancing occasionally at Roger, whose stoic face was hard to read. Were his legs weak-kneed like mine? Eventually the doctor straightened, picked up Steve, who had started to fuss again, and turned toward us. His face softened. Holding Steve in the crook of his right arm and bouncing him gently, Dr. Reedy asked, "What's this little guy's name?"

"Steve!" we responded in unison.

"OK, Mom and Dad, I want to talk with you about Steve's heart. Dr. Tarbox told you he'd heard a murmur, right?"

We nodded. Steve, his face crimson, began to squall industriously. I searched in the diaper bag for a bottle while Roger took our son from the doctor. He held him as Steve began inhaling the contents of his bottle.

"So," the doctor began, "more than fifty percent of babies born with Down syndrome also present with a heart defect and it appears that your son is one of those. I can't be completely certain until we run several tests, but I'm pretty sure Steve has what's called Eisenmenger's syndrome. Have you noticed that Steve's skin looks kind of bluish from time to time?"

I nodded. My eyes filled with tears. This was all over my head and I couldn't connect any of these words to my own child.

"So how serious is this?" asked Roger. It was a good question. I wanted to know too, but I also wanted to shield myself from the answer I somehow intuited the doctor was about to give us.

"AVSD is a pretty significant defect. It is caused by an opening between the upper and lower chambers of the heart and the valve between them, and results in pulmonary hypertension."

My shoulders tightened with fear.

"But right now, Steve is doing pretty well. Someday I suspect we will be able to use surgical intervention to correct defects like this, but we're not there yet." Dr. Reedy assured us that he'd follow Steve closely, order an EKG, and, based on the results, perhaps start Steve on some medication. I asked if the clinic had any information on Down syndrome and he shook his head. "No, at least none I'm aware of."

By now Steve had drained his bottle and fallen asleep. Roger handed him back to me and for the first time ever I focused on the rise and fall of his chest. I hadn't been that concerned when Dr. Tarbox told me he'd heard a murmur. My mother had told me I'd had one as a baby, but the opening had closed on its own. No big deal, I'd assured myself. But now the additional information provided by Dr. Reedy terrified me. An opening between the chambers of his heart? Like a hole? I felt certain I could deal with Steve's Down syndrome. But this heart thing? How long could he live with this condition?

The weight of this information crushed my shoulders like an oversized barbell. And I knew I would feel the burden of this foreboding news every day of Steve's life. Would I ever be able to envision my son becoming an adult?

THREE

The Christmas Story, 1966

After Steve's cardiac assessment, one more hurdle loomed on the horizon—a long-planned Christmas visit in Montreal, Canada, with my parents. As our Convair 880 departed Boston's Logan Airport and gained altitude, a stewardess came by encased in yellow: yellow gabardine short-waisted jacket and straight skirt falling just below the knees, yellow silk scarf tied just so at her neck, and a yellow pillbox hat perched on her lacquered beehive hairdo. "Welcome aboard Northeast's Yellowbird service from Boston to Montreal," she chirped. "I saw you boarding, and I thought you might like this for a souvenir." She handed me an enameled pin in the shape of yellow airplane wings. "Your baby is so adorable! Are you going to be meeting someone special in Montreal?"

She doesn't know, I reassured myself, then forced a smile and answered, "Yes, my parents. They are looking forward to their grandson's first Christmas."

Since Steve's diagnosis, my world had shifted. I now identified myself as the mother of a baby with Down syndrome. Who could tell? Who couldn't? Although my parents had met Steve soon after his birth, I was certain they'd suspected nothing. Roger and I had decided to keep Steve's diagnosis to ourselves until we could tell them in person. I dreaded our arrival in Montreal and the news we were bringing with us.

Dad met us at Dorval Airport. "How is my grandson?" he exclaimed as he eagerly reached for Steve and tickled his tummy. Then he handed Steve back to me and shook hands with Roger.

"Welcome to Montreal! Steve looks great! Nice work!"

Only I understood how much effort Roger put into his hearty reply. "Thanks, Bill, glad to be here!"

On the drive to my folks' house, towering snowbanks lined the brightly lit streets and the illuminated cross crowning the top of Mount Royal Park welcomed us to a winter wonderland. *If only,* I agonized...*if only we weren't about to break my parents' hearts, this would be the perfect Christmas.*

The aroma of my mom's famous french onion soup mingled with the piney scent of fresh cut boughs as we stepped into the foyer where she stood. She enveloped all three of us in her arms. "Joyeux Noël, Feliz Navidad, Merry Christmas!" she said with a laugh.

"Hi, Pete," responded Roger, using the nickname Mom had assigned herself soon after leaving her Cuban homeland for the States in the early thirties. No one in the US had seemed capable of pronouncing her given name, Petra, correctly. Tired of being called PEE-tra she'd simply told folks to call her Pete. Once inside, Roger changed a cranky Steve and prepared a bottle of formula while I wandered alone through the main floor of the townhouse.

In the dining room I gazed at the pinecone wreath set off by gilded walnuts which hung above the cherrywood credenza. As children, my sister, Carol, and I had collected the pinecones and I rubbed my thumbs over my fingertips as I recalled how torn and rough my hands had been once we'd finished wrestling those hard brown fruits onto the metal frame, securing each one with florist's wire. The carved nativity scene Mom had brought from Cuba occupied its usual place in the center of the formal dining table. I reached over, picked up the baby Jesus and held him against my cheek for a moment before returning him to the crib. Moving on I looked up and smiled at the sprig of mistletoe I knew I'd find tacked on the frame of the french doors leading into the living room.

I walked over to the marble-tiled fireplace and let the warmth from the blazing maple logs wrap around me. On the mantel sat the skating scene which Mom meticulously created each Christmas. A small oblong mirror surrounded by cotton batting served as the frozen pond. Tiny houses and evergreen trees—most likely from a model railroad store— spread out in either direction from the pond and exquisite china figure skaters dotted the "ice." I wondered how old these figurines were and where Mom had found them. And I remembered my tenth Christmas when my mother first trusted me with the task of removing the tissue paper wrapping from each individual piece and placing the figures, just so, on the pond. Five stockings hung below the skaters. With a start I realized all were new. Gone were the old, faded, handmade flannel ones, with the names "Bill," "Pete," "Linda," and "Carol." Instead my mother had crafted new needlepoint stockings, each with a different, intricate scene and personalized across the solid red top with "Grandpa," "Grandma," "Linda," "Roger," and "Steve." Mixed emotions coursed through me. One loss, one addition, everything different.

A shimmering tree, whose tip grazed the nine-foot ceiling, stood in one corner. Each individual strip of tinsel hung just so. I smiled pensively. Mom never allowed clumps to be strewn haphazardly on the branches. As children this was the only part of decorating the tree Carol and I tried to avoid…it was just too tedious! Packages of every shape and size, heaped on the plush off-white carpeting, hid the tree's trunk and touched its lowest branches. To one side, on a small mahogany table, my eyes settled on a plate piled with carrots and homemade cookies, along with the traditional note to Santa in my dad's handwriting. A tear tracked down my face and I quickly wiped it away as I heard my mother call, "Linda, come see your father, he's taken over feeding Steve and the baby is about to fall asleep!" I headed back to the kitchen.

I carried a groggy Steve upstairs, laid him in the bassinette my folks had set up in one of the bedrooms, and then joined the adults in the living room. Dad delivered Manhattans to everyone, and we settled in around the coffee table where my mother had set out appetizers—cheese and crackers and her current favorite, herring in sour cream and onions. I fortified myself with a gulp of my drink before setting my glass down. Roger and I locked eyes and he nodded his head imperceptibly. We couldn't wait any longer.

"Mom, Dad." I struggled to keep my composure. "Roger and I have some news to share with you. It's about Steve. He's been diagnosed with Down syndrome."

"Down syndrome? What's that?" asked my dad. "I've never heard of it. When did you find this out?"

But my mother knew about Down syndrome. I could tell. As a brief cloud passed over her face, she looked straight at me. "Tell us what you know, Linda."

Together Roger and I began our well-rehearsed explanation. I started out by saying we'd known about Steve's diagnosis for just a few weeks, but wanted to tell them in person, rather than over the phone. We explained Steve's diagnosis meant he would be mentally retarded and slow to reach key developmental milestones such as sitting, crawling, walking, and talking. We clarified that his heart defect, which we had told them about when they first met him in October, was common for babies born with Down's.

There were things we'd decided not to reveal at this point. We chose not to discuss karyotypes and chromosome abnormalities and simply stated that Down syndrome was a chance occurrence and unlikely to happen again in subsequent births. We didn't share the grim prognosis about Steve's lifespan—that many children born with Down's died before their twentieth birthday due to complications from cardiac problems or infections. We said it was OK to ask questions and that we would try our best to answer them.

"But, before you ask any questions, there is one more important thing for you to know," I said. "Roger and I are in complete agreement on this. Steve will *not* be placed in an institution. We are his parents and we intend to raise him at home, like any other kid. We love our little guy and we are determined to do right by him."

No one spoke. No one moved. Then my mother pushed back her chair, stood, and opened her arms. The rest of us rose and merged into a tearful group hug.

Over the next week my parents' actions reflected their distinctly different personalities. My mother was a whirling dervish of movement and determination. Whenever Steve was awake, she was there, bent over close to his face, talking to him. She seemed to understand intuitively how important it was to offer Steve as much stimulation as possible. She jabbered to him in both Spanish and English, her voice loud, almost strident. Steve responded with smiles and grunts, his eyes fixed on hers, his arms and legs pumping vigorously. Steve and Pete even engaged in a bubble blowing contest with each other. This became their favorite activity, one they repeated several times a day. Each time Steve copied his grandmother she was convinced he was the smartest baby she'd ever seen. Mom exuded confidence. There seemed to be no doubt in her mind Roger and I would be up to this challenge. Like a mother bear with her cubs, Pete made it clear that no one would ever make a disparaging comment about her grandson or lower their expectations for him...not on her watch!

Dad's response was more muted. A loving, sentimental individual, he couldn't get enough of Steve. He wanted to hold him, feed him, and change his diapers. I often found him standing by the bassinette just looking at Steve as he slept peacefully. Initially he had lots of questions. How serious was the heart defect? Would Steve go to school? What kind of a job would he be able to have? Would he get married, have children? Over time the questions stopped, and Dad seemed content just to enjoy Steve's presence, his smile, and the eager way he attacked his bottle.

One day when the two of us were out trudging through the snow-clogged sidewalks, Dad brought up the scholarship he and Mom had established in my sister's name after her death. Carol was a special education major at Lesley College in Cambridge, Massachusetts, when she became ill.

"Maybe someday a student at Lesley who receives Carol's scholarship will be Steve's teacher." His voice trembled and his eyes filled.

I slipped my arm through his as we continued our walk. "That would be really special, Dad. I've been thinking the same thing. Somehow I believe there is a connection between Carol's death and Steve's birth."

"What do you mean?" he asked.

"It's hard to explain," I responded. "But I don't think Steve just 'happened.' Special Education is such a new field. I mean, I'm a teacher and I really don't know much about it. I've never had any students like Steve in my classes. But Carol fell in love with the kids at the camp for the mentally retarded where she worked summers. And that's why she was so interested in becoming a special education teacher. She believed all children could learn. Somehow, I'm certain she knows about Steve and will be guiding me. Ever since I learned Steve had Down's, I've thought about Carol a lot and felt her presence."

Then I had to stop, the raw pain on Dad's face as I spoke about Carol was too much for me to bear. We hugged and then continued our walk in silence. Memories of Carol surrounded us. Tears froze on our faces.

Roger, Steve, and I flew back to Boston on Friday, December 30. Dad drove us to the airport while Mom sat next to him cradling Steve in her arms. A fresh coating of snow sparkled under a bright sun that only gave the appearance of warmth. Outside the cozy confines of the car the temperature struggled to climb above zero. Dad dropped us off at the Northeast sign and headed for the parking garage. We'd checked our bags by the time he joined us at the gate. Only when our flight began to board did Mom relinquish Steve. As the three of us walked out of the terminal, I turned to give one last wave. Pete and Bill were standing shoulder to shoulder holding hands and smiling broadly. What happened when they could no longer see us? Did they turn to each other and begin to cry? Did they admit how worried they were? How would they share Steve's diagnosis with their friends, many of whom were grandparents several times over? Where would they find support and understanding?

The plane hurtled down the runway and I settled into my seat. My arms wrapped around Steve, who, lulled by the plane's engine, had fallen asleep. A blanket of relief tucked itself around me. In words and actions Mom and Dad had demonstrated their unconditional love for their new grandson. I knew they had my back and I felt grateful for their support.

Soul Mates, 1967-68

When Steve was a baby, the lack of readily available information about Down syndrome often left me feeling isolated. Back then, I had one confidant. My childhood friend was both my solace and my soul mate. Her support and confidence in my ability to be a good mother for Steve helped me get through his early years.

I can't remember a time when I didn't know Jane Stephens. Our mothers met while pushing their baby carriages containing their first children, both girls, born just two months apart. Jane and I became inseparable. We played in each other's backyards, attended the same Sunday school, celebrated birthdays together, and as five-year-olds, nervously held tight to our mothers' hands as we entered kindergarten on a September morning in 1945.

We graduated in 1958 from the local high school in Marshfield, Massachusetts, and from our respective colleges four years later. Jane married her high school sweetheart, Kevin Murphy, the youngest of twelve in an Irish-Catholic family, and they moved into a newly purchased house in their hometown. Their first child, a girl, Jamie, was born a couple of months before their first wedding anniversary. Over the next two years another girl, Heather, and then a boy, Sean, followed. Jane declared the family complete.

Roger met Jane and Kevin soon after we moved to the Boston area and the guys quickly became good friends. Kevin easily matched Roger intellectually and brought out his playful side, which too often remained hidden. I was grateful to have my childhood friend in my adult life, but I had no idea how much I would need her once I became a mother myself.

When we'd returned from Montreal after telling my folks Steve had Down syndrome, Jane was the next person with whom I shared my news. She didn't say she was sorry. She just wrapped me in a hug and told me I'd be a great mother. Just what I needed to hear, affirmation from my dearest friend.

Two months later, once Steve and I had settled into a routine, I told Roger I wanted to have another child right away. "Steve will progress more rapidly with a sibling," I told him. Yes, I wanted to give Steve the best possible support, but unspoken was my determination to show myself I was capable of having a typical kid. Jane was the only person with whom I shared this secret.

"I feel like I fell off the proverbial horse and if I don't get back on right away, I'm afraid I never will."

She understood. Totally.

By late spring I was pregnant, and Roger and I began looking at houses. We found the "perfect" one in Marshfield. I was overjoyed to be going home, back to familiar streets and landmarks, back to the beaches I loved. But most of all, relief washed over me knowing that, as I progressed though this second pregnancy, Jane would be close by.

We moved into our modest little home in July and the summer of '67 sailed by—mostly with fresh winds and calm seas. Sunny afternoons were spent with Jane and her kids at Marshfield's town beach. Lugging towels, extra clothing, sand toys, food, and drink, we navigated the sandy path from the parking lot over the dunes to the beach on the other side. As I advanced through the second trimester of my pregnancy, this trip grew harder, but the tramp was worth the effort. The impending birth tightened the connection between us.

With our move to Marshfield four-year-old Heather and one-year-old Steve became devoted to each other, and Heather began most days with a plea to her mother to take her to visit Steve. Jane didn't mind having one less kid to tote around while she ran errands and I enjoyed the company of an "older" person.

One morning Heather burst through our porch door. Her blue eyes scanned the room. "Where's Steve?"

"He hasn't woken up from his morning nap."

Heather's freckled cheeks wrinkled in a frown and her mouth turned down.

"Let's read a couple of books while we wait," I suggested and pointed in the direction of the wooden bookcase I'd set up against one wall. Given our commitment as parents to read to Steve several times a day, we'd accumulated a collection that rivaled the town's small public library. Children's picture books, placed every which way, filled the shelves and spilled onto the floor.

"Why don't you pick a book and snuggle up on the couch with me. I bet when we finish our story time Steve will be up."

Heather perused the bookcase and returned with her choice.

I read the title aloud. "*May I Bring A Friend?*"

Heather's blue eyes widened. "Steve is *my* friend."

I pulled her in close and swiped at my brimming eyes. "I know he is."

Once the story concluded, Heather could be dissuaded no longer. "Can I go watch Steve sleep? I'll go tippy toe and be very, very quiet. I promise."

I nodded and released her from the couch. She scurried toward Steve's room.

Several minutes passed without a sound, so I decided to investigate. Heather stood next to Steve's crib, her strawberry blond hair a mass of unruly ringlets. One freckled hand reached through the crib's slats and I noticed Steve's chubby fingers wrapped around her littlest one. His eyes gazed at Heather. I stood listening as Heather sang "Old MacDonald Had a Farm" in a slightly off-key, whispery voice. Years later Heather admitted she'd woken Steve up.

Jane and her family were my cheerleaders. I needed their support more than ever when Steve turned one. On the day of our son's birthday, Roger was away on business, but I invited Jane and her kids to Steve's party. The previous night I'd been leafing through my Dr. Spock book, a combined exercise in solace and torment. Dr. Spock wrote in soothing tones, reassuring new parents, essentially mothers: "You know more than you think you do." Often, I felt as though he were sitting in the room with me, holding my hand and telling me I was doing a good job. But whenever I turned to the section on developmental milestones, the torture began.

Reading my 1957 edition, with a cherubic baby boy looking out from the pink cover, only served to remind me of all the things my one-year-old still couldn't do. Steve couldn't sit unsupported, pull himself into a standing position, creep, or crawl. And certainly, he wasn't remotely close to walking.

After presents and cake at Steve's party we headed outside for our daily dose of fresh air. Jane helped me move one of the benches back from the wooden picnic table before she settled effortlessly onto the one opposite me. I envied her trim figure, deeply tanned from summer days on the beach. My due date was still two months away. I lowered my ponderous self and sat with my elbows on the table supporting my chin. My eyes stared off into the distance.

"You seem a little sad, Linda," observed my friend. "It's Steve's birthday! What's wrong?"

I told her what I'd been reading and how Spock's words had depressed me.

Jane reached across the table and placed her hand on my arm. "Linda. Put away that silly book! Steve will walk when he's ready!" She glanced over at the nearby apple tree where Heather gently pushed Steve back and forth on a new baby swing Roger had hung just before he left. "Look at him! He's healthy. He's happy. His antics are hilarious. Heather loves him. She talks about Steve constantly."

"You're right about Heather and Steve," I said. "They are true soul mates."

She nodded, took in my belly, and grinned. "And once that baby shows up you won't believe how busy and tired you'll be."

Of course, Jane was right. Michael Andrew Cohen arrived on November 29, 1967. And for many months, I didn't have time to think about when Steve would walk.

When he turned two the following September, Steve still wasn't walking—a monumental disappointment. He was so close! Both brothers were constantly on the move, preferring standing to any other position. Steve watched Michael intently. Sometimes one or both would let go of whatever piece of furniture they were holding and stand wobbling before their legs gave way and they collapsed onto the floor. No matter how often I held out my arms, encouraging them to take a step, just one step toward me, walking didn't happen. Michael was only ten months old, but Steve was two! I was desperate for him to hit this milestone, terrified that it might never happen. How much longer would I have to wait? Not long, as it turned out.

Two days after Steve's birthday, the brothers stood together, hands pressed flat against the Plexiglas panel set low in the frame of the screen door that opened onto the porch. I called this "guarding the castle." I glanced down at my watch…time for *Captain Kangaroo*. I flicked on the TV. Lured by the theme song, Michael pivoted, one hand still on the door and took a step, then another, and another…heading in the direction of the TV. My eyes widened in amazement. I put both hands up to my mouth and stifled a scream. Steve watched his brother. Then he followed him—staggering and swaying, but upright…one, two, three, four.... He reached for his brother's shoulder, grabbed on, and down they both went. I could barely believe what I'd just witnessed. I clapped and laughed and cried all at once. After all, how many mothers get to watch two of their children morph into toddlers simultaneously?

I called Jane.

The boys were walking, I told her—both of them, on the same day! I started crying again. "This will change everything with our kids." In my mind I was already thinking about next summer and our five children romping together on the beach.

Genetic Counseling 101, 1969

One spring day Roger arrived home with a proposal. A Boston medical school was convening a panel on birth defects for third- and fourth-year medical students. This presentation was intended to serve as the students' only instruction in genetic counseling. As parents of a child with Down syndrome we'd been asked to participate. Was I interested?

"What would our role be?"

"Just talk about Steve, I guess," replied Roger. "You know, what it's like to have him for a son."

I didn't hesitate. I'd never really had an opportunity to talk about our son and share our parenting experiences with members of the medical profession. I thought back to the day Dr. Tarbox had delivered his clumsy diagnosis. Perhaps we could save other parents from a similar experience.

Roger and I entered an auditorium packed with over 150 white-jacketed students. As I walked down the aisle, I noted the homogeneity of those in attendance—overwhelmingly male, overwhelmingly Caucasian. Hair styles provided the greatest diversity. While most sported short, well-groomed cuts, some rebels stood out: Beatles-style mop-tops, Elvis pompadours, and a few Afros. The accredited physicians sat in the front rows—silver haired, crow's-feet at the corners of their eyes, wise, all-knowing visages. Roger and I found our reserved seats, and I felt the stare of the man next to me. I nervously fingered the buttons of my cardigan sweater. Did he question my presence among this sea of males? A distinguished gentleman strode to the microphone on stage and explained the presentation would begin with a slide show on birth defects followed by the panel discussion. A large movie screen descended from the ceiling, and the title image from the slide projector, located several rows behind us, appeared: *Birth Defects—An Unfortunate Reality.*

The first slides projected close-up face shots of babies. Many of the heads were enlarged or too small with obvious facial deformities: empty sockets where eyes should have been, protruding foreheads, nostrils without a nose, cleft palates, or a tongue overflowing a mouth. Full body shots showed missing or fused limbs, dark masses that appeared to be misplaced internal organs. One shot was of a baby about a year old with the classic signs of Down syndrome. Her eyes looked dully out at the audience, her tongue protruded out of her mouth, and her legs lay limp and frog-like on the mattress.

Then the shots switched to those of teens or adults, horrible photos of glazed eyes, drooling mouths, naked bodies. In some photos the individuals wore diapers, or a filthy shirt covered with what I imagined was either vomit or feces or both.

Finally, I'd had enough. I couldn't stay there for one more second. This was *not* Steve! I got up, tore up the aisle of the darkened auditorium, pushed open a door, and stepped into the hallway. Roger followed behind me.

For a moment we just stared at each other in the brightly lit hallway, too stunned to speak. Roger broke the silence. "We don't have to stay. We can leave."

"Those photos don't tell the whole story." My voice shook with anger. Visions of our happy, funny, little guy swam in my head. "No!" I squared my shoulders. "No, we can't just walk away. We have to go back in—for Steve's sake." I couldn't let my anger activate my flight response. I needed to advocate for my son, to fight for him and others like him. If I didn't, who would?

"Let's go," said Roger. He reached for my hand and together we returned, strengthen by our resolve to do right by our son.

We took our seats at a long table lined with name cards and titles: Director of the Tufts University Birth Defects Clinic, Pediatrician, Minister, and Director of the Fernald State School (originally called the Massachusetts School for the Feeble-Minded.) Our card read: "Dr. and Mrs. Roger D. Cohen—Parents." I was the only female on the panel.

The moderator introduced each of the panelists and asked who'd like to begin. I simultaneously raised my hand and nudged Roger with my elbow. The moderator nodded at Roger, only Roger. He stood and walked to the microphone. After introducing himself, along with his credentials as a PhD in Sociology, Roger turned the microphone over to me. I hadn't planned a speech. I just spoke from my heart.

I told the audience the photos they'd seen in no way defined our son and I painted a picture for them—a picture I hoped would force these future doctors to question any preconceived notions they may have had regarding their qualifications to advise parents of babies born with birth defects.

I told them that at two and a half Steve was a happy, social little boy with a great sense of humor. I admitted before his birth, I had never seen a person with Down's. Not surprising, I added, since many parents of babies like Steve were told by medical personnel to place their child in an institution, leave them there, and move on with their lives. I looked directly at the physicians seated in the front rows before continuing. Several squirmed uncomfortably. Then I turned my attention to the medical students.

"How many of you have seen or know someone with Down syndrome?" Only a few hands went up. "How many of you have children—babies or toddlers—of your own?" More hands rose.

"I would argue Steve is more like your children than he is different. He laughs when he is happy, cries when he isn't. Every day he learns new skills, though he does need to work harder than his same-age peers to perfect those skills. He understands most of what we say, although he usually ignores us when we tell him 'no!'"

Laughter rippled through the auditorium. I knew I'd made a connection. My chest swelled and my confidence soared. I had something to say to this audience.

"Steve loves most foods, other than vegetables. We read to him several times a day, and he is very clear about which books are his favorites."

I continued by covering the major developmental milestones. "Steve sat on his own at eighteen months, supporting his trunk with his arms. At twenty-three months he cruised from one piece of furniture to another with amazing speed. He took his first steps just two days after his second birthday and now he and his younger brother race around our home with abandon. They are a real wrecking crew." More laughter.

I turned and shot a glance at Roger who nodded and grinned. My shoulders straightened and my voice strengthened. "Don't make the assumption, based on what you've seen here, that the best advice you can give parents of children born with birth defects is institutionalization. Because if you do, the world will be robbed of individuals like

Steve. Do I wish Steve didn't have Down syndrome? Sometimes, but not often. Each of us is born with strengths and challenges. No one is perfect. Educate yourselves about Down syndrome and other birth defects. Think, before you pronounce what these children *won't* be able to do. Don't *ever* take away our hope. Our son is a real person. He is loved and is easy to love. My only regret is I don't have a picture of him with me today to show you. But once today's presentations are over, my husband and I will be happy to meet with you and answer any questions you may have."

An awkward silence filled the room. Then the students erupted in applause. The response from the front rows was more tempered. No one else on the panel spoke for very long, and once the discussion concluded and the lights came on, Roger and I were surrounded by a large group of students. We stayed there for over an hour answering questions.

If a genetic counseling event was held the following year, we were not invited to be part of the panel discussion. In later years I speculated whether any of those students present in the audience in 1969 ever had the opportunity to counsel parents or perspective parents of a child with Down syndrome. If so, I wonder what was said.

I never forgave Dr. Tarbox for the way he withheld Steve's diagnosis from me, but years later I was able to see his inappropriate decision as a gift. For the first two and a half months of Steve's life he was just a baby. A baby who did all the things other babies did. A baby who'd already shown me he could learn, could smile, could recognize his mom and dad. This knowledge and accompanying love provided me with all the strength I needed to move forward.

School Days, 1970-71

Summer arrived and, between us, Jane and I now had six children to supervise on the beach. My third son, Josh, born in late February 1970, dug his toes in the sand while he sat contentedly in his bouncy seat enthralled by the crashing waves and wheeling seagulls. I watched as Michael, Jamie, and Sean ran with abandon through the ankle numbing ocean water. Heather seemed to understand Steve's need to explore his world at a slower, more deliberate pace. She spoke quietly to Steve as together they dug in the sand and unearthed whatever treasures lay hidden below.

Touched by her tenderness toward him, I said to Jane, "Just look at them. He learns so much from her. But come September Heather will start first grade. I wish there were some way Steve could spend more time with other kids, kids his own age."

"What about nursery school?" replied Jane. "There are plenty in town. Why don't you enroll him?"

"Nursery school? Really? Do you think one would take someone like Steve?"

Jane pushed her sunglasses up on her forehead and glared at me. "Come on, Linda! You're a strong woman. You know how to make things happen for Steve."

Yeah, I do, I thought, remembering my genetic counseling lesson. "OK, do you have any suggestions?"

Jane advised me to check out a nursery school near our home, one she'd heard had an outstanding program.

The Steeple School, located on the grounds of Trinity Church, had been in operation since 1963. A phone call confirmed there was still space in the pre-nursery class, and I set up a date to meet the teacher.

Butterflies danced in my stomach as I mounted the steps on a late August morning. Barbara Keith greeted me and led me inside to a spacious classroom filled with natural light. I listened as Mrs. Keith, a fortyish woman with a warm smile and a pixie strawberry blond hair-cut, gave me an overview of the two-day-a-week program for three-year-olds. She spoke with the unbridled enthusiasm of a woman who loved little ones and the opportunity to work with them.

"We see each child as an individual, following their own unique developmental path. At this age there is no 'right' time to learn some-thing, so much depends on the child's interest." I nodded in agreement as I remembered my angst over when Steve would start walking.

"So, what does a typical morning look like at Steeple School?" I asked. I wanted school to be fun for Steve. I didn't want him in over his head.

"Children your son's age learn through play. Most of our time is unstructured. We simply make a variety of activities available: art and music exploration, blocks, dress-up. Our outside time is geared toward large muscle development."

All stuff Steve already did at home with Mike.

Mrs. Keith continued. "As the year progresses, we do build in some structure. We want our children to learn to attend, to develop a span of attention appropriate to their age." I nodded in agreement. "Of course, not all children learn the same skills at the same time," she said. "We expect and value diversity." She paused and looked at me. "So, tell me about your son. His name is Steve, right?"

OK, I thought. *Here goes nothing.* I took a deep breath, nodded, gulped, and began. "Steve is my first born. He will turn three on Sep-tember 27. His brother Michael is fourteen months younger." I raced on. I needed to get Steve's diagnosis out, before I lost my nerve. "But the thing about Steve is…ah…he has Down syndrome."

For a moment whips of silence swirled around the room, broken only by the sound of birds chirping madly outside through the open windows.

"Oh," replied Mrs. Keith. "I've never met anyone with Down syn-drome before and I really don't know much about children such as your son." She hesitated, then leaned in and smiled. "Why don't you tell me about Steve? What's his personality like? What does he enjoy doing? What do you see as his strengths, his challenges? What are your hopes and dreams for him?"

I struggled to hold back the tears which filled my eyes. Folks seldom asked about Steve as just a kid. Usually comments included a qualifier or sympathy. Barbara Keith's response relaxed me, and words tumbled out of my mouth like a rogue wave breaking offshore.

I told her Steve was amazing. He was determined, resilient, and never gave up on himself. "He is a happy kid, with a great sense of humor. He is kind to his brother…well, most of the time," I said with a grin. I paused to take a breath. "He does have delays, especially in language development. He doesn't have a lot of words right now, but he understands everything we say and can follow directions— especially when he knows his mom or dad means business."

"Can you see him as part of a class here this fall?"

"Oh yes! I absolutely can! Steve would love it and I think for the most part he would fit right in. I really do." Did I sound like I was begging? Please lady, just give him a chance.

Mrs. Keith had one more question. "How does Steve feel when you leave him with others? Does he show any anxiety or cry if he knows you aren't going to be with him?"

I laughed. "Steve doesn't care if I am with him or not. He has always been like that. He will go with anyone."

Mrs. Keith leaned back. "I think Steve sounds pretty typical of many of our children when they start out with us in pre-nursery. I'd love to have him join our class."

I floated down the steps as I left. I knew I had just met a very special woman. An angel, in fact.

Long before the terms "accommodation" and "inclusion" became part of special education parlance, Barbara Keith knew how to make things work for Steve. When he and his classmates were introduced to finger paints, he wanted nothing to do with the cool, squishy substance. This was the first sign of his tactile sensitivity, a common trait for children born with Down's. On the day when the class lined up to make handprints for Mother's Day, Steve adamantly refused to put his hand in the pool of white finger paint. Mrs. Keith wondered if he would be willing to make a footprint instead and helped him remove his shoes and socks. Without hesitation, Steve stepped in the white puddle and stomped his bare foot on the paper with a vengeance. Later Mrs. Keith told me once Steve finished, several of his classmates begged to make their footprints.

The following September, Mike joined Steve at Steeple School. On the morning classes began, Steve, almost four, tore across the parking lot, grabbed hold of the railing and two-stepped up the stairs to where Mrs. Keith stood.

"Keiff! Keiff!" he screamed as he wrapped his arms around her knees. The tail of his cotton short-sleeved shirt pulled loose from the elastic waistband of his pants.

His teacher swept our son into her arms. "Stevie! Look at you! You've grown!" Then she lowered him to the ground and added, "We're in the same the classroom as last year. Do you remember the way?"

Steve disappeared through the entrance doors without so much as a backward glance.

I felt a tug on my arm, shifted six-month-old Josh, onto my hip and looked down. "Mommy," said Michael. Freckles danced across the bridge of his nose, his wavy ginger hair temporarily tamed by a vigorous brushing moments before we'd left home. "I don't know where my room is. Can you show me?"

Although he wouldn't turn three until the end of November, Michael was eager to begin this new adventure. He'd spent the previous school year watching his big brother's excitement on school days. Now it was his turn. Clutching his shiny new red lunchbox with a blue Hot Wheels race car, his brown eyes lit up when he saw his teacher standing in the hallway. He peered around her into the classroom, saw some kids, and hurried in. No fuss, no tears...just like Steve. I returned to the car with Josh, pleased his two older brothers seemed so well-adjusted. Good job, Linda.

Especially on days when Steve and Mike attended Steeple School in the mornings, I was often successful in getting all three boys down for an afternoon nap at the same time. One day in late March, I settled into the recliner with a steaming mug of tea and the local paper. An ad in the classified section grabbed my attention. "Wanted: part-time teacher for job-share. Afternoons, fifth grade." This was just what I needed. Something to break up my day, restore the sense of purpose that teaching had given me earlier, and connect me to other adults. Without hesitation I headed for the phone.

The woman who answered explained a teacher returning from maternity leave had decided she didn't want to work full-time. The district had agreed to establish a two-teacher partnership beginning after April vacation until the end of the school year. The hours were noon to 4:00 p.m., *and* the opening was at the South River Elementary School, the same school I'd attended as a fifth grader twenty years earlier! Perfect! That evening I shared my discovery with Roger.

"This would be so great," I exclaimed as I showed Roger the ad. "I'd have enough time to pick up Steve and Mike from school before leaving for work. Then whoever stays with them would get the boys lunch and get all three down for their naps. I'd be home soon after they woke up!"

"You won't net much money after you pay for a sitter," responded my ever-practical husband.

"But that's not the point. You know how much I miss teaching! I'm just not cut out to be a typical housewife." I had no words to explain to Roger how suffocating my isolation felt during the week, especially during the school year when even Jane, who had a full-time job teaching math in a nearby high school, wasn't available to me.

Roger shrugged and agreed nothing could be lost by picking up an application. He really didn't have an opinion about what I did while he was at work. I could stay home or work—that didn't matter to him—as long as I handled the childcare logistics.

Within days after completing the paperwork and dropping the packet off at the district office, I received a call inviting me to come in for an interview with the principal.

During our conversation, I made certain to tell him I was a product of Marshfield Schools. I had a brief opportunity to show some of the materials I had used in my classroom in Syracuse and spoke about my love for hands-on learning. The interview concluded with a promise from him to check my references. "To be honest, we don't have many applicants for this position, given that it's so late in the school year," he commented. "You should be hearing from me within a few days."

I wasn't prepared for my mother's disapproval when I phoned her several days later to tell her I'd be resuming my teaching career in just a few weeks. She knew how much I'd enjoyed teaching in Syracuse, but in her opinion, mothers belonged at home with their young children. Crushed and questioning my decision, I called Jane. I needed her reassurance—badly.

"I've been offered a part-time teaching job in Marshfield," I told her. "However, I just got off the phone with Mom, and she isn't pleased. She thinks I will cause the boys irreparable harm by leaving them with a sitter for a few hours on weekdays. But Jane, I need the stimulation."

Jane laughed. "Believe me, I know exactly what you mean! Why do you think I went back to work! And I heard the same thing from my mother. Just because they stayed home, they think we should too."

I paused before adding, "Yeah, you're right. But damn it. I hate that her approval still is so important to me."

I wasn't used to dealing with disapproval from my mother. For the past four years Mom had been a never-ending source of support, but now? Clearly, she had very specific ideas about the duties of a mother—sacrifice everything for your children. I decided to step past my mother's disapproval for the first time and risk her ire. In future years, situations would arise requiring even longer steps, with more devastating consequences.

Despite my mother's opinion, our family thrived. I returned home each afternoon revived, refreshed, and ready to engage my sons. I loved the new rhythm of my days. As my workload increased, so did my energy level. I felt lighter, happier. Roger noticed and commented on the change in my personality.

But newly placid waters turned into a dizzying whirlpool in May when Roger arrived home from work with some unexpected news.

"I've been waiting for the right time to tell you this," he said after the boys were all in bed. "I've applied for a job in the sociology department at the State University of New York, at Stony Brook, Long Island."

"What! Really?" My jaw dropped. "But that's a long way from here! We'd have to move…leave Marshfield!"

Roger put one arm around my shoulders. I stiffened. He removed his arm. "This is a great opportunity for me."

Everything in me was protesting but I didn't say, *What about me?!* The feminist movement had yet to touch me. I saw my role as a traditional wife and mother. And I was not accustomed to arguing with Roger when it came to his work life. My tiny salary certainly didn't pay the bills. Our family's well-being completely depended on Roger's income and his trajectory, or at least that's what I believed. What I said was, "I see."

"The Stony Brook campus is fairly new," continued Roger. "It's developing a good reputation and attracting a lot of talented people." His voice rose with excitement. "I've enjoyed my time at the community health center, but I really want to work in higher education, and get on a tenure track."

"Oh."

I couldn't believe how the day had turned. Less than twelve hours before, all had seemed perfect. I'd found some balance in my life. Now my life was out of my hands, if it had ever been in my hands at all.

"I should know more about the Stony Brook job before long. They're arranging a visit for me." He yawned. "It's been a long day. I think I'll head up to bed. Are you coming?"

I watched him go and remained on the couch, too dazed to move. Finally, I pushed myself up, walked into the kitchen, opened the refrigerator, and grabbed a beer. *Great! Great for you! But you never asked me if I wanted to move.* I kicked the enameled door shut.

I yanked the tab and took a huge gulp. *You never asked me if I wanted to leave my job and my hometown and my best friend.*

I wiped my eyes with the back of one hand and sat back down on the couch, hard. *You never asked me how moving might impact our sons.*

I tipped the can back and drained the contents. *You never asked me a single question.*

I ended up falling asleep on the couch.

The next morning, and for many days, we tip-toed around each other and the topic of a possible move. I felt the life I'd built for myself over the past two months was on hold, but Roger didn't seem to notice the tension that filled every pore of my body. When he told me his visit to Stony Brook was scheduled for early June, just after Steve and Mike's preschool closed for summer break, I nodded and marked the date on our wall calendar.

Things were still tense between us on Steeple School's last day of classes. Nonetheless, Roger and I stood together and watched proudly as Steve held the flag while the class gathered in a circle, ready to say the Pledge of Allegiance. Dressed in a light blue collarless suit jacket and navy trousers, our son looked quite grown-up at four and a half. He stood straight, shoulders thrown back, a serious look on his scrubbed face. With a nod from Mrs. Keith, the children began, "I pledge allegiance...." I watched Steve's lips moving, and chuckled to myself, imagining how the pledge must sound recited by Steve! At the end of the recitation, Steve turned and solemnly handed the Stars and Stripes to Mrs. Keith. A classmate approached Steve, tapped him on the shoulder, and the two shook hands.

The next day Roger left for a two-day visit to Stony Brook. At home, for our sons' sake, I did my best to keep a smile on my face even though I drifted from task to task in a daze, unable to concentrate. The few hours I had at work provided a welcome distraction. At night, alone in bed, I gave into my pain and let the tears come. I knew a decision about my family's future would be made soon—a decision in which I had no voice.

I saw our future in Roger's face the moment he walked in the door, cheeks flushed and his eyes shining with delight. "They want me!" he burst out. "I've been offered an associate professorship, with a great salary—almost $20,000 plus benefits. I thought I'd begin as an assistant prof, but associate...wow! I'll start off immediately on a tenure track!" His exuberance swirled and bounced off the walls.

"Great," I murmured. "I guess we're moving."

Roger didn't notice my despair. He continued to chatter on about his visit and the prospects ahead. His comments barely registered in my mind as I began ticking off the losses I'd experience as a result of the move. The loss of the hometown of my youth, where I had reestablished myself as a young mother, an adult. The loss of Jane's close presence. The loss of a job I'd grown to love. Suddenly I had to leave the house, to get out, to be alone. The boys were all in their PJs, clamoring for their dad's attention. I kissed them goodnight, asked Roger to read the traditional evening story and put them to bed. Then I fled to the car and headed for the beach, my go-to place when my soul needed soothing. I walked along the shoreline asking myself questions for which there were no answers: Why did our marriage feel so one-sided? Why didn't my voice seem to count?

I didn't return until well after dark.

At the conclusion of my last day of work at South River Elementary I stood in my empty classroom. The slate blackboards were wiped clean, and the plaster walls naked, stripped of student work. I bent over the bookcase, where earlier the students had gleefully stacked their math and science textbooks. I began covering the shelves with brown wrapping paper as instructed in the "Closing Day Memo for Teachers."

When I heard the knock on the wall next to the door, I straightened up and turned around.

"Mrs. Cohen," said the principal as he crossed over the threshold, "I'm so glad you're still here! I was afraid I'd missed you."

"I'm just about done," I replied. "I dropped my grades off earlier with your secretary. Is there something else I need to do?"

"Oh, no...no. Your records are fine, and the classroom as well. I just wanted to thank you for stepping in the way you did. I'll admit some parents were nervous about this job-share position…but you did a wonderful job…no complaints at all…"

"Thank you," I smiled.

"In fact," he continued, "We are going to have a full-time opening this fall in the sixth grade. I know you have three little ones, but I was hoping you might consider applying for the position. We'd love to have you as a full-time member of our staff."

I swallowed hard and my voice caught before I could reply. I hadn't seen this offer coming and that made my response even more difficult. "Thank you for your confidence in me. But as it turns out, my family is leaving Marshfield and moving to Long Island due to a new job opportunity for my husband."

"I completely understand," the principal said, and added, "I'd be happy to write you a strong letter of recommendation."

Of course, he'd understand. In a similar situation, he'd expect the same from his own wife.

Sadness filled me as I drove home. There was no question now how much things had shifted between Roger and me. The equal partnership we'd had during the early years of our marriage, before children, was gone. I didn't blame Roger and I loved my sons. But the price I'd paid for becoming a mother was beyond what I ever could have imagined. Who was I? Who had I become? I had no idea.

For the next three weeks I hired a high-school girl on weekdays to entertain the boys and determinedly went from room to room packing. I focused on the task at hand and did my best not to think too much. Eventually, boxes lined the walls of every room.

On the evening before our move, I pulled into the parking lot of the town beach. Jane was already waiting for me. We'd planned this date in advance and asked our husbands to be responsible for dinner and the kids' bedtime. Jane gave me a hug before reaching back into her car and pulling out a cooler. We each grabbed a handle and made our way over the dunes onto the beach. Neither of us spoke until we'd placed the food on a gray wool blanket and opened our beers.

"You OK?" asked Jane.

"Yeah," I answered. In the evening glow, the contrast sharpened between the cobalt-blue water, the kelly-green spikes of beach grass, and the saffron-gold sand. "Best time to be at the beach," I said softly.

"Absolutely," confirmed Jane. We picnicked in the comfortable silence known only to soul mates.

Later, the two of us walked arm in arm as, in the west, a fireball sank into the marsh lining the South River. The clouds above blushed rose.

"What time do you leave tomorrow?"

I sighed before answering. "Nine. We have reservations on the 2:00 p.m. ferry from Connecticut across Long Island Sound to Port Jefferson. Shit, I can't believe this is really happening."

"Hey," offered Jane, "you never know, maybe you'll be back."

"I don't think so. Both you and Kevin have deep ties to Marshfield. That's not the case with Roger. For him it's all about the job."

Jane nodded. We both understood the futility of the situation. "Yeah, husbands support their families. Wives follow. I wonder if that will ever change?"

"I don't know." My grip on her arm tightened. "I know we'll see each other again. But for now, this is goodbye." I was bereft.

We hugged each other fiercely. Then I pulled away, headed for my car and my last night in Marshfield. The next night our family of five would sleep in our new house in Port Jefferson, New York.

SEVEN

Acronym Land, 1971

We'd decided on Port Jeff for two reasons: its proximity to Roger's work at SUNY Stony Brook (less than five miles away) and its reputation for having an excellent school system. I wasted no time filling out the necessary paperwork for Steve and Michael to enter the kindergarten and prekindergarten programs offered at the town's elementary school with the unusual name of Scraggy Hill.

A week after I dropped off the completed registration forms the phone's ring startled me. As newcomers we had few callers. The voice on the receiver identified herself as an employee at the Port Jefferson school district office.

"Mrs. Cohen, I have the kindergarten registration form for your son Steven in front of me. Your son isn't eligible to enter kindergarten at our school. Perhaps there's been some misunderstanding?"

"Misunderstanding?" What was this woman talking about?

The receptionist cleared her throat. "We don't enroll children with your son's problem in our school system."

Problem? Immediately I felt annoyed. Steve wasn't a problem. He was just a little kid. But before responding hastily, a thought occurred to me. Maybe because Steve had never been to pre-kindergarten she thought he should begin there?

"Well, we didn't have a prekindergarten program in the town we moved from," I responded. Then quickly added, "But he did have two very successful years in nursery school. He knows most of his colors and can count to…"

"Mrs. Cohen, please," the voice interrupted. "Under 'special concerns' you wrote your son has Down syndrome. If your son has Down syndrome, he is retarded."

I shuddered at the sound of that word, a word which was common in special education parlance, but one I'd stopped using. A word none of our sons had ever heard. I closed my eyes while keeping the receiver to my ear and sought calmness.

The disembodied voice droned on. "Our local schools don't accept retarded children."

What? I couldn't believe what I was hearing. Where did she think Steve was supposed to go to school if not in Port Jefferson? The voice continued, "We have a separate centralized program for those children. Our superintendent has instructed me to provide you with the contact information for the Suffolk County BOCES office. Would you like their phone number?"

A dull ache formed in my stomach. This couldn't be true. A separate program? Like racial segregation? I struggled to respond. "Boces? What is that?"

"B-O-C-E-S," she replied crisply. "It's the acronym we use for the Board of Cooperative Educational Services. Why don't you call them? I'm sure someone will be happy to talk with you about the program."

Sputtering, I tried to explain. Steve's younger brother Michael would be entering the prekindergarten program. I wanted the brothers in the same school. But the determined voice cut me off, gave me the BOCES number, and ended the call.

Heart racing, I stood alone in our still unfamiliar house staring at the digits I'd scrawled on scrap paper. How could this be? If Steve couldn't join his brother at the local elementary school, where would he go? I didn't want him to be separated from Michael and later Josh.

Later I shared my news with Roger. He too was surprised and confused. We agreed I needed more information about Steve's options. "Make an appointment with the BOCES district administrator," he advised.

OK, I reminded myself, *I can do this. I know how to advocate for Steve.*

A week later I sat in an upholstered wing chair facing Dr. Richard Levine, PhD, determined to fight for Steve's inclusion at Scraggy Hill. Dr. Levine reached for the file folder lying on his gleaming oak desk, extracted what I recognized as the registration form I'd filled out for

Steve, glanced at it briefly, and looked up at me through thick horn-rimmed glasses.

"I see you live in Port Jefferson, nice little town."

"Yes, we moved there earlier this summer from Massachusetts. My husband, Dr. Roger Cohen, has his PhD in Sociology and is a member of the Health Sciences Department at Stony Brook." Would citing Roger's official status buy me some credibility? Strengthen my female voice and make it heard? I hated pulling the husband card, but I was willing to do anything to make Steve's life better.

Dr. Levine stared at me and my stomach clenched. Instinctively I knew this would be nothing like the casual meeting I'd had with Mrs. Keith. Getting Steve into the Steeple School had been easy. I could feel my self-confidence abandoning me and I longed for Roger's presence.

"And your son...ah...ah...Steven, he will be five in September. When did he first begin receiving EI services?"

"Excuse me? EI services?"

Dr. Levine looked up. "Early Intervention. When did early intervention services begin?"

"You mean his heart catheterization? That was done when he was..."

My inquisitor gave an exasperated sigh and cut me off. "No. No! EI services: physical therapy, occupational therapy, speech therapy."

My stomach ached. I felt so stupid. "He's never had any of those things," I replied. "But he is up to date on all of his shots."

Dr. Levine shook his head and frowned. "It says here that ah...your son...ah...Steve...attended a nursery school for two years. This was a SPED school I assume?"

"SPED?"

"Special Education. Was this a nursery school for retarded children?"

"No," I replied meekly. "Steeple School is just a regular nursery school."

"Hummm," murmured Dr. Levine. He shifted in his chair and leaned forward. "Mrs. Cohen, let me explain a little bit about BOCES and how we operate. BOCES was established in 1948. We are an educational cooperative, serving the fifty-one towns which comprise Suffolk County. Port Jefferson falls within the Brookhaven section which is made up of fourteen school districts." I tried hard to focus. Obviously, he had given this speech many times. "We provide cost-effective educational services for our towns including the education of all retarded children. Our BOCES teachers are specially trained to best serve these students. We have both TMR and EMR classes, beginning with preschool programs. We rent available space from the towns in each district."

My eyes blinked as I tried to follow Dr. Levine's rapid-paced delivery. What the hell was he talking about? What did all those letters mean? My ignorance embarrassed me.

"Excuse me, Dr. Levine. I apologize for interrupting you. But TMR? EMR? What do those letters stand for?"

Dr. Levine's eyebrows rose in disbelief. I slumped in my chair.

"Trainable mentally retarded and educable mentally retarded. Let's see...ah, yes...your son is Down syndrome. Most of our Down's children are EMR."

I nodded to indicate my understanding. When I'd gone to school we'd been assigned reading groups: Bluebirds, Robins, Sparrows. Everyone knew the smartest kids were Bluebirds. So even kids like Steve were separated by ability. But Dr. Levine's next statement sent a knife of fear shooting through me.

"We will need to evaluate your son to be certain."

Oh God! What if Steve tests out as TMR? I thought I'd done my best for him. But what if I hadn't? What if he was behind even his Down syndrome peers? What if he was only "trainable" and not "educable?" What had I cost my son by thinking that my love and advocacy would be enough to guide him through his life?

Dr. Levine stood up. "I have another appointment scheduled, but I'll ask my receptionist to set up a meeting with a BOCES evaluator. She'll explain the testing process your son will undergo." Then he led me out of his office and deposited me in front of the receptionist's desk.

I felt I'd just been through the spin cycle of a washing machine, and stood off to one side, dazed and defeated, not sure of what to do next.

Steve did well during his evaluation and, much to my relief, was assigned to an EMR classroom. On the morning of Steve's first day of BOCES school, when the yellow van (aka the "short bus") pulled into our driveway to pick up Steve, just one passenger was aboard. A little boy peered out the window and my heart leapt when I saw him. Another kid just like Steve! The first kid with Down syndrome Steve had ever met. I obsessed about that little guy all day. How old was he? What was his name? Who were his parents? Would Steve like him? When Steve returned home that afternoon, I stood in the driveway clutching a piece of paper with my name and phone number which I handed to the bus driver.

"Could you please give my contact information to this little boy's mother? We're new to town. I've never met another mother whose kid has Down syndrome and I'd really like to." I didn't tell the driver how much I *needed* to meet this mother.

Later, as I stood in the kitchen getting dinner, the phone rang and I jumped. Could this be her already?

When Ann Patterson introduced herself, I shivered with excitement. I'd been waiting almost five years for this moment. Quickly I learned that she lived in Port Jefferson and Robbie was the youngest of three brothers. He'd been born six months before Steve.

Unfortunately, 5:00 p.m. is the worst time for mothers of young children to try and have an uninterrupted, coherent phone conversation. As much as I wanted to lock myself in a room and talk for hours with Ann, that wasn't going to happen. When she told me she taught second grade at Scraggy Hill, I knew we wouldn't meet until the weekend—four long days away. Ann gave me directions to her house and insisted I bring Steve with me. "Robbie's talked nonstop since I got home from work about his new friend, 'Teve.' I can't wait to meet him as well as you!"

Later I told Roger about Steve's bus mate and the brief conversation I'd had with Ann. He seemed to understand how important this connection could be for me, but really didn't have much to say. His silence told me this was my need, not his.

Time slogged by while I waited for Saturday to arrive. At times memories of the lonely road I'd traveled for five years flooded in. I recalled the thousands of moments when I wondered if I was doing the right thing for Steve; hundreds of times when I'd needed to make a decision without a kindred sounding board; and millions of times I'd worried about Steve and his future. Finally, I would have a chance to know another mother traveling the same road.

Saturday morning, I left Michael and Josh with their dad, and drove across town with Steve to the Patterson's house. I turned onto a dead-end street and scattered a bevy of boys engaged in a whiffle ball game. I recognized the littlest, a towhead with a bowl-style haircut, who waved one chubby hand vigorously. An older boy reached protectively for his other hand and gently pulled him out of harm's way. A petite woman with a pixie haircut stood on a freshly mowed lawn in front of a brick ranch house. Ann beckoned me into the driveway and smiled broadly as she approached.

"Linda! Welcome! Sorry about the ballgame, but all the neighborhood kids regard our road as their private playground."

The door on Steve's side opened and the boy who'd been holding Robbie's hand peered in. "Hey, Steve, I'm Rick, one of Robbie's brothers. Wanna play ball with us?"

Steve had never held a bat or seen a whiffle ball, but he didn't hesitate. He slid off his seat and stood on the pavement. Robbie almost knocked him to the ground as he threw both arms around his new buddy. "Teve! Teve!"

Ann laughed. "Rick's almost twelve and he'll keep an eye on both Steve and Robbie while we get acquainted."

Wow. I forced a smile. A built-in babysitter…an older brother to show Robbie the way! A flicker of envy shot through me.

For the next two hours we sat on her porch stoop and talked nonstop, even as my gaze frequently wandered to Steve. Warmth surged through me as I watched his enthusiastic welcome into the group. We began by comparing notes on our birth stories. Ann told me that within hours of Robbie's birth, their pediatrician told her and her husband their newborn had Down syndrome. I wondered how they'd reacted to this unexpected news.

"We were both pretty upset initially, but the doctor was so positive."

I gulped as Ann continued speaking. Positive? The doctor was positive? That certainly hadn't been my experience.

"He told us about a rotation he'd done as an intern in a medical facility which served children with disabilities. He said he had two families on his caseload, each with a child with Down's, and offered to connect us if we wanted. He *exuded* reassurance and compassion. He gave us hope."

Grief and anger whirled in my head. For the first time I wondered if Steve's pediatrician had ever had a patient with Down syndrome prior to Steve's birth. If not, was that the reason he'd handled the diagnosis so awkwardly? His decision to tell Roger and keep the news from me continued to plague me. I still found it difficult to trust my husband. There was a crack in our marriage that I doubted would ever close. For sure the doctor would never know the damage his advice to Roger had caused.

The more I learned from Ann, the more I realized the profound difference in our experiences. Conflicting emotions tore through me: sadness, confusion, even jealousy. The information and support I'd longed for had been immediately available to her. She'd met other mothers of kids with Down's and Robbie had received all those early intervention services I'd heard about from Dr. Levine. As I listened to her describe the various therapies and the manner in which she was trained to help Robbie, I shifted uncomfortably.

"I was so scared when I found out Steve would have to be tested in order to determine his placement level in BOCES. I was certain I'd failed him," I confessed. Even now, weeks later, guilt made me blink back tears.

But Ann put her hand on my shoulder. "I've been watching Steve today, and I think it's interesting. Although he's had none of the services Robbie enjoyed, it's obvious to me that both boys are similar developmentally. I'm not surprised at all that Steve did well during the evaluation. Give yourself some credit, Linda. You've done a great job."

The way Ann spoke filled me with gratitude. I felt a sudden warmth as my muscles relaxed and released the tension I didn't know I'd been holding. I knew I'd met a mentor and hopefully a friend. On the drive home I heard myself say aloud, "Maybe living on Long Island won't be so bad."

EIGHT

Dark Days, 1974

For the next three years I battled to find my own niche in Port Jefferson. Aside from Ann, connecting with other mothers proved hard. Port Jefferson was a town about the same size as Marshfield but life moved at a faster pace and the women I met seemed consumed by materialism. They hired professionals to coordinate the interior of their homes, dressed in the latest styles, and chattered on about the cocktail party they'd been to on the weekend. Finding women with whom I felt comfortable was difficult. Roger thrived in his professional life and most of our social activities revolved around Roger's colleagues from work—people I barely knew. The brothers, especially Michael and Josh, made friends and seemed happy enough. But I remained on the sidelines, overwhelmed by loneliness and boredom. The days crawled by. I did what needed to be done to keep our family functioning, but I was no one except to my boys. My isolation and anger about BOCES and the segregation it imposed on Steve became too much for me to handle. Finally, I broke.

The day I ran away, a Sunday, began innocently. Roger, as was his custom, had gotten up with the boys and let me sleep in. I don't remember what set me off that day—probably some trivial argument with Roger. But the emotions which propelled me outside and into my car—a blinding despair and anger—were so intense I could not stay in our home. One. More. Second. I'd reached a limit. I couldn't hang on any longer. I hated my life, perhaps even myself, and I had to get out. To escape.

I didn't know where I was heading, but I began berating myself even as I drove. "How can you do this? How can you abandon Steve,

Michael, and Josh?" My guilt overwhelmed me. I knew my sons needed me. But I needed me too. I needed a voice and a life. And right now, I didn't have either. At thirty-three, the pressures of motherhood had stripped me of my sense of self. I longed to find the confident person I'd once been.

Three hours later I found myself standing at the entrance to my parents' home in Chappaqua, New York. Nervously I hesitated before ringing the doorbell. What if my mother answered? Would she let me in? Or send me away? She could be a harsh critic and her reactions to events were often unpredictable. Once I entered their house, I'd have to admit my life wasn't going well. That I wasn't as strong as I pretended to be. Trembling, I rang the doorbell and when my mother opened the door I burst into tears.

"Linda! What's wrong? What are you doing here? Where are the boys? Roger? Are they OK?"

"Everyone's fine," I croaked. "Everyone except me."

I allowed myself a little bit of relief when Mom pulled me to her and led me inside. For the next hour she listened, surprisingly without judgment.

"The only time I have for myself is the two hours in the morning when Josh is in nursery school and that gets eaten up with meal planning, grocery shopping, laundry, and house cleaning—the same things over and over. Most weekdays the only adult conversations I have are with a store clerk or the mailman. And if Roger has a late meeting or is traveling, I don't even have him to talk with at night. The only purpose I feel I have is advocating for Steve, but even there I've failed. He still isn't allowed to go to school with Michael. The only friend he has is the other boy from Port Jefferson who rides the short bus with him to whatever town has space for his BOCES classroom. And the class is located in a different school every year."

I paused to blow my nose with the Kleenex Mom handed me before continuing. "This year is the worst so far. The assigned school is on the other side of the island. Steve and his friend Robbie spend close to an hour on the bus each way." Then I added the most hurtful piece of information. "And the jerk of a principal has roped off a section of the playground for 'the protection of our special guests.' Steve and his classmates have to stay within the boundaries! They can't play with the other kids, nor can the other kids cross the line to play with them." There was so much more I longed to tell her—how I felt so uncomfortable in my role as wife, how I felt my voice didn't matter to anyone—but I knew those were words she wouldn't want to hear. Those were conversations I could only have with Jane.

Finally, I took a breath. My mother sat quietly beside me as a sudden weariness swept over me. My voice lowered. I could feel myself winding down. "My own life has been stuck on pause for so long. Caring for three little boys is a monotonous grind. I feel worthless, without hope."

Mom wrapped me in her arms again, then led me to the guest bedroom and lowered the shades. I fell into a deep sleep.

Over the next two days Mom continued to treat me with kindness and compassion, but also gave me plenty of space. Dad hovered on the periphery with a bewildered expression on his face, clearly unable to comprehend what was bothering me. The respite at my folks' home restored me enough to realize I couldn't allow myself the luxury of indulging my feelings any longer. I needed to return to Port Jefferson. Roger welcomed me home, but like Dad, couldn't understand why I'd felt so troubled. I really didn't want to expend much effort trying to explain. I knew the task of figuring out how to improve the quality of my life rested on my shoulders.

Years later, when I reflected on my mother's understanding during the days I sought refuge with them from my life in Port Jefferson, I wondered: Had she experienced similar frustrations as a young parent? Other than Jane's mother, did she have any friends? In the 1940s my parents didn't even own a car. Dad commuted to Boston every day by train. Along with her Cuban accent, which must have branded her as different, perhaps my mother's isolation had been even more suffocating than mine.

I returned from my parents' house determined to evoke changes in my life. I couldn't do much about Steve's educational situation, but I could attack my isolation and boredom. I knew how to address both.

"I need to take care of myself," I told Roger one evening not long after I'd run away. "I want to go back to work."

Not only did he agree, but he made a surprising offer. "You know, I could arrange my schedule and get the boys off to school in the mornings. Come fall, Josh will be entering prekindergarten at Scraggy Hill and Mike will be in second grade. The three of us can walk to the bus stop together after the BOCES van picks up Steve." He paused before adding, "Actually, I'd like that!"

"Really?" I did a double take. "You wouldn't mind?" A sudden flash of insight blossomed within me. Because Roger had followed the doctor's advice, I had, at times, closed my heart to him. I'd pushed him away and many times had consciously decided to soldier on alone. But Roger was basically a good man. When I asked for help, he was willing. I'd learned how to play the victim role by watching my mother. But here was a dad who seemed eager to participate, just as my father had been. Maybe I needed to look to Roger more.

A few days later I called Ann. From experience, I knew openings were often posted in school offices before appearing in the local papers. Ann agreed to keep her eyes and ears open. Meanwhile I continued mothering my three little boys and thought about how I could involve Roger as a co-parent.

One afternoon in early spring, Roger arrived home with Michael after picking him up at a Cub Scout troop meeting on his way home from work. Michael's face was knotted with concern and worry.

"What's up?" I asked. "Did something happen at Cub Scouts?"

Michael nodded. "Daddy said we'll talk about it after dinner," he whispered.

Later the three of us sat down in the living room. Michael nervously twisted the ends of his yellow Cub Scout scarf.

Roger began by saying when he'd picked up Michael, the den mother, Claire Dorfman, asked to speak with him. He looked at our boy. "She told me there was a problem today involving you and her son Patrick. Why don't you tell us about it?"

Michael's eyes began to fill and spill over. He struggled to speak. A trembling sigh escaped from his lips. I hated seeing his anguish. Then he steadied himself with a deep breath and said, "Patrick and I had a fight. All the kids were outside playing before the meeting started. I punched him in the face and pushed him down. He started to cry and then his mother came out."

"Yup, that's pretty much what Mrs. Dorfman told me," said Roger.

I looked at our son in disbelief. I'd never known him to be violent. Sure, there was the usual pushing and shoving between brothers, but I'd never seen Michael lose his self-control and throw a punch. Ever. What could have possibly provoked him?

"Start at the beginning and tell us what happened," continued Roger. "Why did you hit Patrick and push him down? Do you know why you became so angry?"

"P-P-Patrick s-s-said something mean," Michael sputtered, tears streaking down his face. "H-he c-called Steve a name."

My stomach clenched. I'd continued to worry about Steve's segregation from his age peers; it remained one of my biggest stressors. I knew when people who are different are pushed to the side and not seen, diversity has no value. Fear foments.

"What did Patrick say?" asked Roger gently.

"He called Steve a stupid dummy because I told him Steve liked Batman better than Superman. He said Steve was a retard. I don't know what retard means, but I know it isn't nice."

Shit! For a second I stopped breathing. My heart shattered. I ached for Michael, for Steve, for our family. I couldn't speak through the lump in my throat. For the first time, I considered how having a brother like Steve might impact my other children.

Our son went on to explain that initially he'd ignored Patrick's comment. But when the taunting continued and Patrick ran through his backyard yelling, "Mike's brother is a dummy-retard," he'd snapped. Claire Dorfman heard a commotion and ran outside to find her son on the ground crying with Michael standing over him. When she asked what had happened Patrick told her Michael had started things by calling him names.

"Patrick's mommy got really mad at me and said I was a bad boy. I'm sorry, Mommy and Daddy." Tears puddled down Michael's face and he rubbed at his eyes. "But I didn't call Patrick any names. He called Steve names and I didn't like that."

Roger's eyes flashed. "Michael, you shouldn't have hit Patrick and pushed him down, but..." He hesitated before continuing. "But I probably would have done the same thing."

I placed my hand over my mouth to hide the smile I couldn't contain. But a wave of concern followed.

Poor Michael. I felt so awful for him. Sure, I was proud of him for defending his brother, but he was only seven years old. He shouldn't have to shoulder the same burden of concern his parents did. I carried my little hero to the bathroom, filled the tub, and let the warm water soothe him. In that moment I saw the dual role Michael would hold. He would always be both a middle child and the oldest child.

Soothing myself after Michael's encounter with Patrick proved far more difficult. Outwardly I forced myself to remain calm, but I had trouble focusing and assigned a portion of my clouded vision to the BOCES system. This is what happens, I told myself, when bureaucrats impose their will on kids like Steve and educate them away from their community.

My ever-present Guilt joined in, taunting me: "You've failed not just Steve, but his brother too. Mothers are supposed to protect their children. Always. Under every circumstance."

Recovery for Michael happened quickly. When he said he wanted to quit Cub Scouts and play soccer instead, we let him. But for me the incident only served to point out once again all I disliked about BOCES. I'd long since wearied of confronting the BOCES bureaucracy, but I did want to hold Patrick's mother accountable for his behavior. In the eight years since Steve's birth I'd never faced a situation like this.

I met with Claire wearing an invisible straitjacket to keep my anger in check. When I told her Michael's version of the incident, her first response was she didn't know we had a son with Down syndrome.

Of course not, how could you? He's been hidden from view for the past three years.

Claire said she was "sorry to learn of Steve's condition" and she'd speak with Patrick. Her apology didn't really help. Despite the length of time we'd been in Port Jefferson, to most people, if they knew Steve at all, he remained a strange, funny-looking kid.

Fortunately, a week or so after Michael's brief Cub Scout career came to its abrupt end, a phone call from Ann diverted my anger and despair. An opening had been posted in the Scraggy Hill teacher's room for a sixth-grade position at a middle school about twenty miles farther out on the island. My spirits soared and I wasted no time sending my resume and cover letter to the address she gave me. I got the job.

I taught at this school for three years as the school became recognized for its leadership in middle school education. I worked alongside colleagues who put in long hours and saw teaching as a calling. I grew personally and professionally, which made living on Long Island less of a burden. Working again stimulated my creativity and filled me with purpose. During those three years I stopped seeing teaching as a way of getting out of the house. Teaching became a vocation for me. I became committed to public school education and the concept of providing experiences that served children and their parents.

NINE

Darkness Lightens, 1976-77

As we began our fifth year in Port Jefferson, I hadn't made any headway getting Steve into his hometown school. He and Robbie continued to travel by yellow van to their classroom in a distant town. My expectation that things would ever shift for Steve had all but disappeared.

But then a glimmer of hope broke through the darkness. In December 1975 Congress passed ground-breaking legislation, the Education for All Handicapped Children Act. Also known as PL 94-142, lawmakers had referenced two groups of children: the one million with disabilities who were currently excluded entirely from the public educational system, and a far larger group who had only limited access to public schools. The law proclaimed children with disabilities be placed in the "least restrictive environment possible," one that maximized interaction with non-disabled children. Separate schooling could only occur when the severity of the disability meant that educational goals couldn't be achieved in the regular classroom.

Roger and I obtained our own copy of Public Law 94-142. We spent many nights going through it line-by-line. We both felt certain this new law meant a change for our son. In late January we arranged a meeting with my old nemesis, Dr. Levine. Unfortunately, Roger was unexpectedly called out of town on the day Dr. Levine agreed to see us. I'd already arranged a personal day from school and didn't want to postpone the meeting. Armed with our dog-eared copy of the law, I headed out, confident I would be heard. Now Steve had defined rights, specified in print, signed by the president of the United States!

But Dr. Levine saw things very differently. He felt New York State was in compliance with this new legislation. Unlike disabled children in other states, Steve hadn't been denied an education.

"Your son has not only had total access to a public school program, he's been taught by highly trained individuals. New York State is recognized nationally as a leader in special education." I opened my mouth to speak, but Dr. Levine waved me off. "Yes, PL 94-142 will revise the delivery of our services, but change takes time. We need to proceed cautiously. I would remind you that BOCES was founded to make it possible for small school districts, like Port Jefferson, to combine resources and provide services that otherwise would be uneconomical, inefficient, or unavailable."

My nostrils flared and I could feel my face flush with bitterness. "This isn't about economics or efficiency," I retorted. "This is about my son! We've lived here four and a half years and he's still a stranger in Port Jefferson. One of Steve's brothers ended up quitting Cub Scouts because of the taunting he endured about Steve. Where is your empathy? How would you feel if you had a kid like Steve?"

Dr. Levine glanced down at his wristwatch and said funding to fully support the new legislation wouldn't occur until 1978. He pushed our copy of PL 94-142 back across his desk. "Thank you very much for coming in today, Mrs. Cohen."

I got the message. This meeting was over.

I drove home seething with bitterness at this man's smugness and indifference. I was so tired of battling the male establishment. I knew Roger shared my frustration. Would we ever succeed in changing things for Steve?

Then in the spring of 1977 came an opportunity I hadn't foreseen. After almost six years at SUNY Stony Brook, Roger had earned a sabbatical. Beginning in the fall, if only for a year, we could live anywhere! Roger's requirements were simple: a college campus nearby to support his research and the availability of *The New York Times*. I set my sights on northern New England, an area I'd always loved.

Roger and I had recently visited friends living in Hanover, New Hampshire, the location of Dartmouth College. We liked the town a lot. With a population of 7,000, Hanover had only one elementary school and, unlike New York, no state-wide special education system. Without a BOCES bureaucracy to fight, perhaps there was a chance for Steve to finally attend the same school as his brothers. We both wanted to find out.

I called the Bernice Ray Elementary School and asked to speak with the principal. When Stefan Vogel came on the line, I explained our family was considering a move to Hanover during the summer and that we had three elementary school-aged sons.

"Michael will be entering fifth grade and Joshua will be a second grader," I said.

Mr. Vogel replied that he would mail record release forms to their current elementary school. Then he added, "I thought you mentioned a third son."

I had practiced my speech and was prepared for a battle. But now I had some ammunition. I cleared my throat and words tumbled out. "Steve will turn eleven in September. He has Down syndrome." I licked my dry lips. "PL 94-142 states Steve is entitled to an education in the least restrictive environment. I want him to go to the same school as his brothers and I want him in a regular classroom with typical kids." Then I closed my eyes before asking, "Would that be possible at your school?"

Stefan Vogel didn't hesitate. He assured me he was familiar with the new legislation. "We do have several children with special needs at our school. They are all in regular classrooms and receive additional support from trained special educators in our resource room." A seed of hope tickled my stomach. "We don't have any students with Down syndrome, but our lead SPED teacher comes to us from New York City and I know she has taught children like your son."

Mr. Vogel wondered if Mr. Cohen and I would be coming to Hanover prior to our move and when I said yes, we scheduled a date for a meeting. I should bring Steve's school records and be prepared to discuss his developmental level. And that was that! I hung up feeling amazed, surprised, hopeful, and just a little bit scared.

In June Roger and I drove north to Hanover to meet with Mr. Vogel. Summer vacation had begun, and our footsteps echoed in the empty hall as we followed signs directing us to the main office. I sighed and reached for my husband's hand.

"Nervous?"

"Very." I breathed deeply trying to quell the dancing butterflies in my gut.

In the reception area, we looked through the open door of an inner office and spotted a sandy-haired man seated at a small conference table. A woman sat next to him. He stood and beckoned us in with a wave of one arm.

"Welcome! Mr. and Mrs. Cohen, right?" One hand swiped at the wrinkles of his madras bermuda shorts. "Summer attire," Stefan Vogel remarked as he introduced himself. Roger grinned and tugged at the knot of his tie. "And this is Lois Rowland, our lead special educator."

Lois tucked a stray strand of nut-brown curly hair behind her ear as we shook hands. Seated around the table, we spent the next hour discussing all three of our sons, especially Steve.

I explained although Steve was fourteen months older than Michael, he lagged far behind him, not only in physical size and maturity, but academically as well. Despite his identification as "educable mentally retarded," there was little evidence he'd been exposed to much academic instruction in school.

"Even though Steve's just three months short of eleven, he can't read or add and subtract single digit numbers," I admitted.

Hearing myself say this sent shock waves through me. Once again, I wondered where Steve might be now if he'd been allowed to attend Port Jefferson's school with exposure to typical children. The familiar voice of Guilt whispered in my ear and I shifted uncomfortably in my chair. Have I been a strong enough advocate for him? Should I have fought harder? Should I have taught him myself?

Stefan and Lois completed their review of Steve's records and looked up at us. Hurriedly I broke the silence. "There is no way he would fit in with the kids in a fifth grade classroom," I acknowledged. "Anyway, I don't want him in the same grade as Michael." I paused and then added, "Actually his youngest brother Joshua has also passed Steven academically. I don't want Steve in second grade either." For just a moment a tentacle of doubt penetrated my resolve. What was I doing here? What was I asking for? In what grade did I think Steve belonged? Suddenly I realized that, other than my wish for Steve to attend school with his brothers, I had no idea how to make the experience worthwhile and meaningful, not just for Steve but for everyone else.

Lois responded in her soft earnest voice. "Having Steve at the Ray School will be a new experience for all of us. However, when I taught in New York City, the school where I worked had several children born with Down syndrome." I stopped twisting my watch. My anxiety dropped a few levels. "I know your son can learn. But I feel strongly the most important factor for Steve's success will be the teacher he has, not the grade level he is in."

The next words out of my mouth surprised even me. "Maybe, despite his age, Steve would fit best in a first grade classroom," I offered meekly. "That's about where he is academically, and he is very small for his age. Is there a first grade teacher who might agree to have him?" Startled, Roger swiveled in his chair and looked at me through narrowed eyes as if to say: *Are you nuts?* I felt foolish. My toes curled inside my loafers. An eleven-year-old in first grade?

Mr. Vogel cleared his throat to speak, but Lois replied, "Why don't you give Stefan and me a chance to talk and consider all options? We have well over two months before school reopens."

Mr. Vogel added, "I promise we will get working on this, and notify you soon with our decision. Be assured, *all* of your sons will be students at the Ray School."

My eyes widened and I covered my mouth to hold in the yelp of joy straining to escape. Roger raised his eyebrows and shrugged his shoulders. A smile softened his face. My skin tingled. Euphoria washed over me. I hadn't expected this kind of welcome, encouragement, or collaboration.

We waited until early August to tell the boys about our plans to spend a year in Hanover during their dad's sabbatical. Steve and Josh really didn't understand how long we would be gone, but tears trickled down Michael's cheeks as he absorbed our news.

"I don't want to leave my friends," he croaked. "And what about soccer? Will I be able to play soccer where we're going?"

"You're a pro at making friends," I assured him. "Not only will we sign you up for soccer, but there is a small ski hill practically within walking distance of the house we'll be renting, and a bigger ski area just ten miles north." For the past three winters we'd leased a small cabin in southern Vermont and both Michael and Josh had become accomplished skiers. "No more traveling long hours to ski! *And* Steve will be going to the same school as you and Josh!"

The tortured look on Michael's face showed me he didn't share my excitement about this last bit of news. A whisper of doubt nagged at my conscience. My desire to have Steve in the same school as his brothers was driving our relocation. But I really hadn't given much thought to how this would affect our other sons.

Later, when we were alone, I questioned Michael. "Are you concerned about having Steve in the same school as you? You went to the same nursery school together, but you probably don't remember that."

He shrugged. "I love Steve, but..." Michael rubbed his eyes, struggling for composure.

"But, sometimes having Steve for a brother can be hard, can't it? Like when you were a Cub Scout and Patrick made fun of him?"

"Yeah," replied my nine-year-old, his voice barely audible.

I placed both hands on Michael's shoulders and turned him slightly so we stood facing each other. "Being the 'new kid' is always hard, and it is true that Steve's presence may make it even harder." Michael's eyes bore into mine. "But you know Daddy and I will always be there for you. Right?" Michael nodded. "You aren't alone in this. We are a family and we will tackle this experience as a team."

Michael smiled and moved onto other questions: What was the name of his new school? Would his teachers at Scraggy Hill know he'd moved? Did they know he'd be coming back? Did his grandparents know we were moving? I did my best to reassure him.

TEN

New Kids, 1977

Two weeks later we settled into our rental house within sight of the Bernice Ray Elementary School. Earlier in the summer, as promised, we'd received an information packet from the school which included the boys' class placements and teachers. Steve had been assigned to a first grade classroom with a Mrs. Taylor. The packet also included a personal letter from Principal Stefan Vogel explaining the reasoning behind this decision. Both he and Lois, the SPED teacher, had had several discussions before deciding on Mrs. Taylor for Steve's teacher. She was an experienced educator and children of all abilities were valued in her classroom.

One evening the phone rang. The voice on the other end introduced herself as Margaret Taylor. She wondered if she could visit before school began and meet our family. Really? Relief filled me at the idea Steve would have a teacher who cared enough to do this. We set a date for the following evening.

The next night, after dinner, Steve bolted for the front steps to sit and await his new teacher's arrival. Finally, a car pulled into the driveway and a woman wearing a simple cotton print dress stepped out. Steve ran down the path and wrapped his short arms around her waist.

"You my teacher!"

"Hi, you must be Steve!" Margaret pushed her sunglasses up onto her caramel-colored hair and a broad smile spread over her tanned face. In that instant a bond formed—one which lasted for years.

Inside, introductions completed, we gathered at the dining room table. "Sit here," ordered Steve, pointing to the chair next to his. Michael and Josh sat tongue-tied. A real teacher! In their house! Steve, remembering what we'd practiced earlier, passed the cookie plate to Mrs. Taylor.

"You like cookie? Chocolate-chip. My favorite. I make 'em."

"You helped," corrected Josh.

After a half hour of idle chatter, Roger took the boys to the school playground so Margaret and I could talk privately. In a soft-spoken voice, she admitted to being scared and unsure of her ability to teach Steve. But she and Lois had met frequently over the summer to discuss strategies and she'd read what little she could get her hands on about children with Down's. I admired Margaret's openness and honesty. Several minutes into our conversation, I expressed my concerns about Steve's lack of experience in a mainstream classroom.

Margaret leaned forward, looked straight at me with eyes which resembled pools of chocolate syrup, and said, "This is going to work. I know it will."

"I hope so. I've waited a long time. After meeting Steve, do you think having him in a first grade classroom is the right placement?"

Margaret paused and her face clouded over. "You know, Linda, we're all pioneers here. But I firmly believe Steven belongs with his brothers at the Ray School. From what I've just seen, I think Steve will be very similar to the other children in my classroom—both in stature and development. Years down the road, this may not be the model others will follow. But for now, I think we are doing the right thing."

I nodded in agreement. Steve would fit in better with first graders than his age peers. "Are you concerned what the parents of your other students might think about having Steve in your class?"

"Because of his age, or because he has Down syndrome?"

"Ah...both, I guess." My throat felt dry and I took a sip of water.

Margaret shifted in her seat before answering. "In terms of age, I doubt that will be a factor. Given his size, no one would suspect Steve is almost eleven. And the fact he has Down syndrome is really not anyone's business. But if the issue arises, don't worry, I'll handle it!"

I exhaled deeply and felt soothed by Margaret's quiet fierceness and pluck.

By the time Roger and the boys returned, Margaret had left and three tired little guys were ready for bed. As usual, I said goodnight to Michael last.

"Steve is lucky," he commented.

"Yes, he is," I answered. "Mrs. Taylor seems very nice."

"That's not what I meant, Mom! She's nice and all, but I meant Steve is lucky 'cause he got to meet his teacher. But not Josh. And not me. We don't know what our teachers are like. Or the school. We don't know where our classrooms are or anything!" Michael's frown creased his brow.

"Do you feel like Steve is getting special treatment?" I asked, as guilt surged in.

Michael hesitated. "Maybe...nah...I understand...sort of..." Then he heaved a sigh before continuing. "I hate not knowing what school will be like. Or if I'll be able to find my class. What if I don't like my teacher, or make any friends?"

"I understand how you feel, really I do." I leaned forward and brushed his cheek with one hand. "Daddy and I are nervous too. And I'm sure Josh feels the same way as you."

"But not Steve!" Michael broke into a grin. "Steve never gets nervous about anything!"

"Perhaps not," I answered. I wished I really knew more about what went on in Steve's mind. Michael yawned and rolled over to one side. I swallowed the lump in my throat and silently pleaded to let this turn out for the best, for all my boys.

"Mom?" Michael's eyelids began to flutter. "Mom, can you and Dad call me Mike from now on? I like Mike better than Michael."

On September 7, the boys and I woke up early. Roger had left the day before to return to Stony Brook on business, leaving me to support our sons on their first day in a new school. We were all nervous, but I hid my anxiety from my sons. Mike and Josh tore through their bowls of Rice Krispies and headed to the garage to grab their bikes.

Riding to school without a parent alongside meant independence—an important step for them. Steve and I met his brothers in the driveway. I positioned Steve between the two and stepped back, my Kodak box camera loaded with a fresh roll of film.

"OK, guys—one, two, three—smile!" But no one did.

"Mom, can we go now...*pleeease*?!" Mike's anxiety had caused his face to look pale despite his summer tan. He pressed his lips tightly together. I nodded and they peddled off.

I drove the short distance with Steve, parked, and met his brothers at the entrance. Sensing Mike's increasing apprehension, I headed for his fifth grade classroom first. As we stood in front of room 212, I gave my son a quick hug. He took a deep breath and stepped through the doorway.

Steve was next. Standing at the threshold of Margaret's classroom, she spotted us above the heads of several children and moved toward us. "Hi, Steve, welcome to the Ray School. Let me show you your cubby with your name on it." I blinked back tears. This was really happening! Margaret continued, "You can put your things there and then go play with the other children." Without hesitating Steve put one trusting hand in hers and trotted in. I turned and walked away.

I'd saved Josh for last on purpose. He'd grown into a happy and well-adjusted little boy. He made friends effortlessly. I figured, of the three brothers, he'd have the easiest time being a new kid. As a second grader, his classroom stood just a few doors away from Steve's. "OK, bud, you're next," I said brightly as I moved toward his room. Silence. I looked behind me and there stood my youngest—sobbing, tears pouring down his cheeks. I knelt and pulled him close, momentarily burying my face into his mass of tightly coiled ringlets.

"Hey, Josh, what's the matter? Why are you crying?"

"I-I-I-I'm s-s-s-scared," he stuttered between sobs. "I don't know anybody. I miss my friends in Port Jefferson. What if I g-g-get lost in this school and c-c-c-can't find the bathroom?" My heart wept with dismay. Once again Guilt tickled the edges of my consciousness. What have you done?

"Shall we go find the bathrooms and make sure you know how to get there and back to your classroom?" Josh nodded dubiously.

A few minutes later we stood by the entrance to his room. "Remember? Your teacher's name is Mrs. Brown. There she is, over by the bookcase. Shall we go meet her together?"

"OK," whispered Josh, looking up at me with red-rimmed eyes. He slipped his hand into mine. Minutes later I hugged him goodbye and left, willing myself not to look back. I walked out of the school, climbed into the car, and burst into tears.

Josh's panic left me completely unhinged. Clearly my insistence on uprooting our family so Steve could attend school with his brothers and other typical kids meant I'd asked everyone—my family, as well as the educators here in Hanover—to leap into uncharted waters. Would mainstreaming work? I was asking a lot of Steve's brothers, and this morning had shown me just how scared these epic changes had left them.

ELEVEN

The Dream Year, 1977-78

Despite their initial fears, Mike and Josh quickly found their groove. For Steve, staying afloat in the mainstream took a prodigious amount of effort. Now instead of a small group of eight to ten special education students confined to one room, he was part of a school community numbering over four hundred students. During recess, for the initial week of school, Margaret and the other first grade teachers remained on the playground with their charges. Steve never strayed far from her, unsure of where to go, what to do, in a sea of active children.

As the school year progressed, teaching assistants took over recess supervision. Lois Rowland had anticipated Steve might take longer to figure out this unstructured time, so she'd arranged for an older student to be Steve's playground buddy and teach him the ropes. By October, Steve was happily on his own. As he became accustomed to the routines, his behavior evened out. He learned to wait his turn. His attention span increased as well as his ability to work independently. He accepted the reality that play time didn't happen until he completed all his assignments.

Throughout the year, Margaret Taylor remained Steve's champion. While Steve's strong desire to "be good" and fit in with his classmates sustained him, he also experienced frustration and could be very stubborn. One day, in a fit of pique, he fled into the classroom supply closet and despite Margaret's efforts, wouldn't come out. Knowing she needed to continue with the rest of her students, she told Steve he could remain in the closet as long as he left the door open so she could see him. Time passed and eventually Steve left his sanctuary and approached his teacher.

"Sorry," he mumbled, giving her a hug.

"Hi, Steve, do you feel better?" asked Mrs. Taylor.

At the end of the day, as the class lined up to go home, one little girl approached her. Referring to Steve and the closet incident, she remarked cheerfully, "Well, we made it through another day, Mrs. Taylor!" Then she ran over to Steve, gave him a hug, and told him she'd see him the next day. Triumph lifted me up when I heard this story. I felt I could let down my guard just a little.

The boys' adjustment allowed me to breathe and think about taking care of myself. The father of one of Josh's friends directed the Outward Bound Center at Dartmouth. I'd heard about this wilderness program designed to ask participants to step outside their comfort zones and push themselves both physically and emotionally. When I discovered the center had programs for women over thirty, I decided to investigate. The descriptive brochure promised the opportunity to gain confidence by meeting challenges in a supportive and compassionate group environment and transfer that newly acquired self-reliance to life at home. Immediately I knew this was something I wanted to try.

In early May, I left the boys and Roger—this time planning for my departure rather than running away—and joined nine other women enrolled in a ten-day canoeing expedition—the first time since Steve's birth more than eleven years ago I'd done something just for me. Led by two competent instructors, we camped and paddled on rivers and lakes in the Adirondack Mountains of New York State. I reveled in the physical tests the course offered. These included rock climbing and rappelling, setting up and breaking down our campsite each day, and portaging canoes and all our gear between lakes—including some where ice still clung to the deserted shores.

Just when I thought I was refreshed enough to go back to my life with Roger and the kids, the Solo was announced. Solo—days spent apart from the group—is the hallmark of any Outward Bound course. Solo provides every member with time for uninterrupted reflection, in a safe but isolated location, with just a minimum of supplies. I knew about the Solo but wasn't prepared for what would happen.

The two nights and days I spent alone had a powerful and transformative effect. With only the sounds of wavelets lapping against the shoreline, birds calling, squirrels chattering, and every now and then the eerie cry of a distant loon, I had time to consider what I wanted from my life—really wanted. I spent the days deep in thought. I wrote over thirty pages in my journal.

I was thirty-eight. Roger and I had been married for almost fifteen years. I'd done everything expected of me: birthed and raised children, kept the house, and moved when and wherever Roger's job took him. Sure, I'd had my teaching, but I knew full well my career played second fiddle to Roger's. For the first time I also acknowledged to myself something was missing from my marriage—Roger couldn't or wouldn't provide the emotional support I craved in our relationship. For this I'd always turned to my female friends, like Jane. But now, living in Hanover for the past several months, I'd found a place and lifestyle I loved. The peace in the pastoral countryside of rolling hills, crystalline streams and lakes, and distant mountain ridgelines filled me. I'd met several women who enjoyed the same activities I did: skiing, hiking, camping, running. I felt I'd found a true home.

On my final evening of Solo, as the embers from my campfire pulsed and glowed, I spoke aloud the truth I'd been keeping inside me. "I don't want to leave Hanover." I looked to the stars and asked my questions. "Why does Roger's job dictate our lives? What is my worth as a woman, anyway?" And then, a surprise question which would eventually lead me to truths I wasn't ready for yet: "Why can't I feel an emotional connection with my husband?"

Eventually I doused the flames, crawled under my tarp, and into the comforting embrace of my sleeping bag.

Two evenings later, at a campground just outside of Hanover, our group of tired but proud women gathered around our final Outward Bound campfire. Everyone had a chance to reflect on what they'd gained from the experience. Then, one by one folks stood and headed for their tents. I lingered with a few others listening to the crackle of pine knots exploding and watching sparks rise into a deep velvet sky. No one spoke, but within me the thoughts and questions that had found their voice during Solo continued to twist and turn.

The following morning, after more than a week in the wild, our group returned to civilization. After a much-needed hot shower in the Dartmouth gym, I found a pay phone, deposited two dimes, and dialed our home. I didn't know if I was ready to return to my "real" life, but those doubts vanished when I heard Mike's voice.

"Mommy!" he squealed after I greeted him. "Mommy! You're alive!"

When Roger pulled up to the curb in front of the gym, the boys tumbled out holding their homemade "welcome home" cards. Mike and Josh closed in and began peppering me with questions.

"Where'd you go? What'd you do?"

"Did ya see any bears?"

"Did ya go swimming?"

"Where'd ya go to the bathroom?"

Steve stood off to one side, a bewildered look wrinkled his brow. Then a smile lit his face and he stepped forward. "Mommy," he murmured, "I miss you." He melted into my arms.

Roger claimed to have fared well during my absence. After the boys were in bed, we sat together in the living room sipping beers and catching up. Roger handed me two sheets of lined paper folded in half. "This is for you," he said. "I decided to keep a journal while you were gone."

"Really?" I stared at him pop-eyed. "A journal? That's so unlike you! Have you ever kept a journal?"

Roger ducked his head shyly. "No. Never. But I really missed you and this just seemed like a way to stay connected to you."

As my eyes tracked down the first page, one entry stopped me short.

"I was very depressed on Monday. I ate a lot, and I have more understanding of what you face. It's hard to keep my mind on home, meals, kids, and work."

Welcome to my world, I thought.

Over the next few days, I struggled to return to my routine. My experience had left me unsettled, and yes, fearful of the future. On some level I knew I'd begun to travel on a new path. I knew the woman, wife, and mother who had departed just a week-and-a-half ago had metamorphosed on this trip. I was ready to spread my wings, break free of society's constraints, and follow my dreams. Would I have the courage to make that happen?

TWELVE

Momentous Decision, 1978-79

The end of our year in Hanover was in sight when I sat down with Roger several weeks after my return from the women's Outward Bound course. The stress and discontent which defined my days on Long Island had faded, replaced by quick laughter and close, connected friendships. I didn't want to be anywhere else. I didn't want to disturb what I saw as a positive status quo—not just for me but for our entire family.

Mike and Josh were living the life I'd longed for at their age—easy access to skiing in the winter, hiking and camping during the other seasons. And all three boys were making great friendships. Walking down Hanover's Main Street took twice as long if Steve joined me. *Everyone* seemed to know him. Steve's year at the Ray School had resulted in integrating him and connecting our family to the community beyond my wildest hopes. I didn't want him returning to the BOCES system in New York.

The final narrative reports from both Lois Rowland and Margaret Taylor filled me with elation and gratitude.

Lois wrote: "What can I say except that knowing and working with Steven has been one of the most wonderful experiences of the entire school year.... I feel Steven has helped *us* learn about sharing, caring, and working with one another."

Margaret Taylor began with, "Here I am again trying to express in words Steve's year in our class and in our school community." She ended her page-long handwritten statement with: "Being in our class has helped Steven choose appropriate behaviors. It hasn't all been easy, but we have all gained a sense of 'togetherness.' I love him. I will miss him."

My eyes burned as I read their comments. Thinking back on the endless hurdles I'd faced with BOCES, I felt vindicated. My advocacy for Steve had paid off. The understanding that our family would be returning to Long Island at the end of the school year had never dissuaded either woman from giving their best to Steve. They hadn't judged him by the way he looked, or what he couldn't do. Instead they'd seen him for who he was—a little boy without guile, who loved without reservation, who wanted to please and to learn.

Tentatively, like a turtle poking her head out from her protective shell, I broached the idea of staying in Hanover with Roger. I focused on our sons, especially Steve, and how well they had adjusted. Any mention of my needs—community, authenticity, choice—still felt too self-indulgent and uncomfortable. We both understood staying in Hanover would mean separating Roger from the rest of the family, at least for a while. In return for his paid sabbatical, he owed Stony Brook a year of work.

We agreed, for financial reasons, I'd need to find a teaching job if we were to stay in Hanover. I wanted to return to education anyway. Being a stay-at-home mom didn't work for me no matter where we lived. When I spotted an advertisement for a position teaching middle school social studies in the tiny town of Lyme, New Hampshire, ten miles north of Hanover, I filled out an application and mailed it in. Roger and I decided to let our final decision hinge on whether I got the job.

Some evenings I went to bed feeling certain remaining in Hanover could work for everyone. Other nights I tossed and turned, unable to fall asleep. What right did I have to push for this decision? What was I doing to our family? To our marriage? I conferenced with the Lyme principal and a couple of teachers, was selected as a finalist, and appeared before the school board for the deciding interview.

Ironically, I received the news I'd been selected as Lyme's new middle school social studies teacher on the day Roger and I had planned to celebrate our fifteenth wedding anniversary with dinner at the stately Hanover Inn. We were seated at a table for two in a corner of the elegant dining room. A vase of fresh flowers sat atop the white linen tablecloth while the piano player bent over the keyboard and classical music flowed from his dancing fingers. A waiter in black pants, a crisp white shirt, and a Dartmouth-green tie, took our drink order, handed us each a menu, and lit two tall tapers.

I looked up at Roger. "What are we going to do?"

He reached into his jacket pocket and extracted a small gift-wrapped rectangular box. "First, I want to give you this," he said with a smile. "Happy anniversary! Go on, open it!" My husband reached for my hand. "I thought you'd like this, especially after your Outward Bound trip."

I removed the wrapping and opened the box. Nestled on a bed of cotton batting was a Swiss Army knife with multiple blades and tools. "I love it!" I exclaimed. "It's perfect." Not many wives receive a jack-knife from their husband as an anniversary gift. But to me the present symbolized Roger's acknowledgement of who I was, what I valued. I knew for certain he had me on his radar. Something I hadn't always felt. I jumped up from my seat, moved around the table, and embraced him. A long kiss followed. I didn't care if other diners were watching. "Thanks. I love you," I whispered before returning to my chair.

I handed him my gift and watched as Roger tore open the wrapping to reveal a slim book I'd chosen carefully: *I Wish You Good Spaces: Poetic Selections from the Songs of Gordon Lightfoot.* Roger's face glowed in the candlelight as he read the opening lines of the initial poem aloud. "If you could read my mind, love, what a tale my thoughts could tell."

Then he looked across the table at me. "OK, so what we're going to do is go through with our plan. You take the job in Lyme. I'll go back to Stony Brook."

I gulped. My face flushed. My chest pounded. Had he really said this?

Roger smiled at my reaction and continued speaking. "It's easy to see how happy everyone's been here." I nodded and brought my linen napkin to my brimming eyes. "Recently I've had a series of promising conversations with folks here at Dartmouth. There is increasing inter-est in hiring me to join the community medicine faculty here. Folks are trying to put together a package, but it will take several months before anything is certain."

When we left the inn and walked into the warm June evening, I think we both believed a positive future lay ahead for our family.

With a clear path before us, the long-standing tension between us abated. I alerted the Ray School both Steve and Josh would be return-ing, and Mike would be attending the Richmond Middle School as an incoming sixth grader. Within days I received a phone call from Lois.

She and Margaret wanted to meet with Roger and me as soon as possible. My heart sank. What if they didn't want Steve back at the school?

"Thanks for coming," the two educators chorused as we entered the school's conference room. "We've been talking and have some ideas about Steve's program which we'd like to share with you."

My stomach stopped flip-flopping at their greeting. "Oh," I replied. "I was afraid you might not want Steve here for another year."

Margaret laughed. "Of course, we want him back! We figured you knew that!"

Lois took the lead. She explained they wanted us to consider having Steven do a second year with Margaret. "We realize there will be even more of an age gap, since Steve will turn twelve in the fall, but our thinking is Steve is close to being able to do first grade work, especially in math, and he is familiar with Margaret's routine."

"You know how much I love Steve," added Margaret, "even if he christened me 'Meatball.' Both Lois and I feel staying with me will be best for Steve. He feels safe with me."

I sat back in my chair. "Hey, I don't think either Roger or I need convincing." But I did have a concern. "I'm going to be teaching in Lyme," I told them. "I won't be able to spend much time at the Ray School, like I did last year."

"Steve will be OK," the women replied.

I thought so too.

Roger spoke next. "Not only will Linda be working full-time, but I'll be spending weekdays back in Long Island. Your decision makes sense. Consistency will be good for Steve."

Before concluding the meeting, Lois detailed some of their other thoughts for Steve. The biggest concern, and one Roger and I shared, was Steve's need to be with older children who could model more mature, age-appropriate behaviors. To some extent this occurred in the resource room since the groups there were multi-aged. However, they wanted Steve to have an extra period of PE once a week with a second grade class, and Lois wanted to build in some prevocational tasks for Steve to work on. These would include following three- and four-part directions involving mimeographing and collating work papers and running errands throughout the school. We agreed with their plan and left the building in high spirits.

We called a family meeting, to explain our decision to the boys. I started things off.

"We've decided to stay in Hanover for at least another year and I am going to be teaching middle school social studies."

"Does that mean I am going to have you for a teacher?" Mike's lips turned down, a frown creased his forehead, and his shoulders stiffened.

"No," I said and laughed. "Don't worry, you're safe. I'll be teaching in Lyme, not at your school."

"Good," he muttered, tension escaping his body like the air from an inflated balloon.

Roger jumped in. "During the week I'll be working at Stony Brook, at my old job."

"That's all the way back in Long Island," exclaimed Josh. His eyes clouded. "You can't drive back and forth from there every day!"

"No, I can't," agreed his father. "I'll be staying on Long Island with friends during the week and come up here for weekends and holidays."

Steve sat next to Roger on the couch, following the discussion, his head swiveling back and forth from speaker to speaker as if watching a ping-pong match.

Now, he leaned into Roger and reached for his hand. "I teeny bit worry about you," he said softly.

"Yah, me too," echoed Josh. "Why can't you just work here at the college?"

Roger explained the terms of a sabbatical and his hope that a job would develop for him at Dartmouth.

Josh frowned. "But what if that doesn't happen?"

We both assured the boys everything would be fine. They were too young to worry about such things. We focused on the positives. Steve would return to Mrs. Taylor. Josh's third grade teacher would be a man! And Mike was finished with elementary school. He'd be in a middle school, something which didn't exist in Port Jefferson. Oh, and we'd found a house to rent across the street from the college's practice football field!

"Cool," replied Josh. "Can this meeting be over now?"

Josh's dismissive restlessness left my stomach in knots. Regardless of age he *was* worried about his dad. And probably Mike as well. What would this decision cost our family?

The following nine months proved difficult for everyone. While the boys did well in school, they missed the daily presence of their dad. I had trouble switching gears from weekday single parent to weekend wife. Conflicting emotions warred within me. Gratitude and love for Roger's willingness to step off this cliff with me. Sorrow for his sadness about spending weekdays alone in Long Island. Self-questioning and guilt for pushing for this "adventure." Hopefulness and a shared optimism for our future. And underneath it all, a subconscious awareness which niggled at me—a truth about my sexuality which I couldn't or didn't want to address.

THIRTEEN

Lunch Alone, 1980

In late spring Roger resigned his position at SUNY Stony Brook and began a job in Concord, New Hampshire, with the State Department of Health. He commuted a total of one hundred and twenty miles each day. During the summer we became permanent residents of Hanover and moved into our newly purchased home—the boys' third house in three years.

As the school year approached, I sat down to talk with Steve about his new teacher. After two years with Margaret Taylor a change was due. He would be in a third grade class with Jack Wilde, Josh's teacher from the previous year. I felt having a male teacher would be good for Steve, fewer soft edges along with expectations for more mature behavior. I asked nine-year-old Josh to join us.

"Steve, you are going to like having Mr. Wilde. Remember, he was my teacher last year. He's really awesome," Josh assured him.

"I miss Meatball," insisted Steve, calling Mrs. Taylor by the nickname he'd assigned her. "I sad."

"No, Steve, don't be sad," Josh replied. "You're in third grade now. You're a big guy. And remember, you'll know a lot of the kids. They were in your class two years ago."

Although Steve started the school year stating, "I teeny bit nervous," he adjusted quickly. Third grade reading, writing, and math were too much of a stretch for him. Therefore, he spent much of the morning in the resource room before returning to Mr. Wilde's class in the afternoon for science and social studies.

One day in March I decided to surprise Steve during his lunch time. When I entered the cafeteria, I scanned the various clusters of third graders eating their bag lunches and enjoying their unstructured social time. I couldn't find Steve anywhere. And then I spotted him— a solitary figure seated at a table in the farthest corner—his lunch box opened, and the various ingredients spread around him. His hands clutched two Star Wars figures and he seemed to be engaged in a solo dialogue with the toys. My heart splintered at the sight.

Steve greeted me with a smile and a big hug. "Why you here?"

"Hi, Steve," I replied. "I thought I'd just stop by to have lunch with you. How come you're eating all by yourself?"

"It OK," he said and shrugged. "I happy."

But in that moment, I knew this "least restrictive environment" no longer fit Steve. He was a thirteen-and-a-half-year-old boy in an elementary school. Recently I'd noticed the few stray hairs sprouting above his mouth. His time at the Ray School had run out. I needed to start working on a change. For the rest of the day, the vision of Steve eating lunch by himself sat in my stomach like a lump of sour milk.

When Roger arrived home from work, I barely waited for him to take off his jacket and loosen his tie before describing the scene I'd witnessed. "Steve can't remain at the Ray School after the end of this school year. The gap between him and the other kids is widening. He needs to be with kids his age."

"But he told you he was fine," countered Roger.

"Well *I* don't think he is fine. Maybe he just doesn't have the words to describe how he's really feeling."

This discussion was typical of how differently Roger and I reacted to the same situation. As a mother, I was tuned into the emotional frequencies of all our children—both a burden and a blessing. I saw a wrong and wanted it righted. Immediately. Roger's response was always more measured, more cautious. He was never one to spring into action. He wanted to believe the lunch scene I'd witnessed was just a fluke, but my instincts told me otherwise. I made an appointment to meet with Lois Rowland.

In the conference room I described the scene I'd observed a few days earlier. Lois listened intently. "So, have you noticed anything like this before, or did I just stumble onto a one-time occurrence?"

Lois sighed and leaned forward in her chair. "At this age, children really begin to notice differences—both in themselves and in others. Friendship groups are beginning to solidify. Kids are more aware of the pecking order and how their actions affect their position in that order." She paused for a moment. "I don't think Steven's classmates are overtly mean to him, but they are certainly more aware than first graders of his differences, especially the immaturity he exhibits from time to time."

"And keeping up with the social dialogue during an unstructured time like lunch is hard for Steve," I added. I hoped I didn't sound bitter. "Maybe we should begin thinking about a different placement for the next school year. Maybe Steve needs to be in a setting with older children, so he can model their behaviors. Maybe it's time for Steve to go to the Hanover Middle School."

"I agree with you about Steve's need to be with older children, but Hanover Middle School won't work for him. There is no peer group for Steve there."

I raised my eyebrows. I wasn't sure what Lois meant.

Lois explained she felt Steve would do best in a setting where he could be with other teens with similar special needs. While he should be in a school with exposure to typical teens—kids who were his age peers if not his intellectual peers, he also needed a trained special educator as his classroom teacher. "There is a program like this at the Hartford Middle School, across the river in Vermont. I've heard the teacher there is wonderful. Hanover would pay tuition for Steve to attend and also provide transportation. I can arrange for you and Roger to visit. And I'll go with you, if you want."

Shock and disbelief tore through me. "But Lois, what you're saying feels like a return to the BOCES system we left back in Port Jefferson! I want Steve to go to school in Hanover. This is his community. Why does he not only have to leave Hanover to get an education, but travel to a different state as well? How does this program fit with the 'least restrictive environment' clause?"

"It doesn't," Lois replied bluntly. "And Hanover does need to develop a program to accommodate kids like Steve. Right now, however, Hartford is the closest option. Otherwise you might need to think about a residential school, and I know you don't want that."

I had no response for Lois. Her comment was a punch to my gut. My shoulders hunched and my arms cradled my stomach. Time stopped and I heard the words spoken by Dr. Tarbox so long ago: "You may want to consider institutional placement...." Hell no, Steve wasn't going to be sent hundreds of miles away to live in a segregated facility, isolated from his family and the general population. Any option was better than that.

But I still felt defeated. I'd fought so hard to bring Steve into the mainstream. I knew I had the law backing me up. Legally, I could insist on Steve's inclusion at the Hanover Middle School, but how would that benefit him? Who would teach him? Where would he find friends?

A few weeks later, Roger and I traveled to the Hartford Middle School to observe the Intensive Special Needs (ISN) class taught by a spitfire woman named Sima Paskowitz. Barely five feet tall and just over one hundred pounds, many of the nine teens in the room towered over her. A halo of frizzy auburn hair framed her face and her distinctive accent gave away her New York City roots. Yet with her business-like, bordering on brusque, personality, Sima projected the command of an accomplished conductor directing a finely tuned chamber orchestra. The students were continuously engaged, challenged, and learning. Sima didn't waste a minute. Slowly, I began to see possibilities.

An hour later, when the room emptied and the students, accompanied by Sima's aide, left for lunch in the school's cafeteria, Sima joined us at the table where we were seated. She wiped her palms on her brown polyester slacks, smiled, and said softly, "So, tell me about your son, Steven."

Sima listened closely while I told the story of Steve's twisted educational path. When I described his start at the Ray School as an almost eleven-year-old first grader she raised her eyebrows quizzically. "I really didn't know where he belonged," I said in what felt like an apology. "I just wanted Steve to go to school with his brothers. That's all I ever wanted." Sima said nothing, so I continued. "But now Steve is beginning to develop physically. It's obvious elementary school is no longer an appropriate location for him, but Hanover has no program for kids like Steve at their middle school."

"I understand why you felt the way you did when your family came to Hanover," Sima responded. Her compassionate tone disarmed my defensiveness, and my facial muscles relaxed. "The federal legislation is opening doors, but those doors were tightly shuttered for a long time. Honestly, most school districts in this area are still trying to figure things out."

Roger, who'd said nothing until this point, spoke up. "But doesn't that include Hartford Middle School as well? Yes, at least there is a program here, but from what I've observed this morning your students are still pretty segregated from the typical population."

Sima nodded. "This is only our second year here. Change takes time."

Yup, I thought. *I've heard that line before.*

"I was hired to begin this program by a district consortium of special educators, and I am looking for situations where I can integrate my students. But it's hard. No one knows these children or has had much exposure to kids like them."

I sighed. *Another familiar line.*

Sima continued. "At first the administration tried to put my class in one of the portable buildings. But I refused."

I smiled at the thought of this diminutive woman standing up to the principal and assistant principal—both males. I was beginning to like her! I needed to give her a chance.

"I told them these students, all of whom are between thirteen and fifteen, needed access to their peer group. Modeling of age-appropriate behavior by the school's typical population was critical. Every student in my classroom has matured considerably since we began over a year and a half ago," she stated firmly.

I felt much better on the twenty-minute drive back to Hanover. I would need to trust Sima, just as I had trusted the staff at the Ray School.

Decision made, I now worried about how to convince Steve it was time for another change. He remained blissfully unaware of the disconnect created by a thirteen-year-old attending a facility meant for first through fifth graders. I asked Mike, a seventh grader, to help me. I knew how much Steve admired his "big" brother. Playing to Steve's sweet tooth, we decided on an ice cream date for the three of us at Steve's favorite store, the Ice Cream Machine.

On arrival, Steve stared at the sign behind the counter. The one he knew listed the available flavors. The one he couldn't read. He looked at Mike. "Peppermint stick?"

"It's not on the list, Steve."

"Rats! How 'bout chocolate chip?" When Mike nodded yes, Steve grinned and added, "With chocolate sauce, Cool Whip, and cherry on top!"

Mike, never a fan of sweets, ordered a small dish of chocolate ice cream. We crossed the black-and-white tiled floor and slid into a booth with red vinyl benches.

"So, Steve, how's school going?" asked Mike.

"Good. I like it."

"Remember how I used to go to the Ray School?"

"Yup," said Steve with a nod. Cool Whip ringed his mouth and chocolate sauce dribbled down his chin. I handed him a napkin. Steve continued, "You not go there now. You go to big kids' school now."

"Right! But you are a big kid too! And even though I'm taller than you, you're older! You're thirteen."

Steve swiped at his chin "I know that, Mikey-Boy! I be fourteen my next birthday!"

"So, I think you should go to a big kids' school, like I do."

"You got that right," replied Steve. "I big kid. OK. I go to big kid school!"

And that was all it took! Once again Steve surprised me.

In May, Steve spent a day visiting Sima's classroom. When I arrived home from school, Steve produced a brief note from her indicating all went well. I asked Steve what he thought. He responded, "I like it. I like the big kids." He didn't seem to notice the school wasn't in Hanover, or that several of the teens in Sima's class, including a new friend named Fred, had Down syndrome.

Steve spent four rich years with Sima as his teacher at the Hartford Middle School. Academically he made some gains in both reading and basic math. But now the focus had shifted to life skills. However, Sima's high expectations when it came to age-appropriate behavior brought about the biggest growth in Steve.

Sima may have been small in stature but her belief in her students' capabilities was limitless. Since French language instruction was available to the general middle school population, she insisted that French be taught to her students as well. Steve embraced his French name, Etienne, and engaged in brief dialogues with typical students. Not only did Sima seek out opportunities to integrate her charges academically, but she also welcomed all middle school students to drop into the ISN classroom in the morning before the final bell sounded. A consistent self-selected cadre hung out with Steve and his friends and often reappeared during the lunch/recess period to play games or help Sima's students with reading or other projects. Overnight Steve transformed from a little boy into a teenager, including the use of an occasional swear word.

But this incredible educator also believed learning extended far beyond the classroom walls. When Sima noted one of the school's fifteen-seat passenger vans sat idle during most days, she asked the principal if her class could use it for field trips. Told the school didn't have the funds to pay for a bus driver, Sima obtained her commercial driver's license and she and her students hit the road. They visited bowling alleys, restaurants, and went shopping. On these excursions

Steve and the others learned to function in small groups with limited help from Sima or her aide.

Physically Steve changed too. He grew several inches, and his body thickened as he became more muscular. He started shaving regularly. His voice deepened. If I or anyone else referred to him as a boy, Steve quickly and firmly corrected the speaker.

"I not a boy. I a man."

Steve was right in ways he couldn't begin to comprehend. Behaviors which had upped his cuteness quotient now were unacceptable. Sima insisted that a firm handshake replace hugs. Our family struggled to come up with age-appropriate gifts for Christmas and his birthdays. What do you give a teen who still prefers watching cartoons and playing with superhero action figures? Who really can't read? Who's never learned to ride a bike? Who's never been on a high school sports team? Or gone on a date? Or been part of a band or chorus? Much later, throughout Steve's adult years, the yawning chasm between his age and his behavior would become even more troublesome.

FOURTEEN

Call 911!, 1983

"Mom, wake up! Something's wrong with Steve. He's bleeding all over!" Mike's almost sixteen-year-old face was inches from mine, his eyes wild with fear.

I flung back the covers and raced barefoot toward Steve's brightly lit bedroom. He sat in his bed, wide-eyed, a crimson geyser gushing from his nose, spreading over his Batman comforter.

Mike stammered. "His yelling woke me up. I tried to stop the bleeding, but I couldn't. It just keeps coming and coming."

Steve coughed and blood exploded from his nose. Spittle dribbled from the corner of his mouth and ran down his chin. "I scared! Why I bleeding?" At seventeen he still had complete faith in my ability to protect him.

"Mom, what's the matter?" I turned to see Josh, thirteen, standing in the hallway just outside his brother's room. His unruly curls were matted from sleep. He rubbed his eyes with one hand.

In a quiet voice that belied my fear, I told Mike to go downstairs and call 911. "Make sure you give them our address. Tell them your brother is bleeding. A LOT! We need help right away. Turn on the outside light and wait for the ambulance on the landing. Josh, grab another towel from the bathroom, then go to the kitchen, fill a bowl with ice, and bring it back upstairs to me. Hurry!"

I pinched the bridge of Steve's nose and told him to lie down. Almost immediately he gagged and vomited blood. "Shit, that's not right," I muttered. I pushed him into a sitting position, while I continued to apply pressure to his nostrils. "Tip your head back, Steve, and try to relax. Everything is going to be OK." I glanced at the clock radio on the nightstand: 4:17 a.m.

The whine of the ambulance's siren pierced the night and a revolving red light played a kaleidoscope pattern on the walls of the bedroom. Led by Mike, two burly guys stepped into the room, strapped Steve onto a portable stretcher, hustled him down the stairs and out the door. In the cold darkness, hands strained and guided the gurney toward the opened rear doors of the still running ambulance. As Steve's terrified face disappeared into that gaping maw, I began to crawl in next to my son.

"I'm sorry," said a uniformed attendant. "You're not allowed to ride with us. Meet us at the emergency entrance."

I stepped aside as he vaulted in next to Steve. "Oh…" I sputtered. The doors swung shut. "Oh!"

November's bare treetops glowed red as the vehicle descended our gravel driveway and headed to Hanover's hospital. I turned, raced up the steps, and pushed past Mike and Josh standing stunned and silent just outside the door of our mudroom.

In my bedroom I threw a sweater on over my nightgown, jammed my feet into the nearest pair of shoes, grabbed my purse and car keys, and flew back out the door headed for the carport.

"Mom!" Mike's voice floated behind me, "should I call Dad in Albany?"

In September we'd begun another commuter marriage. Two years earlier the job Roger had been waiting for at Dartmouth College opened, and he'd left his position at the New Hampshire State Department of Health in Concord. We both knew a grant-funded position came with risks, however the opportunity to work at an Ivy League school, in the town where we lived, had great appeal. Our family prospered. Our life seemed perfect. But in early spring came the news that the grant had not been renewed. On July 1 Roger joined the ranks of the unemployed, depressed and destroyed. Finally, in late August, he was offered a position at SUNY's Albany campus, which he accepted without hesitation. I was both relieved and happy for my husband but concerned. We'd agreed that moving the family so close to the beginning of school would be too disruptive. Mike, a high school junior, and Josh, an eighth grader, were old enough to understand our decision. Steve, soon to begin his fourth year in Sima's class, went with the flow. So, Roger found a room in Albany and made the three-hour commute to Hanover on weekends. Our idyllic way of living evaporated. And never was that more apparent than in an emergency like this one.

I skidded to a stop, turned, and faced Steve's brothers, still frozen in place. Illuminated by the porch light, their ghost-like faces seemed to float in the darkness. "No," I replied. "Don't call him yet. Let me get to the hospital and find out what's going on. You guys did a great job. Thanks." Then I added, "Steve's going to be OK. I promise." I knew I couldn't promise this, but I had to leave Mike and Josh with hope.

I careened down empty streets, past shadowy sleeping houses, with my heart thrashing, my body shaking. Was the prediction Dr. Tarbox made so long ago, that Steve wouldn't outlive his teens, about to come true? To whatever life force might be listening, I pleaded silently: *Please. Please watch over my son.* Within minutes I arrived at the hospital and raced into the bright emergency entrance.

Steve lay in a curtained treatment cubicle. A pale blue hospital gown replaced his bloodstained pajamas which sat in a tangled heap on a nearby chair. Medical personnel clad in white hospital scrubs clustered around my son, stethoscopes slung carelessly around their necks. Clear fluid dripped from an IV bag through transparent tubing into his left arm.

"Hi, Mom," croaked Steve. The cotton packed in his nostrils contributed to the stuffy tone of his voice. "I alive. I not die."

With a flick of her head, one of the nurses motioned for me to follow her into the hallway. The hemorrhaging had ceased, she assured me, and, for the moment, Steve appeared stable. Dr. Bill Boyle, Steve's longtime physician, had been notified and was on his way. I nodded and reentered the cubicle.

Steve's eyes locked on mine as I moved toward him. "I scared. Please, I no want you leave me again."

I reached for his hand, bent down close to his ear, and began to softly croon his comfort song. "I love you, Steve, even more than a bushel and a peck." I hugged my son around his neck. Steve sighed and his shoulders slumped. Eventually, despite the glaring lights, eyelids fluttered, and he fell asleep. I sat huddled in the bedside chair, alone with my thoughts. Shit, this is it. This is what that fucking doctor predicted so many years before. Steve's seventeen. He's not going to make it. He's not going to outlive his teens.

A few minutes later, a hand flung aside the cubical curtain. "Steve!" Dr. Boyle's voice boomed. "What are you doing here? The hospital called and told me you said to get over here quick! You woke me up!"

Startled, Steve focused his eyes and replied, "I sorry. I all bloody. I scared."

"Lemme have a listen, buddy."

Bill, a close family friend as well as the boys' physician, rubbed his hands over the chest piece of his stethoscope to warm it before gently reaching inside the hospital gown to place the diaphragm over Steve's heart. As he bent down, a shock of reddish-brown-turning-to-silver hair fell to the side of his high forehead, momentarily hiding the ever-present twinkle in his blue eyes. After listening intently, he straightened his sturdy frame and looked at me. "So...tell me what happened."

I took a deep breath and replayed the scene in Steve's bedroom. Bill listened without interruption. Compassion flooded his ruddy Irish face. When I finished, he said, "Sounds to me as though you, Mike, and Josh all did a great job under pretty trying circumstances." Then he explained he needed to talk with the emergency room physician and review preliminary test results.

When he returned Dr. Boyle informed me he was going to have Steve, who'd drifted off again, admitted to the hospital. He insisted I return home, check in with Steve's brothers, and call Roger. He also promised he wouldn't leave Steve's side until I returned.

Roger arrived from Albany shortly after noon. Steve's eyes lit up at the sight of his father when he walked into his room. "Hi, Pops, you want ice cream?" Roger held him in a long embrace until, with a muffled voice, Steve added, "Move please, I not see TV."

During the next several days, we took turns staying with our son. Steve seldom complained—except for when someone blocked his view of the cartoons that ran continuously on his TV. He didn't seem to mind the nose cannula that delivered oxygen, or the fact he remained tethered to an IV line. Despite being poked and prodded, he enjoyed the attention he received from his family and friends. Dr. Boyle checked in several times a day and Steve's cheery nature, sense of humor, and polite manners (all requests were delivered with a "please" followed by a "thank you") soon made him a favorite of the nursing staff. He especially loved the unending supply of ice cream, always there for the asking.

One morning Bill met Roger and me in Steve's room. He'd written orders for Steve's release. "It's going to take several more days before we get any test results," he said, hands jammed in the pockets of his long white lab coat. "Steve is stable, eating well, peeing and pooping on schedule. His color looks pretty good considering, and there's really no reason to keep him here any longer. I've arranged for oxygen to be delivered to your house. He needs to be on it at night. Once we have some information, I'll call you two and we'll meet to discuss next steps."

Roger and I brought Steve home in a wheelchair. The oxygen tank, attached to the back of the chair, looked like an oversized pistol in a giant holster. Steve loved the huge sign his brothers had created and hung in the kitchen.

"Welcome Home Steve," he intoned. "I read it!"

"Yup," replied Roger. "And look over there," he added, pointing to the dining table where the chocolate cake he'd made sat, along with wrapped gifts from Mike and Josh.

"Cake! And pink balloons! My favorite! We have party!"

As our family gathered around the table to celebrate Steve's return, one thought repeated in my head. Can I do this? Can I give Steve the care he needs? My new responsibilities loomed large.

With Steve home, I tried to convince myself the crisis had passed, and he was on the road to recovery. But one piece of information I'd gleaned over the years was that a significant percentage of kids with Down syndrome developed leukemia. I also knew that unexplained hemorrhaging could be a sign of this disease. I kept my grim thoughts to myself.

FIFTEEN

Death Sentence, 1983-84

Sunday evening Roger reluctantly returned to Albany, but I remained at home. A substitute covered my middle school social studies classes, using the detailed lesson plans I'd worked on over the weekend.

Steve slept in, often not waking before 10:00 a.m. I struggled to keep myself from peeking into his room every few minutes to make sure he was still breathing. He remained cheerful, but weak. Just getting up and dressed left him short of breath and turned the skin on his hands and face blue. The oxygen tank, with the coiled, snake-like tubing resting on top, lent a sinister presence to his bedroom. The bulky wheelchair stood folded in our mudroom, ready to be wrestled down the porch steps and wrangled into the rear of our wagon, for Steve to use any place requiring a walk of more than a few steps.

I had too much time to worry, wonder, and wait for Dr. Boyle's promised phone call. November meant a hiatus between Mike and Josh's fall sport, soccer, and their winter sport, downhill skiing, and without me having to ask, the brothers took turns coming home as soon as school let out. I'd head off for a much-needed run, my major stress reliever. I really didn't mind the frequent interruptions which broke the rhythm of my jogging as friends slowed their passing cars to ask about Steve or shouted inquiries from their yards. News travels fast in a small New England town. Every night, like clockwork, the phone rang at 7:00 p.m.—Roger calling for an update and a chance to talk with his sons. Finally, Dr. Boyle called. He had some results and wanted to meet with Roger and me.

On Saturday morning, November 19, Dr. Boyle met us in his office. I perched on the edge of my seat, clammy hands closed into tight fists, my heart pounding. Roger sat next to me, his face taut, lips pressed together in a thin line. He reached for my hand.

Bill leaned forward, glasses perched on his nose. The collar of a blue pinstriped broadcloth shirt peeked above his navy wool crewneck sweater, an elbow poked through a hole in one of the sleeves. He cleared his throat. "I'll start off by telling you that Steve doesn't have leukemia. With the nosebleed, that was my first concern. Fortunately, none of the tests, including the bone marrow sample, came back positive."

My cheeks puffed out as I released a relieved sigh. Roger gave my hand a reassuring squeeze. "That's good news," replied my husband.

"Yes," agreed Bill. "But you know Steve was born with Eisenmenger's syndrome—a fairly common congenital heart defect for babies with Down's. As a result, he has a hole, or shunt, between the main chambers of his heart."

Roger interrupted. "Yeah, Steve often tells people, 'I handicap. I have hole in my heart.'"

Bill smiled weakly and continued. "Steve's done amazingly well, but the cardiologist I consulted with feels the shunt may be enlarging and led to Steve's hemorrhaging."

A chill tore through me. "How could his heart cause him to bleed from his nose? That makes no sense to me!"

"The results of Steve's CBC led us to that conclusion."

"What's a CBC?" I asked.

"CBC stands for Complete Blood Count. We use the results to evaluate the three types of cells—white blood cells, red blood cells and platelets—that circulate in the blood. In Steve's case the lab's analysis showed his percentage of red blood cells is way out of whack—something in the neighborhood of sixty-five percent. The norm is around forty percent.

"The excess red blood cells are crowding out his platelets and lowering *that* count. Platelets provide the clotting factor in blood. My colleagues and I feel Steve's low platelet count caused the hemorrhaging. Good blood chemistry requires a delicate balance. For whatever reason, Steve's blood has lost this balance. Not a good sign."

My stomach lurched and my eyes began to fill. "What do you mean? What are you saying?"

"A runaway red blood count isn't compatible with life. Unless we can reverse this, Steve will continue to experience more and more bleeds over the next six months or so. Once he starts bleeding internally…"

"Isn't there anything you can do?" pleaded Roger.

Our physician and good friend shifted uncomfortably in his seat. "There just isn't much research on Eisenmenger's, especially with patients in Steve's age bracket."

I knew what Bill left unsaid; most patients with Eisenmenger's didn't live as long as Steve had lived.

Bill continued, "But I've consulted with specialists in other hospitals and we've come up with a plan. I just don't know if it will work."

Steve's treatment plan had a dual focus. First, by providing supplemental oxygen at night, the doctors hoped to increase the oxygen level in his bloodstream and reduce the need for the production of additional red blood cells. That might allow his platelet count to increase and prevent further hemorrhaging. Secondly, regular blood draws, phlebotomy, would also lower the red blood count. An abundance of red blood cells causes the blood to become sludgy, and flow poorly. Steve was at risk for a stroke. The combination of these two approaches might buy Steve some time.

The pessimist in me cut to the chase. "And if this plan doesn't work...If his blood chemistry doesn't balance...?"

"If we can't reverse this situation, Steve probably has about six months to live. I'm so sorry."

Like an eclipse of the sun, a sudden darkness seemed to fill the room. Steve has six months to live. Steve has six months to live. Those six words flashed like a neon sign in the dark recesses of my brain. *From this point on,* I thought, *life will be about getting ready for Steve to die.* How exactly does one prepare for the death of a child? Is it even possible?

There was really nothing more to say. Bill gave us each a hug and we stumbled out of the room.

We got into our car, our silence choking on our unspoken anguish. Roger headed north on Route 10, a two-lane road which paralleled the Connecticut River.

Then, without warning, the volcano building inside of me exploded. "I guess that doctor was right seventeen years ago when he told us Steve was unlikely to outlive his teens." Roger said nothing, but tears coursed down his face. "Shit! It would have been easier to have him die as an infant. How are we going to explain this to Mike and Josh? And our parents? I don't know how to deal with this, damn it." I began pounding my fist on the seat of the car. My right leg began to jiggle as the level of my panic rose. Guttural yells bounced off the interior of our vehicle. Roger remained mute, his lips pressed together in a tight line.

Eventually he pulled off the road onto a worn rutted track. "Let's walk," he said.

A trail led through a needle-carpeted pine grove to a rocky outcrop, before dropping down to the river. We'd been to this spot many times. We stood close together and watched the pewter-colored river make her inevitable way between the sepia grassy banks of late fall. My breath came in ragged gasps. A red-tailed hawk wheeled overhead; in the distance a woodpecker beat a staccato tattoo. We walked several miles and, as always, Mother Earth calmed and quieted me. As my breathing slowed, Roger draped his arm over my shoulders. His gesture comforted me. In that moment I felt connected to him, something I didn't often feel.

Dr. Boyle pushed us to get Steve back into school. "Steve needs normalcy in his life," he urged. "School will be good for him. And getting back to work at the Lyme School will be good for you. You can't dwell on an unknown future."

So, in December Steve returned to school on a part-time basis. He'd been asking daily, "When I go to school? I better. I miss my friends."

I met with my principal. He found a woman interested in splitting the school day with me. She had experience and would teach mornings until lunch. From the time I arrived at 11:30 a.m. until I left sometime after 4:00 p.m., I lost myself in my work. I didn't think about Steve or our family. But when I turned the car south toward home, rivers of grief washed over me.

Steve's quality of life became a huge concern, something I ruminated about constantly. What if Dr. Boyle decides he needs to draw blood more frequently and Steve's veins collapsed? What if just breathing becomes a struggle? What if he is in pain most of the time? None of this was currently true, but these negative thoughts flooded my brain.

Steve tolerated his new normal with courage and grace. He hated the weekly "stupid needles" but he loved teasing Dr. Boyle. Bill always focused intently when his gloveless hands performed the venipuncture. But the technology of the '80s often meant more blood was taken than needed to fill the vials. Once the tubes were filled, he dumped the excess into the treatment room sink and the crimson liquid frequently splattered.

"You so messy," chastised Steve. "You very messy."

Nor did Steve complain each night when I rolled the pale green oxygen tank next to his bed, placed the strapping of the nasal cannula around his head, and gently inserted the two prongs into his nostrils.

"Why I need that?" he asked every time.

"It's to help you get better," I replied.

"OK. Night, Mom."

Slowly life settled back into a rhythm. Gradually, Steve began to make progress. In mid-February Dr. Boyle released Steve from his nightly oxygen tether. Instead, he received oxygen for a half hour in the morning before getting out of bed. Blood draws were dialed back to every other week. Steve's numbers improved steadily, indicating a return to that delicate but necessary balance.

The approach of summer meant six months had passed since Dr. Boyle's prognosis. But I had difficulty letting down my guard. Maybe those aggressive red blood cells were hiding somewhere deep within my son, just waiting before they mounted their final vicious attack. Who could know for sure?

In May I made an appointment to see Bill. For weeks Steve had been asking the same questions. "I go Camp Allen in summer? I see my friends?" Over the past several summers, he'd spent two weeks at this special needs camp. I wanted him to go. I knew we all needed a break. But would he be safe?

"Don't ask me how or why," Dr. Boyle said as we sat together in his familiar office. "But I think I can proclaim Steve cured. The treatment plan seems to have worked. His CBC has been normal for several months now. You can tell Steve, no more 'stupid needles.' Although he still needs to regain some strength, he is on his way. Register him for camp, Linda. He's going to be fine."

No more death sentence? Steve is going to make it? I floated out of Bill's office and called Roger as soon as I got home. While he sounded relieved, he didn't seem to share my level of excitement. Perhaps he'd already come to this conclusion on his own? My run that afternoon seemed effortless.

In June as the school year ended, I resigned from my position at the Lyme Middle School. I made the difficult decision for a variety of reasons—many of those centered on Steve's brothers who'd never been told about Steve's six-month-to-live sentence. Mike, a rising senior who wouldn't turn seventeen until late November, was slated to be the varsity goalie on a talented soccer team. College loomed and I knew I would miss him. During the acute phases of Steve's illness, he had taken on a lot of responsibility, including grocery shopping and even making dinner on the nights when the thought of what to put on the table overwhelmed me. The previous November we'd barely acknowledged Mike's sixteenth birthday. He deserved more from me. And Josh would begin high school, still weighing less than one hundred pounds, gifted in all things athletic, but struggling academically.

Equally important, the past ten months had exacted a heavy toll on me. I felt burned out, a taut rubber band about to snap. The time for being Super Mom had passed. I needed some respite, some space for myself.

Our commuter marriage, with no end in sight, had once again begun to strain my relationship with Roger. Given Steve's illness, we'd never discussed moving the family to Albany. Weekends gave us less than forty-eight hours together—not much time to reconnect, bring each other up to date, participate in family and social events, and make love...something I knew Roger wanted and expected. If Sunday morning arrived and we hadn't had sex, the walls of our bedroom crackled with electric tension. I'd begun to dread the sound of Roger's car as it crunched up the driveway on Friday evenings. Sometimes I heaved a sigh of relief when Roger pulled away on Sunday nights, as the stress, which had been building steadily all weekend, melted like an ice cube dropped into a pot of boiling water. Maybe if the pace of my life slowed during the week, I'd do a better job of accommodating Roger's needs during the weekends. I felt I owed him and our family that much. Life, like Robert Frost's poem, "The Road Not Taken," seemed at a crossroads:

I hoped I knew which path to travel.

SIXTEEN

Turning Eighteen, 1984

One Friday afternoon in early September, Steve stood in the kitchen sorting through the mail I'd just dumped on the counter. Even though his eighteenth birthday was still several weeks away, he was on the lookout for cards.

"Mom! I got mail! This have my name on it!"

"So open it."

His stubby fingers wrestled with the envelope. I turned around as he handed the letter to me. "What it say? I not read."

The official heading of the Selective Service System sent a shiver through me, followed by a strangled snort of laughter. Good grief! This was ridiculous!

"What it say, Mom?" repeated Steve.

"Well, Steve, you're going to be eighteen soon."

"I know that!"

"And when boys…"

"I not a boy, I a man."

"Right. When men turn eighteen, they get a letter telling them they need to register for the draft."

"What that?"

"It's like an invitation to join the Army," I replied.

"No way! I not like guns! I say, no thank you!"

"Let's wait until Dad gets here tonight. You can show him your letter and tell him how you feel." I smiled to myself, imagining my husband's reaction. *This will be good for a few laughs*, I thought.

At dinner I hid my smirk behind one hand as Steve showed the letter to his father.

"Impressive, Steve! I'm sure the Army would love to have you."

Steve repeated his claim about not liking guns. "I say no thank you!"

"Excellent idea, Steve," answered Roger. "After dinner you and I will write a no-thank-you letter to the Army!"

Josh laughed, but not Mike. Now a sixteen-year-old high school senior, his brown eyes clouded, and a hint of a frown creased his brow. I paid scant attention. Although undersized at 5'7" and weighing 135 pounds on a good day, Mike was the starting keeper on the varsity soccer team. He'd earned the position through determined hard work and defended his territory fiercely. I figured he was probably thinking about the next day's game.

Mike headed straight upstairs to his room right after dinner. I decided to check in. "Hey, everything OK?" I asked, poking my head past the open door. He sat perched on his bed, mechanically rubbing oil into his soccer shoes. "You were really quiet at dinner and you don't look very happy now either."

"It won't be that long before *I* get a letter, Mom." He looked up at me. "And I won't be able to say 'No thank you.'"

A knife of concern stabbed me. "But you're not even seventeen yet. There's still a lot of time before you need to face this."

"Not if I want to go to college. I can't get a Pell Grant unless I sign up for the draft. A lot of the guys in my class have already registered."

Mike remained focused on his cleats. Clearly, he didn't want to continue our conversation, and I had to respect his wishes. But I had a hard time falling asleep that night. His words sat in my belly like a heavy stone. So, this is what boys his age discussed? I'd been so focused on Steve's slow recovery from the nasal hemorrhage last November, I hadn't considered what an eighteenth birthday meant to young males. Balancing the needs of three sons was like dancing on steel ball bearings spilled across a newly waxed floor.

On the weekend Steve turned eighteen, we hosted a giant party to celebrate his landmark birthday and his return to health. My lingering memory of Steve's frightened face gushing blood belied the happy guy who now greeted each new guest with whoops of joy and excitement. The boys' friends and ours packed our house.

Ann Patterson and Robbie traveled from Port Jefferson. A brief pang of envy flitted through me when Robbie entered clad in his blue-and-white Port Jefferson High School letterman's jacket—the one he'd received last winter after serving as assistant manager of the boys' basketball team. While it had taken our former hometown longer to implement PL 94-142, now Port Jefferson had moved ahead of Hanover. Unlike Steve, Robbie attended his local high school. The irony made my chest hurt.

Jane and Kevin came from Marshfield, along with their daughter, Heather, now a college student. My heart melted as I watched her and Steve embrace—her presence a strong testimony to the special connection the two still maintained.

"I not know you come!" exclaimed Steve.

"Of course, I came," chuckled Heather softly. "It's your birthday, Steve! I wouldn't miss your party!"

The evening was a joyous one for our entire family. Despite the cacophony of voices that swirled around me, I took a deep breath and felt a kind of spiritual peacefulness. My connection to our many supporters ran deep.

The official status of adulthood took on more interesting implications in mid-October of Steve's eighteenth year. One evening when the picture windows framed the blazing autumn leaves outside, a very disgruntled Steve sat down to dinner.

"What's wrong?" asked Josh—the brothers were always sensitive to Steve's moods.

"Stupid speech on TV," grumbled Steve. "I miss Mr. T. show."

"Campaign speeches! Who was it this time—Mondale or President Reagan?" wondered Mike.

When Steve replied it was the president, Mike did his best to reassure his brother. "Steve, the election will happen soon, and you'll be able to get back to your shows." Mike paused, then his face broke into a grin. "Hey, you know Steve...you could vote! You're eighteen."

"I vote?" Steve's narrow eyes widened. "Yes! I do that!"

I shot Mike a loving smile. I'd never considered that possibility.

Before registering Steve as a voter, I checked in with Hanover's town clerk. I wanted to make certain there'd be no roadblocks to dismantle. She greeted me warmly as I walked into her office and explained why I was there.

"That Stevie! He is such a sweetheart! How is he doing?"

Like most people in town, Jeanette knew about Steve's hemorrhage. I shook my head to release those memories.

"He's doing great. Is there anything in New Hampshire's regulations that would keep him from registering to vote?"

She assured me Steve met all the qualifications: U.S. citizen, eighteen years of age, and a resident of the state. "You just bring Stevie right in here, and we'll get him all set up. Make sure to bring his birth certificate and if you have something addressed to him as proof of residence that would be helpful."

Yup, I thought, *there's the letter from the Selective Service. Good for something.*

The following day after school, Steve and I drove to city hall and Jeanette's office. Steve headed straight for her desk brandishing his birth certificate. "I born," he exclaimed. "I eighteen. I vote!"

As soon as Steve got home, he drew a circle around Tuesday, November 6—voting day—on all five of the calendars he kept on his desk. Steve left nothing to chance.

In school, when Sima heard Steve tell his classmates he was going to vote for president, she developed a unit around the election. She encouraged Steve's friends who were eighteen and older to become registered voters. She provided sample ballots for the class and together the students studied how to recognize the names of the candidates and mark them. Sima also emphasized that voting was both a privilege and a private act. The choice to support a particular candidate was theirs and theirs alone. For Steve and his friends, having a true choice in any matter was something they seldom experienced. The opportunity to pick his candidate filled Steve with pride and self-importance.

One evening at dinner Steve tapped his fork against his glass of milk. "Attention, please! I have announcement!" Assured he had everyone's full attention, he stood up. "Ladies and gentlemen. I vote for Mondale. Mondale for president!" Then he took a bow and sat down.

"Steve," Mike asked, "how did you decide to vote for Mr. Mondale?"

We were all curious. His dad and I were firmly in the Mondale camp, but we'd been careful not to voice our opinions within earshot of our son. Steve had told us many times, "Voting private. Paskowitz say so."

Steve explained that he'd kept track on his calendars of every TV show he'd missed due to campaign speeches. He'd lost more shows to Reagan than Mondale. Thus, Steve had thrown his support to the less intrusive candidate!

No one laughed. Then Mike added what I had been thinking. "Sounds like you've made your decision, and your reason makes as much sense as anything else I've heard." Steve beamed. I glanced around the table, drinking in this moment.

Roger brought home a Mondale campaign button for Steve. Every morning, as he dressed, I helped him pin it to his shirt. He proudly wore the image of his candidate but wondered about the two donkeys (which he called horses) placed on either side of Mondale's portrait.

Monday evening, November 5, Steve reminded his brothers several times, "Tomorrow voting day. Tomorrow I vote." He was keenly aware the next day he would be doing something neither one of them could do.

Late the following afternoon, Steve sat beside me as I backed our Ford wagon down the driveway and headed for Hanover High School's gymnasium, the town's official polling place. Dusk was rapidly approaching, and a biting wind created mini-tornados of dead brown leaves as I parked.

Steve did a double take when we entered the gym. Parka-clad voters navigated slowly through a maze defined by sections of rope looped through stanchions. I directed Steve toward the serious-looking woman seated behind the placard labeled "A-F."

Steve stepped forward and announced, "I Steve Cohen. I vote."

If the gray-haired official behind the table noticed anything different about the five-foot-tall young man, bundled into a navy blue parka with a New England Patriots cap sitting atop his dark brown hair, she kept her face neutral. She found his name, and without hesitation handed Steve his ballot.

Steve stared at the folded paper in his hand. "Now I vote," he declared.

I pointed to an empty booth. "Do you want me to go with you?"

"No way! I a man. I do it myself."

As he slid the red-white-and-blue-striped curtain closed, I hardly noticed the other voters who moved around me. I didn't hear the muted voices in the crowded gymnasium. Instead I focused on the pair of slightly bowed, jean-clad legs with the rolled-up cuffs behind the curtain. My heart swelled and I swallowed hard. I thought about obstacles faced and opportunities denied over the last eighteen years. Steve's vote was only one among millions, but it was a vote of an eager, proud, and plucky participant with a huge heart.

Steve's sneakered feet shifted from their pigeon-toed stance and pivoted. The curtain swayed and Steve emerged beaming. "I done, Mom. You go now."

I moved toward the booth with a deeper appreciation for our country and the democratic process. As I marked my ballot, I realized that I had just witnessed my son take an important step toward adulthood.

"I hope Mondale win," said Steve as he and I drove home. I couldn't tell him then what I, and just about everyone else in America, knew—not a chance!

While Steve's eighteenth birthday gained him the right to vote, Roger and I didn't realize that, in the process, we'd lost our parental rights. But thankfully Sima knew. She alerted me. We needed to file for legal guardianship.

I called the county probate office and began one of the more bizarre journeys of my life. The clerk who answered the phone confirmed that yes indeed, when Steve turned eighteen the right to make decisions regarding his education, finances, medical care, and so forth belonged exclusively to him. Did I feel the individual in question was competent to manage all aspects of his life? Hardly. After hanging up the phone I calculated just how many days had I been Steve's mother. The answer: 6,750. But now I needed to go to court to legally continue in that capacity. I hadn't had much time to ponder the whole concept of guardianship. In reality Steve was just a day older. But now the rules had changed. I couldn't shake the feeling that the court date constituted a test of my parenting.

On the designated day, my mood matched the dreary late November landscape as the three of us made the forty-minute drive to Haverhill, New Hampshire, and the Grafton County Courthouse.

Inside, the receptionist took our names, and soon a gray-haired woman dressed in a black skirt with a matching suit jacket approached us. She smiled warmly and introduced herself as Mrs. Bennet, Steve's court-appointed attorney.

"Cool," exclaimed Steve.

Roger and I had painted a broad-stroke picture for Steve of what would happen. Because he'd turned eighteen, the law required he decide if he wanted us to continue taking care of him and making decisions for him. The determination would be made in a courtroom. In front of a judge. He would have his own lawyer. "I like it," he'd told us. "Whole truth and nothing but the truth." Now Steve rose from his seat and disappeared with Mrs. Bennet through a set of swinging doors.

We met our attorney, Mr. Clark, for the first time in a small conference room. Dressed in a rumpled suit, the folds of his neck strained at the collar of his dress shirt. His meaty hands shuffled though a morass of papers until he found what he was looking for. "Ah," he breathed. Speaking rapidly, he assured us he'd filed all the necessary documents and stated the hearing would probably last less than an hour. "This really isn't a big deal."

You have no idea how big a deal this is, I told myself.

I'd never been in a courtroom before and my nerves jangled and rubbed against each other as we entered the dark-paneled room and moved down the inclined carpeted aisle, led by Mr. Clark. Two mahogany tables stood in front of the railing which marked the end of the public viewing area. Mr. Clark pointed to the table on the right and we took our seats.

Within minutes Steve and Attorney Bennet sat in their seats on the left side. I swallowed hard as I looked across the aisle at our son. Was I seen by the court as Steve's adversary? Steve smiled and waved. The court stenographer entered and sat at a table below the bench.

A uniformed officer strode in and drew himself to attention. His voice echoed in the vast quarters: "All rise."

A door opened in the dark-paneled wall in the front of the room. A distinguished-looking judge entered in his black robe and took his place behind the bench. I reached for Roger's hand. Everyone sat down.

Steve grinned and shifted in his seat as the judge banged his gavel.

Roger muttered, "This is ridiculous."

But I reacted very differently. My hands felt clammy. My eyes blinked rapidly. The scene before me sped by at a pace I could barely follow. A sudden, illogical fear gripped me. Was my son about to be taken from me? A kaleidoscope of events paraded before my eyes. Over the past eighteen years I'd made a ton of decisions for Steve, especially in the areas of his education and his heath. Had those been the right decisions? The judge's somber voice penetrated my anxious fog.

"Will the respondent please stand?"

Steve's attorney cued him, and he jumped to his feet.

"Please state your name."

Steve frowned, crossed his arms in front of him, and shook his head. Attorney Bennet rose and spoke quietly to her client. Steve's head moved from side to side. I began to get up, but Roger put his hand on my knee.

"No, stay down. This is going to be good. Let them figure this out."

After a whispered conversation, Steve's counsel cleared her throat. "Your Honor, if it please the court, my client refuses to speak until he's been given the oath."

The judge looked flustered. "But that's not necessary in this case."

"I understand, Your Honor, but my client thinks it is."

My inner turmoil evaporated. I lowered my head and tried to swallow my laughter.

The judge reached under the bench, produced a bible, and intoned the oath: "Do you solemnly swear to tell the truth, the whole truth, and nothing but the truth, so help you God?"

"I do," exclaimed Steve. Then he added, "Amen!"

"Thank you, Mr. Cohen. You may be seated."

"You welcome, Judge!"

The magistrate smiled and turned his attention to Roger and me. Anger rose inside me when he said, "Will you both explain your relationship to Mr. Cohen?" I wanted to say: *I'm his mother, for fuck's sake!*

"Mother," I muttered.

Several questions followed. Roger provided the answers as my brain screamed against the utter ridiculousness of this inane procedure.

"What is the nature of your son's disability?"

Really? Wasn't that obvious?

"Do you feel your son lacks the capacity to make his own decisions?"

In certain cases, hell yes.

"Are you capable of fulfilling the duties required of a guardian?"

Apparently, since we'd been doing so for over eighteen years.

"Do you understand as guardians that you will be under the supervision of the court?"

Are you serious?

Satisfied, the judge looked across the room at Steve. "Mr. Cohen, do you agree to have the petitioners appointed as your legal guardians?"

"What that mean?" asked Steve.

Mrs. Bennet spoke in his ear.

Steve grinned. "No way!"

I looked at Roger. Fear rushed back in. *What?!*

"Is there someone else you'd prefer?" asked the judge.

My lips trembled. What was going on?

Steve stood. "I want Madonna and Mr. T!"

Strangled laughter from both Roger and me earned a reproving glance from the beleaguered magistrate. "I'm afraid that's not possible," he replied. "Will your parents be OK?"

"Rats! OK, I take Mom and Pops."

"Thank you, Mr. Cohen." Then the gavel sounded, and court was adjourned.

The sun was setting as we pulled out of the parking lot and headed south to Hanover and home. Steve, seated between us on the front bench seat, asked, "I do good?"

Roger laughed and draped his right arm over his shoulder. "You were great, Steve! Awesome, in fact! I'm sure the judge will remember you for quite some time!"

Steve sighed and leaned his head on my shoulder. "I have fun," he murmured. Within minutes the car's motion lulled him to sleep.

I looked across him toward my husband. "Hey, Rog, what did you do with the no-thank-you letter Steve wrote to the Selective Service?"

"Huh? I threw it out."

"What about the draft notice?"

"That too. What made you think about that stuff today?"

"I guess I'll always feel this whole guardianship thing started the day Steve got that letter." I paused and then asked, "Wait? You threw out the draft notice?! Isn't that illegal?"

Roger took his eyes off the road to glance in my direction. "You really think the Army is going to go after Steve? There's got to be a few perks for having Down syndrome!"

"But it's not going to be the same for Mike. Or Josh, either, for that matter. They could be drafted. They could end up going to war."

Suddenly I fast-forwarded to the not-too-distant future, when first Mike and finally Josh would turn eighteen. I wasn't questioning my decision to have more kids after Steve's birth. I knew while Steve's younger brothers had helped him, the learning had gone both ways. But having Steve for a sibling hadn't always been easy. After all, Mike had been involved in a fight because of Steve. And Josh? My youngest wore his heart on his sleeve. His concern for his oldest brother was always with him. They would make their own decisions, ones that I might question, but couldn't legally oppose. Eventually they would leave the nest to pursue their own independent lives. Steve had required so much of my attention and time. Had I done enough to prepare his brothers once they legally became adults?

Dusk closed in and Roger reached for the knob that controlled the headlights. A cone of light illuminated the deserted country road. "You're right," he said. "But for today, Steve's guardianship hearing is all I can handle." With that he turned on his favorite classical radio station. He was done with the discussion even if I wasn't.

On the drive home, my mind continued to process the day's events. Once more the scene tilted. Anxiety flooded me. My legs felt restless. I couldn't get comfortable. I had just signed up, along with Roger, to assume complete responsibility for all Steve's affairs. Always. Meeting his needs as a child had never seemed hard. But would I be able to meet Steve's needs as an adult? What would that look like? Would Steve live at home forever? Would he ever have a job? What if his CBC became imbalanced again? Could Steve come back a second time? A jolt of fear stabbed me. Anxiety turned to agitation. *Jesus, Linda! Stop it. Slow down!* I closed my eyes, took several deep breaths, and focused intently on the soothing sounds coming from the radio. *Stay in the present*, I counseled myself. *That's all you can know for now.*

SEVENTEEN

Adjustment Needed, 1985

Supporting someone like Steve called for endless acuity. As with his brothers, change was a constant in his life. But with Mike and Josh I'd set them on course and as long as the wind blew from the same direction, I watched them sail away. For Steve the waters were far more turbulent. The winds swirled and seldom remained steady for long. His sails required constant trimming.

By spring of 1985 Steve's stamina was close to normal and he'd returned to a full-time school schedule. He'd spent four years with Sima Paskowitz, and the class continued to be based at the Hartford Middle School. Come September Steve would turn nineteen. Roger and I held renewed hope for his future. It was that hope which led me to meet with Sima in early April.

I arrived at the Hartford Middle School during dismissal time. Steve was already on the short bus which transported him back and forth from our Hanover home. As I headed toward the entrance, I watched the hordes of children—twelve- through fourteen-year-olds—surge out of the building. Compared to Mike and his friends—all high school seniors—these students looked so young. Sima was waiting for me in her empty classroom. We exchanged the usual pleasantries, and then I began.

"Sima, first of all I just want to acknowledge again how much Steve has progressed with you over the past years."

Sima smiled, unfolded her hands on the student desk where she sat opposite me, and said softly, "But…"

"Yeah, but...," I replied. "Over the past several months Roger and I have finally allowed ourselves to imagine Steve as an adult. Something we've never really done before."

Sima's eyes moistened. "And what do you both see?"

"We're hoping someday Steve will have a job and maybe eventually live on his own."

Sima nodded. "And for that to happen, his educational program and placement need to change."

I relaxed. *Yes, she gets it!* I'd worried Sima would feel we didn't appreciate all she'd done for Steve.

"Your goals for Steve are reasonable. And I am so glad you see a future for Steve beyond living with you. Many parents can't envision that. They are content to have their children remain with me here until they age out after their twenty-first birthday."

"That's not what Roger and I want for Steve," I replied. "He's learned a lot with you, but now he needs exposure to older students, as well as job and life skills training."

"You're absolutely right," answered Sima. "He needs to be in the Diversified Occupations program."

Sima had begun taking her students across campus to the high school DO program three afternoons a week. DO provided an opportunity for students with mild developmental disabilities to engage in hands-on exploration leading to entry-level employment in fields such as culinary arts, greenhouse operations, and health services. A second component focused on Activities of Daily Living (ADL) skills: grocery shopping, basic cooking, laundry, and housekeeping.

"Do you think Steve could be successful in the DO program?" I asked.

"Yes. Some adjustments will need to be made to accommodate him." Sima paused and a frown passed across her face. "But those changes are past due."

"So how do we make that happen for Steve?"

Sima leaned in toward me. "Ask for a change of placement at Steve's annual Individual Education Program meeting. I know it's a cliché, but the squeaky wheel does get the grease!"

On the morning of the IEP meeting, Roger and I arrived at the Hartford Middle School ready to fight for our son. Unlike many dads of this era, Roger seldom missed one of these sessions. Although I'd always done most of the weekday parenting, I never needed to ask him to attend a school function for Steve or his brothers. Once the date was on the calendar, Roger found a way to be present, even if, as in this case, it meant making the three-and-a-half-hour drive from Albany the night before.

We walked into a sterile conference room and were greeted by the other attendees—Sima, the middle school guidance counselor, and the special education directors from both the Hanover and Hartford school districts. IEP meetings were the only times we ever saw the latter two. By now, I'd learned what to anticipate at these gatherings. Although parents were supposed to have a voice in the development of their child's IEP, I knew the document had already been written. The expectation was we would go along with the recommendations and make few, if any, requests for changes. I suppressed a smile. Not this year! We were about to dump something very unexpected onto their collective plates.

Copies of Steve's IEP for the upcoming 1985-86 school year were passed around and Hanover's SPED director, Dr. Robert Height, professionally attired in a navy blue suit, opened the meeting. First came a summary of Steve's present levels of performance (or PLOP!), followed by a list of measurable goals. I sat quietly waiting for what I knew was coming: the placement decision for the next year. Steve's recommended placement was the same as it had been for the last four years: "Intensive Special Needs class with as much mainstreamed activities as possible." That was my cue.

"Actually, my husband and I want a change of placement," I stated. "Next fall we want our son based at Hartford High School and enrolled in the DO program." I smiled, displaying a confidence I didn't feel, and looked around the table.

The SPED director from Hartford raised his eyebrows. Sima and the guidance counselor smiled and nodded their heads. Dr. Height tugged at his tie and shifted uneasily in his chair. Technically, since Steve's place of residence was Hanover, this gentleman was responsible for our son's educational program. "I thought you and Dr. Cohen were pleased with Mrs. Paskowitz's instruction."

I took a deep breath and fingered the string of brightly colored beads of my necklace which lay against my white cotton-eyelet blouse. *Here I go—ready or not.* "Our request is based on Steve's age, not Mrs. Paskowitz's competence. He should be in a high school, not a middle school." The director's mouth turned down and a frown creased his brow. I ignored his obvious displeasure. "As an adult, I want him to have the skills to live as independently as possible. And I want him to have a job. The DO program can help him achieve those goals." Then I added, "Do you really feel individuals in their late teens and twenties belong in a middle school?"

Ever the diplomat, Roger adjusted his glasses and jumped in. "I believe Linda's point is well taken. Steve needs to be in a high school environment in order to mature. I think we would all agree that while Steve is capable of learning, acquisition of new skills takes time for him. And time is running out. We feel placement in the DO program affords him the best chance to move toward independence on all levels."

Roger reached into his worn leather briefcase and removed the *Parental Rights in Special Education* document. "I know you are all familiar with our rights as parents, but just allow me to read the first sentence under Least Restrictive Environment." He paused momentarily and began. "'You have the right to have your child educated to the fullest extent possible in the same environment as non-handicapped children.'" Roger removed his glasses and looked around the table. "How many non-handicapped eighteen- and nineteen-year-olds are being educated in this middle school?"

His question quivered in the air and the room remained silent.

Dr. Height found his voice and began to speak. Rapidly. "Oh. Well. We weren't aware that you wanted a change in placement. We really can't do anything this late in the school year, and..."

I couldn't hold my frustration in check any longer. I put my copy of the IEP down and broke in. "I'm sure you remember less than two years ago we were told Steve might not live another six months." My chest clenched. "We didn't fight like hell for his recovery only to have him parked in the intensive needs class until he ages out after his twenty-first birthday. By law Steve is entitled to three more years of public school education. He needs a program which will give him the skills to function as an independent adult." I grabbed a much-needed breath before finishing. "I won't sign off on this IEP as it is written." I raised the document and brandished it in the air. "Steve deserves more, much more."

The director's face flushed red. His eyes refused to meet mine as he cleared his throat. "I see. Well, uh...uh...Mr. and Mrs. Cohen...," he stammered, "I could share your concerns with the DO instructors. Also, we will need to do some further assessment of Steven to ensure we develop a suitable program for him." His colleague from Hartford nodded vigorously. "How about we write in an addendum to the IEP?

One outlining the steps we will take to provide Steven with a curriculum more in line with your and Dr. Cohen's wishes for your son?"

I nodded curtly and added, "Let's get started."

By the end of the meeting the typed IEP included the following hand-written amendments: "Schedule a vocational evaluation, and a full psychological evaluation over the summer. Schedule an IEP meeting in the fall to write DO transition plan." Roger and I signed the IEP, knowing Steve might never become a high school student. We still had a prodigious battle on our hands.

"These meetings leave me feeling angry and frustrated," I sighed to Roger on our way back to Hanover. "It seems like the special education system is always one step behind where Steve needs to be."

I was so tired of fighting the educational bureaucrats and once again Guilt sat on my shoulder. How had I failed to noticed Steve's sails needed an adjustment? I'd let him remain in elementary school for too long. Now I'd repeated my mistake with middle school.

In June, Mike donned his maroon cap and gown and graduated Hanover High School. As he received his diploma, a shiver of unease caused me to tremble slightly. Of course, I was proud of Mike, but I also shared the familiar conflict mothers experience as a child fledges and gets ready to leave the nest. At summer's end Mike would head off to college. And with his departure, once again the question of whether the rest of the family should stay in Hanover would rise to the surface.

Roger had been living and working in Albany during the week for two years. With financial help from his father, we'd recently purchased a three-story brownstone in the heart of the city. Currently he lived on the first floor and rented out the other two levels. But the long-range plan was to convert the building back to a single-family residence. We'd both agreed Mike should complete his education at Hanover High School. Now, it seemed equally important for Josh to continue at Hanover High with the friends who'd done so much to support him during Steve's illness. And really, neither Roger nor I was eager to move Steve out of Hanover. We wanted him under Dr. Boyle's care. We also wanted him stay with Sima as his teacher and hoped her class would move to Hartford High School. But once Josh graduated high school in three more years and Steve aged out of the school system at twenty-one, what then? For me, remaining in Hanover indefinitely didn't seem feasible. Roger would want and expect me to join him in Albany.

Becoming Real, 1985

Once Mike's graduation was over, I pushed aside my thoughts of an eventual move. In January I'd enrolled in a graduate-level course in general counseling. I'd enjoyed the intellectual challenge and decided to pursue a master's degree in Guidance and Counseling. For the first six weeks of summer I'd be commuting daily to Plymouth State College in New Hampshire, an hour's drive from Hanover. Both Mike, seventeen, and Josh, fifteen, had jobs in two of the town's restaurants. I didn't want Steve spending long days alone at home while his brothers worked and I was in class. Roger offered a solution. Steve could live with him in Albany Monday through Friday and attend a day program the city ran for disabled teens and adults. That arrangement left me with the freedom to come and go as I pleased, something I hadn't had for years.

In July I called a friend I'd met over the winter during the counseling course and suggested we meet for dinner followed by a movie, *Prizzi's Honor*, a mafia tale staring Jack Nicholson. Sitting in the darkened movie house with Maggie, our knees brushed together, and an intense tingle moved up from my groin toward my stomach. I ignored the sensation. But when our legs touched a second time and I felt the tingling again—and again, and again—I had to wonder. What the hell was going on? I knew I'd never felt this level of arousal with Roger.

The drama on the screen ended, the lights rose, and we headed for the lobby. But within me the drama continued to play. For years I'd had little desire for sex with Roger. Internally I'd felt dead for a long time. Now the intensity of the rush I'd just experienced left me reeling. A part of me wanted more.

"Did you like the movie?" I asked.

"Yeah, I did. Where'd you park?"

"I walked," I replied.

"Do you want a ride home?"

"Sure, that'd be great."

As Maggie's car pulled into my driveway, I asked politely, "Do you want to come in for a glass of wine? Steve's spending the week in Albany with his dad. Mike and Josh are hanging out with friends."

Inside we sat on the living room couch sipping chilled chardonnay, talking about the movie, and the summer courses I was taking. And then...

Maggie reached over and began fingering the edge of my short-sleeved blouse. Her blue-black curly hair framed the bemused smile on her face, while her deep brown eyes bore through mine. Her hand slipped down my arm to my wrist and rested there.

Shit! I thought. *What do I do now?!* I did nothing. Didn't move away. Didn't move closer. Kept one hand on my wineglass and the other in my lap. I didn't dare look at her.

"Gee, you have amazing eyes," she said. "Are they hazel?"

"Yeah." They could have been neon purple for all I knew at that moment.

We both heard a car door slam and footsteps on the porch. Maggie snatched her hand from my wrist. The door from the mudroom flew open and Mike bounded in.

"Hey, Mike. This is my friend Maggie."

Mike ducked his head, mumbled a greeting, and fled up the stairs to his room. Maggie glanced at her watch, drained her glass, and stood up.

"Gotta go."

I watched from the porch as she climbed into her Toyota sedan and backed down the driveway. Then I stood there a while longer, staring into the quiet, starry night accompanied by the crickets' chorus. I felt confused, surprised, *and* turned on.

Within weeks I was a woman in lust. And scared. Really scared.

With Maggie conversation was easy. I felt heard and understood. I loved holding her in my arms and being held by her. My desire for sex became insatiable. And during the week, while summer school was in session, finding time to spend with Maggie was easy. Her name began creeping into family conversations, but as far as my sons and husband were concerned, Maggie and I were "just friends."

By the time my classes ended in mid-August, Roger had figured things out. We were staying at the iconic Hotel Saranac in upstate New York, gateway to the Adirondack wilderness. The following morning, we planned to head out on a three-day canoe trip with another couple from Hanover through the legendary St. Regis Canoe Area. I'd considered trying to pull out of this adventure which had been planned months before but couldn't figure out how to do so. During dinner with Roger, as my anxiety built, I uncharacteristically pushed my food around, unable to force much into my churning stomach. We headed for our room after finishing our meal and I quickly got into bed.

"Are you OK?" Roger asked as he began undressing. "You seemed kind of distant at dinner."

"Huh?"

"I asked you if you were OK." His eyes bore into mine.

"Oh. Yeah. Yeah, I'm fine."

Roger, clad in his boxers, stood at the foot of the double bed and stared at me intently. "Are you sleeping with Maggie?" His jaw trembled.

"NO!"

Roger said nothing but continued staring at me.

"Yes," I admitted.

"Shit!" The word exploded out of his mouth and bounced off the wallpapered walls. "I knew it." He reached down, grabbed one of his shoes, and flung it. The sneaker skittered across the wooden floor and came to rest under the curly-maple antique nightstand.

"Roger," I stammered, "I'm sorry! I didn't mean for this to happen!" Guilt and self-loathing flooded me. In that moment I wished I could rewind the tape back to before I'd ever invited Maggie to join me for dinner and a movie. What had I done? What would happen now?

Tears poured down Roger's face. I waited for my tears to arrive. They never did.

The night seemed to last forever. Neither of us knew what to do. We knew of friends who'd had affairs, but not a same-sex one. Characteristically Roger didn't have much to say after his initial outburst and fell asleep soon after getting into bed. I tossed and turned, searching for understanding and found none.

In the morning, we met our friends at the designated put-in to begin our canoe expedition. The rigors of the next three days provided a welcome distraction. We talked some on the four-hour drive home but returned to Hanover uncertain of what to do next.

For a while I actually thought I could continue the two relationships. Roger didn't try to keep me from seeing Maggie. Probably he knew that wouldn't work. Maybe he hoped my involvement with her was "just a phase." Maybe I did as well.

August 31, the day Mike had been eagerly anticipating, finally arrived. I kissed him goodbye as he got into Roger's car and the two of them began the 1,300-mile drive to Macalester College in St. Paul, Minnesota. There the coach of the Division III soccer team was eagerly awaiting the arrival of his new seventeen-year-old goalie.

Mike's departure left a huge void. No matter how many times I walked past his unnaturally sterile room—with the neatly made bed and the silent stereo system—I couldn't quite believe, deep down, he was gone. Steve commented frequently, "I miss Mikey-Boy."

School began for Steve and Josh. I too returned to work—this time as the sixth grade social studies teacher at Hanover's middle school. My brain raced overtime and returning to the classroom provided me with a much-needed focus.

Most weekday evenings I found a reason to head to Maggie's house for a couple of hours; "grocery shopping," "a meeting," "a book to pick up at the library." I hated lying to Josh and Steve. Skulking around left me feeling dirty and ashamed. But to finally experience my true self at age forty-five was so powerful. Authenticity trumped guilt. Every time.

As the leaves turned and September drew to a close, I came to a reluctant decision. During the past two months I'd lost over twelve pounds. I was sleeping with Maggie during the week and Roger on weekends. I had no idea where the affair with Maggie was headed, but I knew the twenty-one-year marriage to Roger was over. I was a lesbian. Early on a Sunday morning Roger and I went for a walk. The morning mist rose from the Dartmouth playing fields and wet leaves squished under our feet. Neither of us spoke. I think we both knew what was coming.

Finally, I stopped walking and broke the silence. "I can't do this anymore, Roger. I can't stay married to you. I want a divorce."

This time we both wept. We talked about how to tell our sons.

Sunday morning, October 13, dawned crisp and clear. Peak foliage had passed and spent leaves fluttered to the ground. Roger and I called Steve and Josh to our bedroom. I'd told Roger I'd begin the conversation. Since I'd been the one to ask for the divorce, I felt that was the least I could do. I'd practiced my speech several times, but that didn't help. If I'd been a guitar, I'd have snapped every string. For the first time in nineteen years I found myself wishing I didn't have children. Somehow it seemed that would make things easier.

The boys walked in and looked around, unsure of why they were there. I pointed to our bed.

"Can you guys sit down over there? Please?"

Steve plopped down and Josh lowered himself uneasily next to his brother—almost protectively. His eyes showed concern, but I doubted he had any idea of how his life was about to change. Roger pulled the maple rocking chair from the corner and sat in it, head down, avoiding his sons' eyes. I remained standing, took a deep breath and looked at the brothers. Steve stared at me, his face placid and filled with trust. A trust I didn't deserve.

"Hey, guys, this is really hard. But Dad and I have agreed we can't stay married anymore." My voice cracked, but I continued. "And there's something else. I've fallen in love with Maggie. That means I'm gay. I've asked your dad for a divorce." Roger continued looking at the floor.

Steve spoke first. "I know what divorce mean. Big fight." My comment about my sexuality was lost on him.

"No," responded Roger. "Mom and I didn't have a big fight. We just can't stay married." His face revealed none of the pain he must have been feeling.

"Rats," replied Steve. "I sad."

My stomach roiled. Bile rose to my throat. But I also knew Steve couldn't completely take in what was happening. Not so with Josh.

He stood up facing us. Tears streamed down his flushed cheeks.

"Dad and I love you both," I choked on my words. Nothing I could say felt adequate. I wanted to disappear.

Josh stepped forward, hugged us both, and fled into his room. Roger and I let him go.

Steve stood and looked around. "Josh OK? I hungry. We have breakfast soon?"

Later, when Josh wondered if Mike knew, we told him we'd decided to wait until his brother came home from college over Christmas break. We wanted to tell him face-to-face.

Somehow, we all survived. Steve continued to be based at the Hartford Middle School despite the IEP meeting Roger and I had attended last spring. Josh struggled in the classroom but found relief on the varsity soccer team. Roger continued to live and work in Albany, but rarely missed one of Josh's games, even the weekday ones. Most weekends he came to Hanover and I stayed at Maggie's house. Over Christmas Mike absorbed the news of our divorce with little visible emotion.

NINETEEN

Power Struggle 1985-87

When Steve began his 1985-86 school year, not only was he still in the intensive special needs classroom in Hartford Middle School, but he had a new teacher. Sima Paskowitz and her family had returned to the New York City area. Like her predecessor, Sarah Knapp had a master's degree in special education. A New Hampshire native with an engaging personality and a trigger-quick sense of humor, she had an uncanny ability to find something unique and special in every student in the class. She quickly pegged Steve's outgoing personality as his greatest strength. I liked her.

We met at the end of the first marking period in late October to discuss Steve's progress. Sarah greeted me warmly as she held up Steve's IEP folder.

"When I went over your son's paperwork, I noticed that an addendum is to be added this fall for the purpose of transitioning Steve to the diversified occupations program. How is that going?"

"Slowly," I replied. I didn't add that I'd spent much of the summer focused on myself, my affair with Maggie, and my new identity. For the first time in almost twenty years, mothering was not the central focus of my daily life. A rush of guilt tunneled in. "Steve met with an examiner from the Vocational Assessment and Career Center in late August. And he also had an evaluation to determine his IQ. Both reports were sent to Dr. Height. Have you seen those?"

Sarah replied she had not.

I continued. "The vocational assessment stated that Steve should finish his public school experience with a program that combines prevocational, life skills training, and functional academics. That's exactly what I have been asking for!"

Sarah nodded. "And what about the cognitive testing?"

"Nothing new there. This is the second time the same psychologist has evaluated Steve. She is a family friend and knows him well." I sighed and my shoulders slumped. "Steve's full IQ still comes in at 61, but she doesn't feel that is an accurate reflection of Steve's ability."

I hated the labels attached to IQ numbers. That's all an IQ was—a number. I knew Steve's score, topped by almost ninety-seven percent of the typical population, classified him as "borderline low." The test purported to measure reasoning and problem-solving abilities, but it didn't measure Steve's determination, resilience, or the way he viewed life without filters or prejudice—skills some of the world's smartest lack.

Sarah assured me she'd ask to see the reports and push folks to get the addendum written. I felt heartened by her support. I didn't have a lot of strength or the motivation left to continue to fight the turtle-like pace of the educational system. Instead I was expending much of my energy on my concerns for Roger and our sons in the wake of the divorce papers I'd just filed.

Finally, in January, Dr. Height called me into his office and handed me the promised addendum along with Steve's new schedule. Now he would spend his mornings in the middle school with Sarah Knapp and afternoons in the high school's DO program. Better, but still not what I wanted. I wanted him in the high school full time.

Five months later, near the end of the school year, I received a letter from Dr. Height's office announcing a significant program change for Steve and his classmates. At the start of the next school year, Steve, along with most of his buddies of appropriate age, would be based at the high school. No more nineteen- and twenty-year-olds in the middle school! Sarah Knapp would move over with them as part of the DO teaching staff. A certain degree of smugness coursed through me. "Finally," I exclaimed. Finally, Steve and his friends would be where they belonged. I hoped it wouldn't be too late for them to learn the skills they needed to function outside of a sheltered middle school environment. Most had just a couple of years before turning twenty-one, when they would age out of public school education.

The same month I received notice of the change in placement, I walked into the conference room at the Hartford Middle School for Steve's annual IEP meeting. I was alone. For the first time since we'd begun attending these meetings almost ten years earlier, Roger was absent. I missed his support, but I understood. For him, the pain of our separation and impending divorce was too raw. I was now a single mother. That reality overwhelmed me as I took a seat at the table between Sarah Knapp and the guidance counselor—Steve's allies.

The special education bigwigs were already seated. I picked up the IEP in front of me and flipped to the last page to see the all-important placement decision. My eyes lit up. "Hartford High School. DO math and reading. Vocational training in school and in a community-based work situation." This made everything official.

As the assembled parties went through the individual educational plan page by page, I noticed the goals for Steve now focused on acquiring work habits needed for future employment in the community, as well as developing skills needed for increased independence in daily living. Instruction would include use of a pay telephone, simple first aid techniques, and trips to a bank, post office, and grocery store. Steve would also learn how to fill out personal ID information on an identification card.

"This all looks great," I said. "These are exactly the skills Steve needs to learn." I understood I could teach Steve how to perform all of these tasks, but Steve was a teenager. Mom had lost the credibility that school-based lessons still had. Pleasing his teachers remained important to Steve. "But I am most excited about the community-based work experience. Can you tell me more about that?"

The DO site coordinator explained that after the first semester, he would review Steve's progress with his teachers and together they would look at a listing of local businesses willing to serve as training sites for DO students. After agreeing on an employment opportunity which aligned with Steve's strengths, Steve would go through a typical application process supported by one of his teachers. Eventually Steve would train at his job a couple of days a week, for a few hours each day.

I nodded as the coordinator concluded his explanation. "Usually our DO students go through several on-site work explorations before graduation. If they demonstrate particular aptitude or interest, occasionally a job offer is the end result."

I floated out of the meeting. *At last*, I thought, *my voice has been heard*. Once again, my hopes for Steve soared. Anything seemed possible! He was eligible for two more years in the public school system. I pictured him marching down the aisle in a blue gown, a graduate of the Hartford High School Class of 1988, the same year Josh would graduate from Hanover High School.

Like any new program, things sounded better on paper than they turned out to be in real life. When I met with Sarah in the fall of 1986, I asked her how things were going.

"Steve and his classmates are in the right program, but it's going to take a while before all the needed adjustments are in place," she responded.

"What do you mean?" I asked.

Her eyes clouded as she continued. "These teachers aren't used to teaching kids like Steve."

"Kids like Steve?" I frowned. "You mean kids who *look* like Steve? Kids with Down syndrome."

Sarah nodded. "They'd never state it that way—but yes. The diversified occupation teachers have never worked with kids who don't look typical. I keep pleading with them not to lower their expectations based on appearance. I don't want them excusing immature behavior or goofing off. And recently I've seen some progress, but we're not there yet."

I appreciated Sarah's frankness. But what did that mean for Steve? "I'm afraid time is running out for Steve as far as public schooling goes. He's recently turned twenty. Next year his youngest brother Josh will be a high school senior and once Josh graduates and leaves home, Steve's life will really be different." *Mine too,* I thought. The freedom to live my own life appeared tantalizingly close. So much depended on what Steve could achieve during his last two years in public school. "Do you have any suggestions for how to help Steve develop the skills he needs?"

Sarah did. She told me about her former employer, United Developmental Services, or UDS, the local agency which served area adults with developmental disabilities.

"Even though technically Steve can continue in school for one more year after this one, he can also simultaneously receive services through UDS. You should begin working on a transition plan with them now." We'd lived in Hanover for over ten years, but I'd never heard of this organization.

Sarah gave me the contact information and within a month Steve became a UDS client. A meeting was scheduled for Steve and me to meet his case manager. We'd only been sitting in the agency's waiting room for a few moments when a lean and lanky guy entered. I took note of the fact he approached Steve first, not me—an important move.

"Hey, Steve. My name is Robert Vaillancourt. Welcome to UDS. I'm going to be your case manager." Steve jumped to his feet and shook Robert's extended hand. "Did you bring anyone with you today?"

"Yup. This my mom."

"Great! Let's go into my office and get acquainted." And that's how Robert entered our lives.

After an initial discussion with Steve about his interests, Robert sent him off with the UDS recreational director to meet some other age peers who were hanging out in the day room.

"I like short meeting," Steve commented over his shoulder. Robert and I both laughed.

"You just scored big points with Steve," I said.

Robert shared a bit of his professional history before asking me the now familiar question—what were my goals for Steve. "I want Steve to have a job and eventually move out of our house. I've been saying this for a while now, but I'm not sure Steve is any closer to meeting these goals than he was a couple of years ago."

A smile creased Robert's angular face. "Let's get started on changing that."

Shortly after Christmas Steve began a training program at the local newspaper where he joined a small group of cognitively disabled adults collating and inserting items into the paper before distribution. Once a week, after a full day of school, I drove Steve to the *Valley News* plant and dropped him off in time to punch in by 5:00 p.m. Three hours later, I returned to pick up a tired but happy son. After completing his second week of work, he burst out the door of the plant and ran for our car.

"Mom, Mom, look at this!" Breathing heavily, Steve slid into the front seat. In his hand he clutched a legal-sized envelope.

"What's that?" I asked.

His stubby fingers reached inside the envelope and pulled out a check. "Paycheck! I get paid! See my name? S-T-E-V-E-N-C-O-H-E-N! Like Mike and Josh! I work, I get money!" He paused to catch his breath and leaned in to look closely at the check. "I not know how much," he added.

The following afternoon Steve and I headed to the bank. There he proudly showed the teller his check.

"I work. I get paid," he announced as he stood at the window.

At $1.75 an hour, the amount for two work sessions wasn't much, but that made no difference to Steve. The understanding teller handed Steve his ten dollars in one-dollar bills and the change in an assortment of nickels, dimes, and a single quarter. Later he called both his father and Mike at college to share his big news. When Josh got home from soccer practice, Steve proudly showed him his money—the dollar bills lined up in a row, all facing the same way, and the change sorted by type. Soon Steve was able to correctly count his money. He now had a reason to learn that skill.

When the program ended in April, Steve was devastated. He thought he'd been fired.

In August, Robert called and asked me to meet with him. The air-conditioning in his office provided blessed relief from a late-summer heat wave. Robert motioned me toward a chair and began.

"We are starting a new program in a few weeks. We've been given an opportunity through the Hanover Food Co-op to place a work enclave in their store. I thought you might be interested in this for Steve."

I wasn't familiar with the term "work enclave," so Robert explained. Sally Page, who had led the group at the *Valley News*, felt that placement had looked too much like a sheltered workshop model. She had high expectations for her clients and wanted something that would provide greater visibility. A long-time resident of Hanover, Sally was a dynamo in a small package and recognized the co-op for what it was—Hanover's unofficial meeting place. She'd lobbied the co-op's manager and then met with the store's board of directors. They'd agreed to her proposal to bring her clients into the store.

"What would the work entail?" I asked Robert.

"Initially Sally will take a crew into the co-op in the mornings and teach them how to clean the employee locker room and break room. They will also clean the office area. She hopes some folks will demonstrate enough ability to work on the floor of the co-op—stocking shelves, pricing items, and perhaps even bagging groceries."

"That sounds great, but the hours won't work for Steve. He will be in school," I replied.

"Based on the work Steve did at the *Valley News*, his name has been mentioned as a potential candidate. Sally told me she knows your family well and admires all you've done for Steve. She thinks he has untapped potential and would really like him on the crew. This is an opportunity for him that may not come up again any time soon." I gave a silent thanks that Roger and I had kept our family in Hanover despite the heart-wrenching separations our choice and Roger's work had imposed on our sons. Robert continued, "You know, there is no rule that says Steve needs to remain in school until he ages out. That decision is really yours."

I called Roger that evening. Although we'd been officially divorced for six months now, and he wasn't physically present, we continued to make parenting decisions together. Roger's heart had yet to mend and my identity as a lesbian still felt very new. But our commitment to our sons remained firm. On that there was no disagreement or hostility toward each other.

We quickly agreed that pulling Steve out of school and letting him try Sally Page's program was a good gamble.

The following day I sat down with Steve. "We need to have an important conversation, a big talk."

Steve asked, "It be long talk?"

I smiled and shook my head. "Do you remember Mrs. Page? The lady who helped you with your work at the *Valley News* this winter?"

"Yup! I like her. She nice! She pay me! I call her Sally."

"Sally likes you too, Steve! And guess what? She has another job for you!"

"What that?" wondered Steve.

"The job is at the co-op, where we do our grocery shopping. But there is one problem. For this job you would be working days, not nights. So, you wouldn't be able to go to school."

"I like school. I like my friends. I miss them."

"Yeah, I know. You have some really good buddies there, but..."

"Mom?" Steve interrupted me. "I get paid?"

"Oh yes, Steve. You would get paid. Sally would pay you."

"I not get paid at school."

"Nope, you don't." I knew the wheels were turning.

"OK. I like money. I like pay. I do it."

Steve successfully completed a trial week at the co-op. He loved the work and Sally commented on how quickly he'd made friends with several of the co-op's employees. On August 30, 1987, I sent a letter to Dr. Height, advising him our son would not be returning to the Hartford DO program for his final year of public schooling. We cut our ties with the Hanover School District and made the switch to UDS and their adult services program on a full-time basis. A month before his twenty-first birthday Steve's long and twisted public school education road ended. Ahead of him stretched new adventures.

New adventures seemed a possibility for me as well. After two years my amazing, wonderful, tortured affair with Maggie ended, and I was devastated. I wallowed in anguish for several months. But I'd begun to accept myself and my sexuality. Over time my pain lessened. Serenity and calm filled my empty spaces. Who knew what might lie just beyond the horizon?

TWENTY

Graduation Day, 1987

Josh planted the idea in my head one night as he and I sat down to dinner, just before the start of his senior year at Hanover High School. "I can't believe it," I'd commented. "My baby—a senior!"

Josh grinned. At seventeen, he was a compact wiry bundle of energy, his curly brown hair cropped close. "Well, I can! Seems like I've been waiting for the right to use the senior lounge forever." But even as Josh reveled in the thought of this privilege, his faced clouded. "But..."

"But what?"

"I kinda feel bad for Steve. Because he's left school and is working at the co-op, he's going to miss graduating. That's not fair. The plan was we were both going to graduate high school the same year."

My heart melted. I reached across the table and placed my hand on Josh's tanned arm.

"You're always thinking about Steve, aren't you?"

Later that evening I sat alone in the living room waiting for Steve to get home. A UDS staffer had taken Steve and two other adults out for pizza and a movie. I thought about Josh's comment. Steve...graduating? I doubted the thought was on Steve's radar. He rarely expressed any regrets about the past. Instead Steve lived in the moment, which now meant working at the co-op. But for me, who had navigated years of advocating for him in different education systems, and for his brothers, who had cheered him on, a commencement ceremony would feel cathartic. I heard a car door slam and Steve entered.

"Hi, Mom, I home."

"Hey, Steve, I can see that! How was the movie? What did you see?"

"We see *Masters of the Universe*. I like it! He-Man kill Skeletor." He began brandishing an imaginary sword, reenacting the duel, complete with sound effects. "And I sit next to my new friend Belinda," he added smugly.

"Cool, Steve. Did you say 'thank-you' to your driver?"

"Yes, I did. I say it. I go to bed now. Work tomorrow." Steve gave me a hug and headed upstairs.

Over the next few days Josh's sensitivity about Steve missing his high school graduation continued to haunt me. A plan began to form and swirl around in my head. I called Roger.

"With Steve's twenty-first birthday coming up at the end of September, I'm thinking…why not make it a joint celebration, a birthday party with a graduation ceremony?"

"Tell me more," Roger said.

"We could arrange for a band, one that knows 'Pomp and Circumstance.' I could ask Steve's former teachers Margaret Taylor and Sima Paskowitz to speak and contact the folks at DO and see if they can come up with some kind of diploma. The 27th falls on a Sunday, so we could plan something for around 5:00 p.m. And…"

Roger caught my excitement and offered ideas of his own. He suggested several possible venues, reminded me of a local band we both liked, and then came up with the answer to the puzzle that stumped me.

"I can take care of getting a gown and mortarboard," he stated.

"Really? Where? September isn't exactly the season for graduations, but Steve needs the full outfit."

Roger offered to contact a female professor and ask to borrow her regalia. "She's pretty short. Her gown should work for Steve."

"Great! Let's make this happen," I replied.

The last weekend of September turned out to be perfect in every way, including the weather—the quintessential New England autumnal riot of colorful maple, oak, and birch leaves under cloudless azure skies.

Roger stayed at our house, sleeping in Mike's empty room. Steve and Josh loved having him there and even I felt relaxed in his presence. Roger had begun dating a woman named Polly. I felt happy he'd found someone. With no tension between us, it was easy to focus on being parents to our sons.

Sunday morning Josh and I left to set up for the party at the Kiwanis Club in a nearby town where we'd rented the large event room. Steve was still asleep, and we left Roger contentedly sipping coffee and reading *The New York Times*. Several hours later we were done. Josh and I lingered a moment and admired the transformation we'd accomplished.

"Mom, this looks great! Steve is going to love it!"

I slid one arm around his waist. "Yes, he will. And remember this all started with the comment you made while we were having dinner." Then we headed home to shower and change into our party clothes.

Cars began pulling into the Kiwanis parking lot at 5:00 p.m. sharp and soon the eclectic aromas of various potluck offerings wafted throughout the room. In the kitchen I loaded the oven with casseroles. Beef stew and spaghetti and meatballs simmered on the stove. I glanced through the serving window where appetizers covered one table—deviled eggs, chips and dip, popcorn, cheese and crackers.

In the alcove The Flames began tuning up—acoustic guitar, bass, sax, and a riff from the drummer. "Testing, testing, testing," repeated the vocalist as she checked the mic. Then Josh's voice floated through the sound system. "OK, everyone. I just saw my dad's car pull in. Get ready...Steve is here!"

Clad in khaki pants with a light tan jacket covering his blue short-sleeved shirt, Steve entered the hall. Cheers and spontaneous applause greeted him. Although the party wasn't a surprise, for a moment he appeared stunned as he stood under a rainbow of streamers which crisscrossed the room. When he spotted the bouquet of pink balloons (his long professed favorite color) surrounding an extra-large gold one with the word CONGRATULATIONS, a wide grin creased his clean-shaven face.

I heard him exclaim, "Cool! I like it!"

Steve spotted one of his buddies from the DO program and ran to meet him. "I miss you," he exclaimed. "I not see you."

I stood alone in a corner, a plastic glass of white wine in my left hand, and watched Steve disappear as folks crowded around him—Hanover friends, several young adult clients from UDS including Belinda, Sally Page, members of her work enclave, along with a few regular employees from the Hanover Food Co-op. Heather, who now managed a home for adult women with developmental disabilities in western Massachusetts, found Steve and the two exchanged a long hug. I scarcely heard the din of happy voices. An invisible bubble enclosed me as I watched the scene play out before me.

Time stood still. *Twenty-one years ago...it's taken forever and flashed by in an instant.* I continued to reminisce. *It's been tears of sorrow and of joy. It's been failure and success...fear and relief...never-ending advocacy...grit, determination, and courage.*

Roger moved in beside me. "Wow, did you ever think we'd get here? This is amazing. You've done a great job, Linda."

My bubble burst and I looked into my ex-husband's shining brown eyes, his bushy Afro tinged with gray. "We both have," I replied. I swelled with pride. I felt a cocoon of peacefulness settle around us. I could tell Roger felt it too. I reached for his hand. No further words were needed.

Fifteen minutes later I gently separated Steve from his admirers and guided him to the small room where I'd hung his graduation outfit. His father helped him slip into the black gown and lovingly placed the mortarboard on his narrow head. Steve's almond-shaped eyes opened wide as he viewed himself in the full-length mirror hung on the back of the door.

"It real! I graduate!" Suddenly his lower lip began to tremble.

"What's the matter, Steve?" I asked. "What's wrong?"

"I teeny nervous. I never graduate before."

"I know, but this is going to be fun," replied Roger. "Remember when Mike graduated?"

Steve's shoulders shuddered and tears spilled from his eyes. "I miss Mikey-Boy. He not here. He in college. I wish he here."

"We all miss Mike, Steve," I assured him. "He misses us too. Remember the card you got from him in yesterday's mail?"

Steve used the hem of one sleeve to wipe his face. "Yes! He send me money. He say buy a Bud Lite!" His brothers had made certain that Steve knew turning twenty-one meant he could legally buy beer.

The door opened a crack and Josh peeked in. "All set, Steve?"

"I ready, I graduate."

"OK then," said Josh. "I'll tell the band to start playing."

As the sax wailed the first notes of "Pomp and Circumstance," I gave Steve one last hug. "Here you go, buddy. Happy graduation! Dad and I will wait for you up by the band."

Slowly, our son made his way up the aisle formed by his friends. The tassel on the mortarboard swung from side to side and hands touched Steve on the shoulder or offered up a high-five. As Steve moved ever closer, he seemed to part the scenes drifting by my eyes: the dark paneling of the doctor's office where I first heard Steve's diagnosis; three-year-old Heather standing by his crib and singing to him softly; Steeple School; Josh in his bathing suit pausing to help

Steve over a sand dune; Mike punching out the kid who called his brother a name; Ray School; Hartford Middle School; Hartford High School. The endless meetings. The long string of acronyms: BOCES, EMR, TMR, INS, PLOP, DO, IEP. I glanced up at Roger. Behind his glasses, his eyelids blinked back tears.

The music faded out, and Margaret Taylor stepped to the microphone. She recalled Steve's pioneering days at the Ray School and how just last year a five-year-old little girl, born with Down syndrome, began kindergarten there. "You helped make that happen, Steve, you and your parents."

Sima Paskowitz spoke next. "Remember, Steve, when our class had French lessons?"

"Yes, I Etienne," interjected Steve.

"And then the whole class went on an overnight trip to Montreal to practice our French words," continued Sima.

Warm gratitude moved through me. The steadfast belief in Steve's ability to learn held by both women meant so much.

The formal part of Steve's graduation concluded as Steve's guidance counselor from middle school—one of Steve's loyal supporters—presented him with a rolled-up certificate, stating Steve had attended Hartford High School. Steve threw his mortarboard into the air, stepped out of his gown, grabbed the mic, and yelled, "Now, we dance!"

The dance floor filled as The Flames covered many of the top hits: "Purple Rain," "Up Where We Belong," "Survivor," "Jump," "Time After Time," and Steve's all-time favorite, Michael Jackson's "Beat It." Steve alternated between dancing and singing with the vocalist in an off-key monotone. When I heard the opening notes of "Wake Up Little Susie," a '50s standard, I grabbed Roger's hand and pulled him onto the floor.

"Mom, I need you." Steve found me on the dance floor.

"Hey, Steve, what's up?"

"I want ask Heather to dance with me."

"So, go ask her, Steve, I know you're not shy."

"I need slow music. I ask the band?"

I nodded and then watched as Steve approached the band leader who bent down while Steve spoke into his ear.

The crowd formed a circle as Steve, smiling broadly, searched out Heather and led her onto dance floor. As the opening chords of "That's What Friends Are For" broke the silence, Steve wrapped his arms around Heather's waist and the two began to sway back and forth. Heather's long curly locks tumbled down over her shoulders. She towered over Steve, but she placed her arms around him and closed her eyes. Jane and Kevin stood next to Roger and me and the four of us watched our children. I swallowed hard. As the song ended the band segued into Starship's "We Built This City." Heather and Steve began to rock, joined by just about everyone else.

The festivities continued and I returned to my observation bubble. Lately I'd begun to sense my time in Hanover was coming to an end. I fully expected Josh would move out of the house after he graduated next June. His departure would leave a huge void in both Steve's life and mine. Robert Vaillancourt and I had already started to discuss independent living options in the area for Steve. We'd agreed an apartment with space for a typical roommate/caregiver was the ideal situation. Tonight was an opportunity for me to pull back and watch Steve function in a community which loved and supported him. I needed to believe I could move on and Steve, like his brothers, would be fine without my daily oversight.

Steve's voice brought me back to the present. "It time for dessert!" Roger walked out holding a huge sheet cake covered in vanilla frosting, with chocolate lettering: "Happy Graduation and 21st Birthday." One corner was decorated with a mortarboard and two long-stemmed roses—pink, of course. The band began to play "Happy Birthday" and I moved to stand next to Roger as he placed the cake on the table. Steve stepped forward to blow out the twenty-one candles which blazed around its edges. Josh's soccer buddies waded through the crowd offering goblets filled with sparkling white grape juice, while Josh took the microphone.

"Come on up here, brother." Josh looked down at the index card he held in one hand. "Don't worry, Steve. This will be short. I just want to speak for Mike and me and tell you, you're the best big brother we've ever had! Even though we don't always agree with your taste in music, you keep us laughing with your silly jokes and sayings."

"You got that right, 'Shrimpo,'" Steve grinned.

Josh smiled and continued. "Sometimes your stubborn streak shows through, but usually you are happy and smiling. And most important of all, you've always been there on the sidelines, cheering for us. So now, I'd like everyone to raise their glasses and join me in a toast: To Steve...big brother and best friend...I love you, buddy!"

"To Steve!" The room echoed with the sound of a collective toast while Roger and I wrapped our sons in a family hug. I felt Mike's presence—a thousand miles away at Macalester College. Waves of emotion crashed over me: love, gratitude, and most of all a feeling of fulfillment, of affirmation.

My advocacy for Steve had helped me find my voice. In doing so I'd begun to understand the true meaning of self-care and self-love. Recognition and acceptance of my needs wasn't a selfish act—a belief I'd learned from my mother. No, to be fully human meant I needed to care for myself before I could care for others. Years would pass before I truly understood Steve's gift to me. But as the party wound down and guests began leaving, I took some comfort in knowing our family had survived divorce and my coming out. No matter what the future brings, I told myself, I will always treasure this night.

Thoughts While Running on a November Morning—1987

Sometimes—not often—I think of what he might have been.
He might have been an architect
But he builds incredible structures out of blocks.
He might have been a commercial artist
But people prize the drawings he's done for them.
He might have been an author
But he loves to visit the library and "read" books.
He might have been an athlete
But he's the official score-keeper, play-by-play announcer and
    cheerleader at his brothers' games.
He might have been a politician
But he voted for his candidate in the 1984 Presidential election.
He might have been an actor
But he cracks us up regularly with his comic routines.
He might have been a veterinarian
But he sees redeeming features in his cat that no one else can.
He might have been a minister
But his compassion and concern for others is easily evident.
He might have been a teacher
But in his own way he has taught us much.

One thing I've never wondered about
Is why he is.
For he has already made his contribution
To this world in a way
Most of us can only hope to do.
And I know that long after he is gone
He will be remembered by those he touched.
And all of us will have been enriched for having known him.
And thank god—whatever and wherever she is—
For having set him here among us.
For in this imperfect world
Perfection wears many guises.

PART TWO
ADULTHOOD
1989–2015

TWENTY-ONE

Guilty Freedom, 1989

The tires of my maroon Ford wagon hummed along as I approached the western terminus of the Massachusetts Turnpike bound for Albany, New York. Mileposts slipped by at a steady rate of one a minute, farther and farther from Hanover, the town which had embraced our family for over twelve years. In the passenger seat slumped Steve, twenty-two, his dark brown hair cut short and much coarser than the fine strands of his childhood. At 5'0" he'd long since reached his full adult height but carried his weight of 115 pounds well. Occasionally the eyelids of his almond-shaped eyes fluttered, and a gentle snore escaped his parted lips. Unlike me, he appeared to be at peace on this late July morning. Unlike me, this journey held no special significance for him. He understood today he was moving into a group home in Albany, not far from the three-story brownstone where his dad lived. Over the past four years his two younger brothers had graduated high school and left home. Why not him?

I allowed myself a wry smile as I thought back on the recent flurry of activity and comments Steve had made during his "goodbye tour."

"Today my last day at work. I say goodbye to all my friends."

"Today my last time to see Dr. Who." (Steve's nickname for our family physician, Bill Boyle). "No more needles."

"Today I see *Back to the Future Part II,* my last movie in Hanover. They have movies in Albany?"

We were already behind schedule, our start delayed while Steve searched for his cat, Dubie, who wasn't moving with him, to give him one last hug. Finally, we'd rolled down the driveway as Steve pumped his fist and called out, "Goodbye Hanover! Get ready, Albany, here come Steve!"

I'd done my best to hide my doubts and concern from my son. The decision to have Steve leave the town which had held him close through good times and bad had been a wrenching one for me. My hands tightened on the steering wheel and my eyes began to burn. "Fuck," I muttered. "I can't believe I am doing this." Searching for calm, I slipped a tape into the cassette player and let my thoughts drift.

As I'd expected, life changed profoundly for me once Josh graduated high school in June 1988. That October he'd departed for Bozeman, Montana, to work at a ski area, leaving Steve and me rattling around in our four-bedroom house. Within months, Hanover, for me, no longer seemed a place of opportunity and promise. Now I felt trapped, stagnant, and alone. I wanted to be done with active parenting. I needed to become something more than a mother. I longed for a fresh start, for a chance to begin the next chapter of my life, whatever that would be. A path began to take shape—stay in education, but as an administrator. Move away from Hanover, from my life as Linda Cohen. Live more authentically as Linda Morrow, my original surname.

All Steve's life I'd focused on inclusion and normalization. I'd moved mountains to get him to where he was now. I'd never considered institutionalization for him. I'd gotten him through the public school system. But for most of Steve's life I'd believed Dr. Tarbox's prediction—that he was "unlikely to outlive his teens." I'd hardly dared to dream about what Steve's life as an adult might look like. Then came Steve's nasal hemorrhage and Dr. Boyle's statement: "If our treatment plan doesn't work, Steve may only have six months to live."

But Steve had proven to be amazingly resilient, and with his twenty-first birthday, I'd let myself believe, really believe: He's going to make it! A troubling question followed that realization, however. Would Steve live with me forever? I didn't want that. Not for him. Not for me.

I'd never let his Down syndrome define Steve. Grown men didn't live with their parents. But in the late 1980s most adults with Down syndrome *did* still live with their parents or in large institutions. I should have begun planning for Steve's adult years—and my freedom—long ago.

For more than a year I'd worked diligently with Robert Vaillancourt, Steve's case manager at United Developmental Services, to craft a safe residential environment for Steve. I wanted him to live in an apartment like most of his age peers with a "typical" roommate to provide the oversight he needed. But creating something that didn't exist took time, and I hadn't allowed enough.

Recently, after two decades as an elementary classroom teacher, I'd accepted the position of associate principal at a K-8 school in Lyndon, Vermont, a small town sixty miles north of Hanover. I couldn't keep Steve with me and take the job. I'd called Roger and asked him to start exploring options for Steve near his home in the Albany area. I'd never imagined that my departure from Hanover would force Steve's life to be completely uprooted, but that's how things had turned out. I shivered, despite the summer heat.

Three hours later I snuck an occasional glance at my handwritten directions as I navigated Albany's busy streets, and at last pulled up to the curb of the group home Roger had found. Steve had spent a trial week at Albany City Hostel in early May, but I'd never laid eyes on the place. My son yawned and stretched his arms.

"We here?"

"Yup, buddy. We're here. At your new home." Roger stood on a weed-choked lawn in front of the three-story brick building. "There's your dad, waiting for you." I scanned the gritty-looking residential neighborhood. Would Steve be safe here?

"Pops!" Steve clambered out of the car. "I here!"

I exchanged an awkward hug with Roger. His unruly Afro contributed to his slightly rumpled look. My brown naturally curly locks showed flecks of gray. Age had added a few pounds to both our frames. Our son stepped toward the front porch where several individuals lounged in worn wicker chairs. "Hey, Steve," called a young man. "I 'member you."

The resident director, a heavyset woman, greeted us with a friendly smile and offered a quick tour of the first floor. Steve and Roger lagged behind as we walked into the large common room furnished with overstuffed couches and easy chairs. A large console TV occupied one corner. Cartoons flickered across the screen, despite the absence of an audience. An in-progress jigsaw puzzle covered most of the surface of a card table. Simple board games, "Connect Four," "Chutes and Ladders," "Sorry," filled the shelves of a low bookcase. Steve learned to count playing these games with his brothers. I did my best to conjure up a happy scene of Steve and his new friends socializing here.

Across the central hallway, two rectangular oak tables, each with seating for ten, took up most of the dining room. I wondered what mealtimes looked like here. Did the residents converse with each other? Or just eat in silence? Whatever happened would be a far cry from our intimate family meals—a time to share the events of each member's day, to take a collective pulse.

We stepped into the kitchen. A padlock clamped the handles of the large refrigerator and a similar lock secured the door of the pantry. Steve either didn't notice or didn't understand he would no longer have unrestricted access to snacks. A dark-skinned man, cigarette dangling from his lips, labored at a metal prep table chopping vegetables.

"This is Bruce, our chef," chirped my guide. "Looks like you're putting together the macaroni salad for lunch." Bruce nodded and caught the ash from his Camel before the spent tobacco landed in the stainless steel bowl filled with cooked pasta. I winced. Back in Hanover our home was smoke free.

Behind me Steve piped, "Hi, Bruce! I hungry. When we eat?"

Back outside, Roger and I quickly unloaded Steve's meager possessions from the Ford's cargo space. The information packet I'd received weeks before was very clear about what Steve could bring. His clothing filled two suitcases. A single plastic container held his personal items: clock radio, cassette player and tapes, night light, bath towels, and bedding, including his Batman comforter. We followed our son up the central staircase to the second floor. Wheezing slightly, Steve pointed up the stairs to the third floor.

"That for the ladies. Can't go there." The four bedrooms assigned to the eight male residents circled the landing. Steve led the way to a door marked Room Two. "This my room," he announced. "I share with Mark."

At least he knows the guy who will be his roommate. I longed to know the selection process. Had any thought gone into this match, or did Mark just happen to be the one whose room had a vacancy?

Furnished simply with twin beds, matching maple nightstands, a pair of desks, and two three-drawer dressers, the space looked like a typical college dorm room. But this wasn't for four years. This could be for life. That realization curdled my stomach. A twenty-something pimply-faced male employee with long oily hair appeared and introduced himself.

"I'm going to help Steve settle in while you and your husband meet with our director," he said to me. I didn't bother to correct his assumption.

Steve shot me a panicked look. "Mom! You leave now?" I assured him his dad and I would find him once our meeting concluded.

In the director's office I produced a three-inch binder containing the required information. Robert Vaillancourt had compiled a client review. For three years he had guided Steve through his transition from school into the adult world. The review included a copy of Steve's most recent individual service plan, the ISP. Robert also added an eighteen-page skills inventory, a recent assessment of Steve's competency in every conceivable situation. A comprehensive medical report, written by Dr. Boyle, contained records dating back to 1977 when our family moved to Hanover and he first began treating Steve. Last night I'd composed a three-page typewritten letter of my own, detailing Steve's various idiosyncrasies—things only a mother could know—and clipped it into the front of the binder. I held the heavy notebook out to the director with a somber carefulness as if I were handing her an overfull cup of coffee. Don't spill this, lady. I've filled it to the brim. Nothing can go to waste. Casually she set it down on her desk. I flinched.

"I will review this within the week," the director assured us. "This information will form the basis of the care plan we develop for, ah...," she paused and looked down at her intake sheet, "ah...for your son Steve."

"I have some additional information for you," I replied. "These are two letters of recommendation from the Hanover Food Co-op, where Steve has worked weekdays for the past year and a half. After completing their training program, he became the first person with developmental disabilities hired directly by the co-op."

"I see. That's interesting, but the day program our clients attend includes a sheltered workshop."

What? Steve was now a *client*? And a sheltered workshop instead of a community-based job? I cringed and looked at Roger. "You didn't tell me that." My eyes narrowed.

"I didn't know," he responded.

I pulled my arm back. My hand still clutched the glowing reports from Steve's supervisors at the co-op. In this moment I wanted to run from the director's office, get Steve, and drive him back home.

The director continued. "Mrs. Cohen, you haven't provided me with your son's medications."

I replied Steve had been taking daily meds on his own for several years. But the director shook her head. Self-medication wasn't allowed at Albany City Hostel. I pressed my lips together. This woman didn't know my son. She had a stock answer for everything. Anger and fear filled me as I looked at her stout authority. Like a thief she seemed determined to steal every last vestige of Steve's hard-won independence. I turned to Roger for support, but he avoided my eyes.

I looked down at my remaining piece of proof of all Steve had become, an article from the *Valley News*: "Independence: Steve Cohen Has His Own Life to Lead." The full-page spread touted the gains he'd made in his personal life and included two photos of Steve taken at work. My shoulders sagged. I refolded the article and returned it to my purse, defeated and deflated. I'd failed my son.

In the hallway outside the director's office, I faced Roger and poured out my frustration.

"How did we end up here? This place is awful! How could you think this place is OK for Steve?" I knew I shared responsibility for Steve's arrival at the group home. I just didn't want to admit this.

"Linda, I did the best I could. This is a city, not an Ivy League town. Options are different and limited here."

Guilt slammed into me and refused to budge. This was not the right place for Steve. But I was up against a wall. I had a new job and was moving in three weeks. I had no options whatsoever. I stared at my ex with cold flinty eyes. "Roger, you've got to step up here," I pleaded. "You need to keep a close eye on Steve. I'm counting on you. And so is our son. Please, please watch over him."

I wiped my tears and tried to ignore the ones streaming down Roger's face. "Fuck!" I looked away. "I need to find Steve, say goodbye, and get the hell out of here!"

I rearranged my face to reflect a calm I didn't feel and set off in search of my son.

On the drive back to Hanover, Anger joined Guilt. Seated on my shoulders, the two clawed at each other.

"This is all your fault," growled Guilt.

"No way," snapped Anger. "I've spent twenty-two years nurturing, mothering, and advocating for Steve. It's my turn now."

"But that's what mothers are supposed to do."

"Not forever. I never signed up to do this forever. I want a life. I want my freedom!"

For the first time I'd relinquished the control I'd latched onto when Steve was born. And look what happened! I jammed Joan Baez's *Blessed Are...*tape into the cassette player to drown out my demons.

TWENTY-TWO

Yard Sale, 1989

By the time I arrived back at my house in Hanover I'd worked myself into a lather. I saw the gray Ford van in the driveway, and relief mingled with my tears. Sue's here!

Soon after our family moved to Hanover, I'd joined a local woman's softball team. Of the eight teams in the league, only one sported full uniforms. The other teams made do with matching T-shirts and hats. Maybe it was the uniforms, or the fact that the Oxbow team always won, but I'd found their players very annoying, especially their catcher—a strong, athletic woman named Sue. Always smiling, laughing, and chatting me up when I came to the plate. Very distracting!

Since we were both educators, occasionally I saw Sue in a professional capacity at local workshops and conventions held around New England. In those venues I found a kindred spirit and came to understand that we shared many values. Like myself, Sue felt schools should work for kids, not for the convenience of teachers or administrators. We both championed the underdog, kids who didn't fit the traditional school mold. After my divorce from Roger, and my affair with Maggie ended, I'd often joined her, along with a half dozen or more single women, at loosely organized Sunday night gatherings held at a Hanover restaurant. Within the group there was an unspoken assumption we all belonged to the "same church." But everyone was deep in the closet. In the late '80s I felt uncomfortable using the term *lesbian*. It left me feeling dirty, open to scorn and ridicule. I was still too raw, too scared. Having Sue as a friend was fine, but nothing more. At least not yet. Fortunately, she was patient and willing to bide her time.

Now Sue stood at my door as I made my way up the porch steps. She was there to give me moral support because I'd expected this to be a hard day, though not as hard as it had turned out to be. Her deep tan glowed, and her brown eyes sparkled behind her ever-present glasses. At forty-five she was four years younger than me.

"Hey, welcome back. How did things go?"

"Awful," I replied. "I feel as though I've abandoned Steve. Maybe even ruined his life. I never should have left Roger in charge of finding a place for Steve to live in Albany."

I gave Sue a quick hug and moved past her into the house. Worry joined Guilt and Anger and my body ached as the trio waged battle. Although I'd blamed Roger for the shortcomings of the group home, in truth I knew I was at fault. Throughout Steve's life I'd been his leading advocate. *Now what have I done?* I'd put that advocacy to the side to focus on my own needs, that's what. As Sue headed to the kitchen to get us both a beer, I curled into myself and collapsed onto the couch.

"Hey, Linda? Linda? Are you OK?" Sue's voice pulled me out of my despair. I looked up at her as she handed me a sweating bottle of Michelob Light.

"I said your name several times before you heard me. Where were you?" asked my friend.

"Oh." One hand unconsciously went to my chest and covered my heart. "Back in the past. In a very dark place. Kinda like where I am now."

Sue cocked her head, sat down next to me, and sent me a quizzical look. "Want to tell me what's going on?"

Sue and I had never talked about personal stuff. She knew I was the divorced mother of three sons—one with special needs—but not much else. I took a few seconds before responding. I wasn't used to people asking about my feelings. "For most of my adult life I've followed a very prescribed path: college, marriage, children. I didn't think too much about what I did, I just drove the bus straight down the road, no detours." I could almost see myself behind the wheel. "But now…it's like the hub of the wheel shattered and spokes are flying every which way. Leaving Steve today in a place I know isn't right for him…I don't know what to do. And I'm responsible for the damage. What a mess."

Next I filled her in on the event I always revisited whenever I thought about Steve—his nasal hemorrhage. Sue listened without interruption until I finished the story. It seemed as if I'd been talking for hours when I finally ran out of steam. My eyes burned and my nose continued to run as I looked up at my friend.

"That must have been terrifying," she said. "But obviously the doctor was wrong. Steve seems fine now."

"Yeah. The treatment plan worked and after a year Dr. Boyle pronounced him fully recovered."

"No wonder leaving Steve at the group home was so devastating for you," responded Sue. "Your plate's been really full for a long time."

I gave Sue a weak smile. I had little knowledge of her past. I knew she'd lived in several different states, teaching physical education in public schools, before moving to a small town a few miles north of Hanover. Like me she'd earned a master's degree in school counseling, and recently completed a Certificate of Advanced Studies program in educational administration. Currently she served as director of curriculum in a nearby regional school district. She'd never married or had children. But she knew how to change a tire and check the oil. Carefree and always ready for adventure, the back seats in her van had been replaced with outdoor lounge chairs. An ice-filled cooler held the beer. Both the chairs and the drinks were considered necessary accouterments for the spontaneous road trips she often made with a gang of work colleagues.

A year earlier, when I'd told Sue of my interest in becoming a school principal, she'd assumed the role of mentor. She'd supported and encouraged me as I gained the necessary credentials to move from my seventeen years of classroom teaching to the administrative position I'd be starting in a couple of weeks.

Now sitting on the sofa in a pool of tears, the new job ahead of me didn't occupy a place in my mind. All my thoughts focused on Steve— only Steve. I knew I couldn't leave him at that group home. Not forever.

"Here's the worst thing," I said ramping myself up even more. "According to the director, Steve's only work option is the sheltered workshop run by the day program all residents attend. A sheltered workshop! That's not a job!"

"Linda, that's sounds awful. You have every right to be upset. Do you think once folks get to know Steve that might change? I've seen him at the co-op. He did a great job there."

"Who the hell knows? Arggggggg!" The mountain of crumpled Kleenex beside me signaled I needed to shift gears. I took a few breaths to bring my agitation back to a manageable level. "I can't keep talking about this right now, Sue. I'm just wiped."

"I'm not a mother and I can't imagine what you must be feeling," said Sue. "But I've been around Steve enough to know you've given him a strong foundation. He may be more resilient than you think." Sue's focus on the positive reminded me how much I'd been looking forward to the adventure ahead of me, a new town and a new career.

"I hope you're right. Anyway, I can't turn back now. I've accepted the Lyndon job, found a place to live and rented the house here." I yawned before continuing. "But the logistics of moving just seem impossible. Even though I'm renting this place partially furnished, there's still so much crap I need to clean out. I don't know where to begin."

Sue's eyes lit up and she grinned. "Sounds like a yard sale to me," she laughed. "Want some help?"

My burdened heart lifted just a bit at the thought of not being alone with all I had to do. "Yeah," I agreed. "That will be a good distraction, a step toward shedding my old life in preparation for my new one." I yawned again.

"You look exhausted," observed Sue. "Let's schedule the sale and then I'm going to head out. You've had a long day."

We set a date for the following weekend and Sue left. That night I cried a bit more, but I also felt something new dawning: a hope for happiness.

Sale day dawned bright and sunny as my lawn and driveway filled with the accumulated contents of twenty-two years of family life. Large pieces of excess furniture—the boys' twin beds, our ratty hide-a-bed couch, oak dressers, the maple rocker—drew in customers. Of course, there were the usual yard sale suspects: outgrown or unwanted clothing, threadbare towels, worn sheets and blankets, books, assorted toys. Business maintained a brisk pace. I didn't mourn the departure of each item. In fact, each sale left me feeling a bit lighter and moved me closer to the dream I was chasing.

By early afternoon the furniture had gone, scooped up by young lovers setting up house or students who needed odds and ends for their dorm rooms. I smiled watching excited kids depart shouldering outgrown skis or wheeling the perfectly good bikes abandoned by Mike and Josh. But a flotsam of small items remained. "There is still too much stuff here," I groused to Sue. "I just want it gone."

"So, put out change blankets."

"What are those?"

Sue explained. "Put out three or four blankets, marked with large index cards: 'twenty-five cents,' 'fifty cents,' and so on. Sort what's left accordingly. You'll be amazed."

In a couple of hours, we declared the yard sale over. What remained could easily be stuffed into a couple of large leaf bags and taken to the dump. But one big problem remained. Miller. The dog. Mike's beloved dog. Named for the beer.

All summer long I'd nagged Mike and Josh. "You guys need to do something about Miller. Talk to your friends. Find someone to adopt him. I'm going to be working long days in Lyndon. He's not coming with me." But my pleas fell on unresponsive ears. And when the brothers departed for college and work, Miller remained in residence.

"Uh, 'cuse me, Miss? Is the dog for sale?"

I glanced at the unshaven man standing next to me, hands shoved deep into the pockets of his baggy khaki trousers. He pointed to Miller, who after spending most of the day greeting customers with barks and vigorous tail-wagging, now lay sleeping on the twenty-five-cent blanket.

"You want to buy the dog?!"

"Yup!"

I asked him to wait and quickly walked over to the carport where Sue stood filling bags with the sale remains.

"Sue! That guy over there wants to buy Miller!"

"He *is* on one of the change blankets," she replied.

"Yeah, the twenty-five cent one. But I hadn't planned on selling him!"

Sue reminded me how much I'd been stressing about the dog. "This is your chance," insisted my friend. "You're moving in a week. Pass this up and you might be taking Miller with you."

So, for a quarter, Miller, attached to a leash, ambled down the driveway and jumped into a VW Bug with his new owner. "So long, Miller," I whispered as they drove off. "I did love you. Really."

Yard sale over, I treated Sue to dinner and drinks before she headed home. Alone in my house, walls whispered, and my footsteps echoed as I wandered from room to room, followed by Steve's low-maintenance cat, Dubie, who would come to Lyndon with me. Empty surfaces, freed of knickknacks, and blank walls devoid of photos and art, stared back at me. Miller's food dish and water bowl sat forlornly on the kitchen linoleum.

Upstairs the boys' bedrooms stood vacant—three empty nests. An open footlocker sat on the wooden floor in each one, filled with mementos of my sons' childhoods. I entered their rooms, pulled a blue-covered baby book from each trunk, and retreated to my bedroom where I sat on the edge of my bed and lost myself in those treasured memory books. I fingered the ID bracelets clamped onto my wrist the moment I'd entered the hospital to give birth. I reread congratulatory telegrams. My eyes scanned lined pages where my handwriting detailed vital birth statistics, hospital roommates, names of visitors, and their birth day gifts. These volumes also proclaimed acquisition of developmental milestones. Graphs revealed gains in height and weight. Photos of birthdays, hand-drawn Mother's Day and birthday cards spilled out as I lovingly paged through each album.

Going through Steve's book, I chuckled when I come across the dime wrapped in clear plastic. The one he'd swallowed the summer before his third birthday. The emergency room doctor had instructed me to check his diapers until it passed, which it did after several days of smelly investigation. I fingered a paper plate where Steve's small footprint, in white paint, showed clearly on a circle of blue construction paper pasted in the center of the plate—the Mother's Day gift he'd made years ago as a young student at the Steeple School.

Finally, after a flood of yawns in the dimming light, I returned each album to the appropriate trunk, closed the lid, flipped and pulled the clasps tight. A holy act. That night Dubie and I slept curled together.

The following day I took care of one last remaining piece of business. In probate court, I petitioned to change back to my original surname after twenty-six years of being Linda Cohen. I emerged from the courthouse that morning into the brilliant August sunshine, feeling I'd reclaimed an important piece of myself. My Linda Cohen life was over. Ahead lay my rebirth as Linda Morrow, an adventure I couldn't wait to begin.

TWENTY-THREE

New Beginning, 1989

The drive from Hanover, New Hampshire, to Lyndon, Vermont, takes just over an hour, a straight shot north on I-91. Although the topography of the two towns is somewhat similar, the relatively short distance of sixty-five miles transports you from affluent, liberal Hanover, home of Dartmouth College, to the tri-county area of Vermont known as the Northeast Kingdom, a land of small, isolated, politically conservative towns surrounded by open fields and dense tracks of mountainous hardwood forests. Lyndon is the second largest town in the Kingdom.

My two-bedroom rental house sat on a dirt road and looked across a valley to the looming presence of 3,200-foot Burke Mountain. I settled into my new environment and got busy meeting people. I couldn't have known when I accepted the job as associate principal of the Lyndon K-8 elementary school system that I would be landing in the perfect place to begin this next phase of my life. Gone was the relentless political correctness of Hanover, replaced by a population of 6,500 souls consisting of farmers, loggers, and business people—folks whose roots went back several generations. However, over the years an eclectic community of free spirits, aging hippies, and artists also made their homes in the area. Pretentious individuals were hard to find. Regardless of political persuasion, everyone seemed to embrace a "live-and-let-live" lifestyle. I hoped it wouldn't be hard to find a place I could belong.

I was, after all, changing more than just my job in this move. I'd spent most of my adult life married to Roger, something that'd never seemed quite right to me. I'd assumed the disconnect was my fault. But when I'd had my first lesbian experience with Maggie, the clouds of self-recrimination parted. Finally, I could breathe. I understood I wasn't attracted to men, at least not in the way a married woman should be. But at forty-nine I was still coming to terms with my sexuality. Now this remote area of Vermont represented a fresh start for me—a place where I'd have a chance to live honestly. Here everyone seemed comfortable in their own skin. I wondered, could I learn to be comfortable in mine?

In early September, soon after school began, Jean and Meg, two teachers who were also partners, invited me to join them for a late afternoon swim at Lake Willoughby, a glacial body of water framed by steep granite cliffs surrounding a mostly unpopulated shoreline. When we arrived at the public beach at the lake's southern end, Jean pointed to a path that disappeared into the woods. "That leads to the nude beach about a quarter of a mile away. Do you want to swim there?"

Really? A nude beach? That would never fly in Hanover! It had been years since I'd gone skinny-dipping and then only with close friends. But now I wanted to fit in, and nudged by curiosity, I nodded. We headed down the path. As we walked, doubts assailed me. Should I be doing this as a new administrator? What will people think? At the shoreline, I quickly shrugged out of my bathing suit and dove in. In crystal-clear water, swimming naked among a variety of ages and body types, my concerns evaporated. No one gave the lack of bathing suits a thought. This was freedom!

That evening I crawled into bed and pulled the blanket up to my chin as a cool breeze rippled the curtains of my open window. This Kingdom place felt very different from anywhere I'd ever lived. Maybe here I could pay less attention to what others thought and simply just be me.

Over the next several weeks the numerous challenges of my new position consumed me, and I did my best to compartmentalize my concerns for Steve as I learned the ins and outs of my new community, my new job, and most importantly myself as a person without children in my care.

Sue's support, both professional and personal, remained a source of comfort. We stopped tiptoeing around our shared sexuality. I felt safe and secure in her arms. Besides, Sue wasn't asking for any long-term commitment. She'd just begun considering a move into the uppermost echelon of public school administration—a superintendency. She had no idea where she might end up. Meanwhile she continued to live in her home about forty-five minutes from Lyndon. We spent most weekends together at either her house or mine, a welcome respite from our busy workweeks.

Finally, in mid-October I came up for air and arranged for Steve to visit me during the long weekend when Vermont schools closed for the state-wide teachers' convention. On Thursday morning I left to meet Roger and Steve at a prearranged time and place halfway between Albany and Lyndon. In northern Vermont most of the hardwoods had lost their leaves but farther south the fall foliage remained in full glory. But even on the ninety-minute drive, my thoughts focused on work, and I paid scant attention to the changing scenery.

When I pulled into the parking lot of the convenience store in Brattleboro, Vermont, and spotted Roger's car, Principal Linda Morrow vanished. I morphed into MOM. Steve and I hadn't seen each other in over two months, the longest we'd been apart ever. Steve exploded from the passenger door and we held each other in a tight embrace between the two vehicles. I inhaled the scent of my son's freshly washed hair and relief surged through me. Someone was making sure he bathed regularly.

Steve's voice, muffled against my chest, floated up to me. "Mom! I so happy! I miss you!"

"I missed you too, buddy," I choked out.

Roger and I exchanged brief, perfunctory greetings, confirmed the time for Sunday's exchange, and then Steve and I headed back to Lyndon.

"I miss you a lot, Mom," repeated Steve. "How your new job?"

"My new job is great. I'm really busy though. What about you? How do you like living in Albany?"

"It OK," he replied without much emotion.

I pressed a little more. "What about your roommate? Are you and Mark friends?"

"He OK."

Hmmm. Steve sounded flat. I probed again. "How do you like living so close to Dad? Do you see him a lot?"

"Sometimes."

My concerned heightened. Where was my happy-go-lucky guy? My jokester? My always enthusiastic son? I decided to switch topics.

"So, are you excited to see my new house?"

"Yes! I sleep in my own bedroom? I see my cat Dubie?"

Ahhh, that's more like the Steve I know and love.

"I see my friend Sue? What we have for dinner?" Soon the barrage of questions ceased, and Steve fell asleep for the remainder of the trip.

He awoke with a start when I pulled into White's Market, Lyndon's locally run grocery store. "What this?" he wondered.

"I thought we'd stop at the store and you could pick out what you wanted to have for dinner tonight."

"Yes!" Steve pumped his fist. "They have cheesecake?"

I laughed. "I don't know, Steve. White's serves a different cliental than the co-op." I immediately regretted mentioning his former place of employment.

"I miss my job," he replied, his eyes cast downward, lower lip trembling.

Guilt flooded me. *I bet you do.*

Steve quickly recovered from his own sadness once we entered the store. He spotted a container of Ben and Jerry's Chocolate Chip Cookie Dough in the ice cream section. "My favorite!" he exclaimed and tossed it in the basket to accompany his chosen menu of cheeseburgers and fries.

Back in the car, we arrived at our destination in less than ten minutes. Steve hopped out of the car and headed for the door. "You give me tour?"

"Absolutely!"

As we stepped inside, I pointed out the kitchen to our left and the dining room on our right. Next we walked past the full bath and into the living room. Steve noticed the extensive deck wrapping around three sides of the house. "How I get there?" I pointed to a door along one pine-paneled wall. Steve opened it and stepped out.

"Cool," he announced. Then he turned and walked back inside. "Where the bedrooms?"

"This way," I said with a smile and headed up the stairs leading to second floor. At the top I indicated my bedroom to the right and the half bath directly in front of us. "And in here," I said looking left, "is the guest bedroom where you'll sleep."

Steve looked in, saw Dubie curled tightly on one of the twin beds, and rushed to his side. "My cat!" He lay down next to his pet and buried his face into Dubie's long gray and white fur. "I miss you," he murmured.

Saturday morning Sue arrived and received a big hug from Steve. During my last year in Hanover, she and Steve had bonded quickly. She understood Steve's speech, got his jokes, and, most importantly, shared his taste in movies—something I most certainly did not. Matinee dates became a frequent occurrence for the two: *Beetlejuice, Crocodile Dundee II, The Blob*—horror, adventure, sci-fi…it didn't matter, they saw them all. And every time they'd left for another show, I breathed a sigh of relief and gratitude for the precious hours of solitude Sue gifted me.

Over the long weekend I observed Steve closely. Since so much time had passed since I'd last seen him, I wondered if fresh eyes would reveal something I might not notice otherwise. Even though he'd surpassed his predicated life expectancy, I remained vigilant when it came to Steve's physical health. His heart function remained a special concern.

On Sunday, after a filling breakfast at the infamous Miss Lyndonville Diner, Steve and I, along with Sue, headed south to meet Roger. As we swung onto the interstate, Sue turned to Steve. "So, Steve, did you like your first visit to Lyndon? Did you have fun? I sure did."

"I do," responded Steve. "I have fun." He paused before adding, "I wish I stay one more day."

Guilt stabbed me. What was happening at that group home? My voice cracked. "I'm sorry, buddy. But I have to work tomorrow."

"I know that. I just wish. When I see you again?"

"Christmas," I replied. "You're going to spend Christmas with me. And your brothers will be in Lyndon too!" I smiled. I knew Steve would mark a big *X* on the five calendars he kept on his desk as soon as he entered his room at the group home.

"I miss Mike and Josh." Then, as the opening notes of Prince's "Batdance" sounded on the radio, Steve added, "My favorite!" and leaned forward to crank up the volume. *Saved by the music*, I thought— from Steve's honest feelings and from my own consuming guilt.

Reassured that he would see me again in December, Steve agreeably switched to his father's car when we arrived in Brattleboro. Sue and I headed back to Lyndon.

"How are you doing?" asked Sue as I turned onto the highway.

"OK, I guess. But Christmas seems a long way off." I sighed.

"What's that sigh all about?"

"Just thinking. It was over Steve's first Christmas that Roger and I told my folks about his diagnosis."

"That must have been hard."

"The timing was horrible," I answered. "Especially coming so soon after my sister's death."

A shiver ran through me as I relived that awful day. I gripped the steering wheel hard and kept my eyes on the road.

"Anyway, the bond between Mom and me strengthened after she found out about Steve. His diagnosis awakened her sense of social justice and support of the underdog. She championed every aspect of my advocacy for Steve. So yes," I concluded, "telling my folks about Steve was hard. But that doesn't begin to compare with what I'm dealing with now."

"You mean Steve living in Albany in the group home?" Sue questioned.

I nodded. "Seeing Steve and hearing him say he wished he could stay longer…that just breaks me. I'm a mess." Tears began sliding down my face, the ones I'd been holding back. "I've fought so hard to normalize his life. Now look where he is."

Sue put her hand on my shoulder, but I shrugged it off. This time my guilt refused to yield to Sue's concern.

"I wonder," she said tentatively, "is there any part of Steve's situation you have control of? Anything at all you can improve for him?"

My head suddenly cleared. The fog in my brain parted and lifted. I knew what I needed to do.

The following week I made an appointment to meet with Robert Vaillancourt, Steve's former case manager at United Developmental Services. He and I had worked so hard to create a residential placement in Hanover so Steve could remain in his community and flourish. We'd been close to creating something new and innovative, when my move to Lyndon forced us to drop the idea after several months of brainstorming.

Maybe we'd given up too soon. Maybe we could still make that happen.

TWENTY-FOUR

Course Correction, 1989-90

Once I scheduled an appointment with Robert Vaillancourt, I felt a snippet of hope. Although no longer officially Steve's case manager, he assured me that he wanted to develop a residential option for Steve. I was relieved to know I still had a teammate in Robert, but I also had a job which required my full attention. Somehow, I needed to figure out how to juggle both responsibilities.

Becoming a school administrator meant developing a perspective that extended far beyond the narrow confines of a classroom teacher. In the fall of 1989, Lyndon students were housed in five separate locations throughout the town. My base was the Lyndon Center School, attended by children in kindergarten through third grade. My boss, the principal, had his office at the Lyndonville Graded School, the designated building for sixth, seventh, and eighth grade students. We both shared supervisory responsibilities for fourth and fifth graders whose classrooms were located at the Lyndon Corner School. The two one-room schools still in operation also fell under my jurisdiction. My swimming buddy, Jean, taught kindergarten at the Squabble Hollow School and a teacher named Kathy instructed a combined first-second grade class at the Red Village School. Confusing? Inefficient? Awkward? Yup. But change loomed on the horizon. Passage of a bond vote meant construction had already begun on a consolidated K-8 school.

But for now, getting to know the students and teachers meant traveling between various buildings. I didn't mind. I had a new set of wheels! On my early morning run, a few weeks earlier, I'd had an exquisite epiphany. I was no longer a hands-on mother! The Ford wagon could go! I called Sue. I'd never bought a car on my own, but I knew she had. We agreed to go car shopping over the coming weekend.

On the drive up to Berlin, New Hampshire, land of multiple car dealerships, Sue quizzed me.

"Do you know what you want?" she asked.

"Nope. I just know I don't want anything that can transport a load of kids. Maybe something sporty?"

We stopped at a Plymouth lot and began walking around. A salesman suggested we consider a Fury model: two-door, bucket seats. Sue's eyes landed on a black one with a turbo-charged engine. "Oh! You should test drive that one," she exclaimed.

"Why?"

"You'll see," she assured me.

Off we went and as we approached the first hill I pressed down on the gas. "Holy shit!" I yelped as the car shot forward.

Sue burst into laughter as I clung to the steering wheel.

I settled for a fire-engine-red model with black bucket seats and a traditional engine. On the way home we laughed and giggled. I felt light-headed and liberated.

By late November I knew most of the students by face, if not by name. I especially noticed the pigtailed girl at the Red Village School, with the distinctive facial features so much like Steve's. Her name was Jennie and Kathy was both her teacher and her mother. Curious about their journey in this small town, I wanted to connect with her. I wanted to offer Kathy—both as a mother of a child with Down syndrome and as an administrator—the support I'd lacked when Steve was young. One day I dropped by the school, told her briefly about Steve and suggested we meet over coffee. We set a date for the following week at the Miss Lyndonville Diner.

I was already at a table when Kathy walked in. She headed toward me, exchanging greetings with virtually every staff person and customer in the dining area.

"Wow," I said with a smile. "Obviously you are pretty well known here."

Kathy brushed a strand of her wavy brown hair away from her glasses as she slid into the red vinyl-covered booth opposite me. "My family has lived here for three generations," she chuckled. "I'm whatcha call a real Vermont native."

"I hope you don't mind being seen with a flatlander."

"I'll try not to hold that against you," she said and grinned.

We ordered our drinks and began comparing notes as mothers who belong to the same club often do.

When did she get the diagnosis? Right after her baby was born.

How old was she then? At thirty-six, Kathy was an "older" mother.

Did she have any other kids? Nope. Jennie was Kathy's only child.

Heart defect? Jennie's heart was fine.

Karyotype results? Triosomy-21. Just like Steve.

Support services? Some. Kathy had been given a book about Down syndrome by her family doctor, and he'd connected her with a social worker.

I told Kathy in my almost twenty years as a teacher I'd never taught a child with Down syndrome. "In fact, I've never worked in a school system that's had a kid like Jennie in attendance. Was it hard to convince the district that she belonged in the classroom with her peers?"

A cloud passed over Kathy's face and she paused before responding. "So how much do you know about my story?"

I shrugged. "Nothing."

Kathy's face relaxed. "No, I didn't have any problems getting Jennie into the Lyndon school. The hard part came before that."

I shot Kathy a puzzled look and sat back to listen as the waitress set down our steaming mugs of coffee. Kathy explained she hadn't been married when she found out she was pregnant. "I wasn't sure I wanted to marry Jennie's dad. But when we got the diagnosis after her birth, the guy turned tail and left town."

"That must have been hard. But maybe good riddance?"

"Yes to both," Kathy responded. "My parents stepped in and offered to care for Jennie during the day. At the time I was teaching in a town north of here. When the position at Red Village opened, I applied and was hired. This is my dream job. I went to school here as a kid and now Jennie is doing the same thing!" Kathy's eyes blazed and she leaned forward. "All the kids at Red Village live in the neighborhood. Jennie grew up playing with them and I didn't want to take her away from her friends. When she turned five and started at Red Village, the district provided an aide for her and she's been with me ever since."

I smiled across the table. I was happy for her and glad she had the gumption to fight for Jennie. "Good for you," I replied. I recognized myself in this woman—a fierce advocate for her child. Kathy's shoulders and face relaxed. "Advocacy isn't always easy, is it?"

"Probably a little easier now than when you started?" suggested Kathy.

"Yeah, I had some tough battles. The attitude toward children born with birth defects was pretty dismal in the mid-sixties."

"I'm sure. I can't imagine what you encountered."

Memories came rushing back: the pediatrician's withholding of Steve's diagnosis; the unavailability of surgery to correct Steve's congenital heart defect; my "genetic counseling" talk with medical students; the segregation BOCES imposed on Steve and others like him. Even Steve's placement in a first grade classroom as an eleven-year-old felt like a relic from a distant past. So much had changed. Kathy listened intently as I filled her in on some of my experiences.

Eventually the diner began to fill with dinner customers. I glanced at my watch. No wonder! It was almost 6:00 p.m. "Gosh, I'm sorry. I've talked your ear off. I didn't realize it was so late. You must have to get back to Jennie."

"No, that's OK. She's with my folks. So where is Steve now?" asked Kathy. "Does he live with you?"

"No." I lowered my eyes. In seconds I transformed from confident mentor to guilt-ridden mother. "No, right now he is living in a group home in Albany, New York, not too far from where his dad works. I knew I couldn't bring Steve with me to Lyndon when I accepted this job. But I'd hoped to keep him in Hanover, where he and his brothers grew up. However, time ran out before I could develop an appropriate living situation for him." I hoped Kathy wouldn't judge me.

"I can't imagine Jennie not always living with me."

I nodded. At this point in her life I understood how Kathy felt. But, years from now...would she still feel that way?

I paid for our coffee and left a generous tip for our waitress. Outside we stood for a moment beside our respective cars.

"I'm still trying to bring Steve back to Hanover," I said. "I worked too hard throughout his childhood to give him the life I felt he deserved. There are sixteen residents in the group home. It's too much like an institution." My eyes filled, I couldn't go on.

Kathy put her arms around me. She wasn't judging. She was empathizing. "I'm glad you're here in Lyndon, Linda. I feel like you will always have my back."

"I will," I muttered as I returned her hug.

"I'm sorry you're struggling with Steve's placement. I hope I get to meet him someday. And I hope you'll be able to move him closer to you." I nodded as Kathy stepped back. "Keep me posted, Linda," she added, climbing into her car. "Someday I may be in your shoes."

On my way home, my disquiet continued. Raising Steve and his brothers had seemed easy compared with the never-ending guilt I felt now. Back then I'd just been a typical mother, full steam ahead, the pause button pushed on my own personal life. But now? Now most women my age enjoyed a degree of freedom I yearned for.

As I reached my house, the Fury's headlights picked up the season's first snowflakes drifting lazily down from an ink-black sky. Christmas wasn't far away. This would be my first holiday season with no children living in my home. I looked forward to their upcoming visit.

I loved the cacophony and chaos my three sons brought with them during the week they spent with me. Mike and Josh liked the house well enough but expressed relief they'd grown up in Hanover rather than this rural outpost. They both vied for a chance to drive the Fury and pronounced it "totally rad." Steve never strayed far from Mikey-Boy and Shrimpo. One evening the three left me behind and headed out for a "brothers only" meal. A warm glow filled me as I watched my fledged and fully grown children interacting with each other. This felt so right. This was the way life should be.

I took advantage of Mike and Josh's presence and pestered them with questions about Steve. How did he seem? Did they notice any difference in his breathing? Had he shared anything about his life in Albany? But except for stating he could use a haircut, both brothers assured me Steve was fine. "Stop worrying so much, Mom! Get on with your life! Steve's OK!" I wanted so much to believe them.

But in early 1990, I began getting frequent reports from Roger about Steve not feeling well. Nothing to be concerned about, he assured me—just headaches or an upset stomach. On visits to Lyndon Steve continued to say: "I wish I stay one more day."

My work with Robert to get Steve back to Hanover took on an increased urgency. What I envisioned didn't exist, but I didn't think I was asking for anything outlandish. I longed for Steve to share an apartment with someone who could provide daily support. Ideally the apartment would be in Hanover's downtown core, a location attractive to potential caregivers, perhaps an individual connected with Dartmouth. Once in Hanover, Steve could return to his job at the co-op, learn to cook simple meals, and take public transportation. He would be able to enjoy the kind of life his brothers and their friends saw in their futures. A home with his own bedroom, access to snacks and a say in menu planning, spontaneous pizza and movie nights, perhaps the comfort and companionship of a pet dog or cat.

One May afternoon as my first year as a principal began winding down, Roger called. Steve had been admitted to an Albany Hospital. His complaints about not feeling well had increased. Extensive testing revealed nothing of significance and a couple of days later he was released. But I felt certain I knew what was wrong—Steve was depressed. Worry seared through my body. I felt responsible for his decline both physically and emotionally. I needed to step up my efforts and get him back to Hanover. I couldn't fail Steve. I had to get things right. Steve deserved that.

During the summer, while Robert and I worked feverishly to accomplish our mission, New Hampshire's state-run institution, the Laconia State School, was still operating, albeit with far fewer residents than the 1,100 children and adults with disabilities who'd resided there in 1973 when enrollment was at its highest. Beginning in the 1980s New Hampshire had begun reducing the population by creating group homes in local communities. In the Hanover area, UDS had established three such homes—all initially garnered opposition from nearby neighbors. Now I wanted to push the envelope even further. We needed to find a place for Steve to live and someone interested in living with him.

Robert began using his extensive network and our first break occurred in late August with the identification of a potential caregiver. Jim Mitchell taught sixth grade at the Hartford Middle School, the same school Steve attended years before. Jim came highly recommended by the school's guidance counselor who remembered Steve. When Robert and I met with Jim, he was forthright about his interest.

"My prime motivation is to save the money I would earn for a down payment on a house. What you've described to me sounds ideal. I can keep my job and bank the monthly salary of $1,100 tax-free." He paused before continuing. "But don't get the wrong idea. My colleague at work has given me a pretty good sense of Steve and his personality. He's filled me in on his use of humor. And he also told me about the medical event when Steve was seventeen and the determination he displayed during his long recovery. I think we'd get along pretty well."

The more the three of us talked, the more I liked Jim. In his mid-twenties, he was a great peer for Steve. I appreciated his frankness and his easygoing demeanor. He lived in a single room with a month-to-month lease while he looked for something larger but affordable. He was willing to wait until we found the right place.

In October, I signed a lease on a spacious three-bedroom apartment just a block off Hanover's Main Street. Steve moved out of the Albany City Hostel just before Thanksgiving and spent a couple of weeks living with me in Lyndon. On December 5, I took the day off from work, loaded Steve and his meager belongings into the car, and headed south to Hanover. He remained awake for the sixty-minute drive and chattered excitedly.

"I have my own bedroom? I see my friends at the co-op? I get my own snacks?"

As we pulled off the interstate and crossed the Connecticut River into New Hampshire, Steve pumped his fist and shouted, "Look out, Hanover, Steve Cohen is back!"

Yes, indeed, I thought as I wiped a tear. *After a year and a half, you are back where you belong. This nightmare is over.*

TWENTY-FIVE

Settling In, 1991

Steve quickly transitioned into his life in Hanover thanks to the individual service plan, or ISP, compiled by Robert and his team. The team included Steve, myself, and, for the first time, Sue. Steve's voice was fully evident in the client profile section of his ISP. His list of "likes" included having money, his stereo and TV, working at a job, bowling, toys, and beer! Only four things made him sad or unhappy: not being understood, fighting, meanness, and thunderstorms.

But how do you support a twenty-four-year-old adult with Down syndrome to live his best life? Someone with an IQ in the low sixties? Someone who lacks the mathematical skills to ensure he's received the correct change when making a simple purchase? Someone whose reading is limited to key survival words? Someone whose speech is difficult to understand?

The simple answer? Surround him with others who care about him, are kind, know how to set limits, believe he can learn new skills, and have copious amounts of patience. Federal and state funding helps as well, especially at the state level. And here we were fortunate. New Hampshire ranked high in monies available to the disability population.

In addition to Jim Mitchell's monthly salary as Steve's live-in caregiver, Steve's ISP also provided him with the services of a job coach and a community access person. Unfortunately, Steve's position at the Hanover Food Co-op was no longer available. Soon after Steve moved to Albany another person with developmental disabilities replaced him. But the employment developer at UDS found him a part-time job at Hanover's Grand Union supermarket. A job coach trained Steve until he demonstrated the competency to work on his own. Steve quickly claimed the title of "chief bagger."

Pearl, a lovely older woman, was hired as Steve's community access liaison. She met Steve weekday mornings at his apartment to help him plan his day. The activities included ensuring Steve knew the safest walking route from the apartment to the Grand Union. Pearl also oriented him to the downtown Hanover area so Steve felt comfortable accessing stores on his own, drove him to monthly check-ups with Dr. Bill Boyle, and transported him twice a week to a local gym to work with a personal trainer. Over time Pearl and Steve became close friends and he often joined her for a family dinner at her home.

One May evening, I answered a phone call from Steve.

"Hi, Mom, you see it? I famous!"

"I'm sure you're famous, Steve, but what am I supposed to see?"

"This! The news! My picture in it! On the front page! With Jim!"

I reminded Steve I couldn't see through the phone. Was he holding Hanover's local paper, the *Valley News*?

"Yes! I in the paper," he repeated.

"That's great, Steve. But I don't get the same paper here in Lyndon. You need to mail your copy to me so I can read all about you."

"OK, I do that. I tell Pearl. She help me."

Days later, I eagerly tore open the envelope addressed to me in Steve's bold printing. Under the photo of Steve and Jim, the headline read: "Wanted: The Best of Friends—Agency Seeks Homes Willing to Care for Retarded Residents."

The lengthy story featured comments from the UDS director of supported living. She explained Steve's community-based living arrangement had proven so successful that the agency was in the process of closing two of their three group homes.

A gentle warmth filled me. I'd been part of forging this trail for Steve and now for others too. I recalled Steve's days at the Steeple School with Barbara Keith. Just as she had adapted her classroom activities for Steve, Robert and I had creatively cobbled together an arrangement far better than the quasi-institutional setting of a group home. The model we'd developed now not only had an acronym, EFC for Enhanced Family Care, but more and more families wanted a similar living situation for their loved ones. We'd begun a trend which over the years would be recognized as "best practice" not only in New Hampshire, but across the country.

The next day I duplicated the article on the school's copy machine and mailed it to Jane. Then I placed the original clipping, with others I'd saved, in Steve's baby book.

When my second year as associate principal in Lyndon concluded in late June 1991, my life seemed just about perfect. I had a job that challenged and inspired me. I loved all that living in the Kingdom had to offer: easy-going people, outdoor opportunities galore, peace and serenity. Steve continued to thrive in Hanover. And my relationship with Sue had deepened.

Sue was now a school superintendent in a geographically huge district whose fourteen schools sprawled along the Canadian border in the wildest and most remote part of the Kingdom. She'd rented out her house, moved in with me, and commuted to her office twenty-five miles to the north. We became an official couple. We began looking for a place we could buy together.

In October, Sue and I met with a lawyer in his office to finalize the purchase of our brand new home. He explained in order to get both our names on the deed as shared owners, something we'd insisted on, we'd be signing as tenants in common. Neither of us had ever heard the term before, but he told us this was our only legal option.

"I don't have many clients who are unrelated and want to own a house together."

I tried not to roll my eyes. Using the cover of the table, Sue reached over with one foot and gently nudged my leg. We sat side by side and signed our names on multiple documents.

Back in the car Sue and I began to giggle. Tenants in common?! What a mouthful. We'd begun referring to each other as "sweetie," and now we'd purchased a house together. I wondered, what should I call Sue when we were in public?

"So, from now on should I refer to you as my tenant in common when I introduce you to someone?" I asked.

Sue snorted.

"We have no official status," I said, "and you sure as hell aren't my girlfriend. That sounds weird and too much like high school."

"How about 'friend,'" Sue suggested.

"No! Even worse! 'Friend' feels deceitful and diminishes the depth of our relationship."

Eventually we decided on "partner."

We awoke the following morning to a leaden sky and a fierce downpour. But nothing could dampen our excitement. A century-old

stone wall lined one side of the dirt road. A break in the wall marked
the driveway leading to our new three-bedroom, two-bath home on a
ten-acre parcel just outside of Lyndon. We turned in and parked our
cars next to the U-Haul van we'd dropped off the night before. Its interior brimmed with the contents of each of our homes. Ahead of us
lay the task of merging a collection of furniture, treasures, and trap-
pings that stretched back over fifty years for me and just a bit less for
Sue. It was a far cry from my experience of partnering with Roger,
when we'd depended on wedding gifts to set up house. Now I was an
adult woman in a relationship with another adult woman, buying a
home on my own salary in equal responsibility with my partner.

Many hours later we sat together in the living room on a couch from
Sue's house, exhausted, but satisfied. Piles of unpacked boxes littered
the hardwood floor. They'll still be here in the morning, I mused.

Sue draped one arm across my shoulders. "Tired?"

"Yeah," I answered. "Really tired. But happy too."

"Yup, same here. But I'm ready to call it a night."

We'd spent the afternoon setting up our bedroom. Now we rose as
one, turned out the lights, wrapped our arms around each other's
waists, and headed down the hallway. At the entrance to the bedroom
we stood for a moment taking it all in. Against one wall sat our new
queen-sized bed. On the opposite wall stood the antique three-drawer
pine dresser my parents had purchased at auction in Marshfield almost
forty years earlier. Along another wall we placed Sue's dresser, also
an antique, but larger with an attached mirror.

We looked at each other and grinned. I reached for Sue's hand and
held it tightly. "Wow, sweetie. This looks amazing."

Neither of us had any idea it would be more than twenty years before we moved again. We only knew we were glad to be home and
with each other.

TWENTY-SIX

Tangled Emotions, 1992

Sue and I set to work to make our house a home. As 1992 began and winter clamped down hard, we enjoyed the warmth of our woodstove and learned the importance of keeping an open path to the woodpile. During the week we saw very little of each other. Sue's commute meant she left while I went out on my early morning run and most evenings she didn't return to Lyndon until well after dinnertime. We made time to reconnect over the weekend before disappearing again into our demanding jobs.

Early one April morning, the ringing of the phone woke me. I shot a quick glance at the clock radio: 5:46 a.m. I extracted one arm from under the comforter's warmth and grabbed the receiver.

"Linda, this is your Pa," said my father, calling from my parents' home in Whispering Pines, North Carolina, where they'd retired. "The hospital just notified me. She's gone."

My eighty-year-old mother, my brilliant, feisty, tortured mother, *mi madre cubana,* had died. The news wasn't a surprise. Several years earlier she'd been diagnosed with leukemia, but after a lengthy remission, the disease had returned and she decided not to seek further treatment. Two days earlier Dad had called to say she'd been admitted to the hospital. I thought of my last phone conversation with her in late March, her voice weak, her thoughts distorted. I'd told her I wanted to see her. She'd told me not to come. Her rejection hurt, but I didn't spend energy trying to change her mind. Over the last several years our relationship had been strained. We both knew she was dying and if that's the way she wanted to play it, I'd respect her wishes.

Mom had always been a huge presence in my life—both my champion and more recently my adversary—but her hair-trigger temperament always kept me on edge. I could never see her eruptions coming. As she'd aged, her depression, which began after my sister's death, deepened and she'd become more and more of a contrarian to those around her.

Two days later Dad met me when I landed in Raleigh and I stayed with him in North Carolina for several days. I tried to sort out my tangled emotions. I looked within me for sadness at her passing, for tears.

But those tears never surfaced, not even at the backyard memorial celebration attended by my parents' many friends. Why couldn't I feel anything? Wasn't a daughter, especially the sole surviving one, supposed to feel enormous grief when her mother died? Why couldn't I cry? All I found was relief that my battles with her were over.

When I came out to her as a lesbian at age forty-five, Mom stopped talking to me for more than two years. I reached out to her repeatedly, but she wouldn't take my calls. Each time I phoned, I prayed for my dad to pick up. If Mom answered, she'd hang up as soon as she heard my voice. Whirlpools of confusion swirled within me. I couldn't understand her reaction, the intensity of her anger. Why did she care so much about my sexuality? I was an adult, capable of supporting myself. I'd raised my sons and stayed with Roger far longer than was good for either of us.

During the time Mom and I remained estranged, Dad was hospitalized with a severe case of shingles. Until he recovered enough to call me from the hospital, I knew nothing about his illness. Furious with Mom for keeping this information from me, I knew I had to stand up to her. I dialed their home and when she answered I laid into her.

"Don't hang up, Mom. This has gone on long enough," I started. My body stiffened with tension, but I kept going. "You never let me know how sick Dad was. That's not OK. No matter how you feel about me, I deserve to be kept informed about my father." Mom didn't apologize, but she did promise to stop hanging up on me and keep me apprised of Dad's recovery. I'd never challenged my mother before. Maybe I should have, but I'd always been too scared to take the risk.

After confronting her, things did change—somewhat. But I still had to be careful. I couldn't mention Sue's name in letters or over the phone without engaging her rage. Years passed but I clung to the hope that our mother-daughter relationship might be repaired. Her death ended that dream.

One summer evening Jim Mitchell called. He and Steve had been housemates for three years and he had exciting news to share. True to his initial plan, he'd saved the money he'd earned as Steve's caregiver to make a down payment on a house. And he was getting married. To a woman with a four-year-old daughter. He and his fiancée wanted Steve to live with them. Before telling Steve of the changes ahead, Jim wanted to get my OK.

My OK? What choice did I really have? Every time Steve visited Sue and me in Lyndon he bubbled with happiness. He loved his job and referred to Jim as "my idol." He'd reestablished himself in Hanover and frequently saw people from his childhood. But Jim's news delivered a sobering realization. The model Robert and I'd developed for Steve would always require my vigilance. Caregivers would need replacing, along with, perhaps, Steve's place of residence. I understood in many ways, that for as long as both Steve and I were alive, I would always be a hands-on mother. That was my reality.

Steve seemed happy in his newly constituted family, but I continued to worry. In my perfect world he and Jim would have continued their bachelor life in Hanover forever. Just how long could Steve remain with Jim and Denise? Would having a grown man in the house with her young daughter really work? And what if they decided to add to their family?

I checked in with Jim and Denise regularly. Everything seemed fine, but I could feel the winds of change coming. I thought the change would involve Steve, but that's not what happened.

TWENTY-SEVEN

Despair to Hope, 1993-94

A mysterious melancholy dropped out of nowhere (seemingly) and enveloped me as I began my fourth year at the Lyndon Town School. Initially I ignored it. I didn't dig in or examine. I didn't seek help. I just plowed forward with work.

As an administrator I'd learned to keep several balls in the air at once but pleasing all the various constituencies I served proved far more difficult. Frustration mounted as parents, teachers, and school board members realized if they didn't agree with a decision I made, they could jump the chain of command and speak directly to the principal. Sometimes he began reversing my findings without consulting me. The more often he undermined me, the more powerless I felt. Once again, the patriarchy loomed.

Each morning I awoke feeling sluggish and leaden. Tears flowed freely, but without understanding. I sank deeper and deeper into a dark void. At work I struggled to keep my emotions in check, but on weekends I gave in to my desolation, and anguish spilled over. The most trivial incident—a poor shot on the golf course, a misplaced gardening tool—set me off. I lashed out at Sue, the only person with whom I felt safe. My skin couldn't contain the molten lava boiling within me. Anger or a deep pulsing sadness seemed the only emotions I could access.

Sue expressed her concern. She'd never seen me like this. Get help, she urged but for a long while I resisted. I'd always seen myself as strong and competent. Shame engulfed me. Finally, I made an appointment with my physician. She prescribed an antidepressant and referred me to a therapist.

It took a while for me to see the therapy sessions as a gift to my-self, but, with professional support, I began taking stock of my life. Were the expectations which I'd unthinkingly submitted to while growing up in the fifties now bubbling to the surface? Was the contin-uing power of the patriarchy strangling me? Maybe my constant concern for Steve had cracked my stoic exterior? Perhaps I still need-ed to fully grieve my mother's death and come to terms with the knowledge I'd never receive the approval I'd longed for from her? Or was I genetically predisposed to hopelessness?

Slowly, very slowly, the dark cloud over me parted and once I gained the rim of depression's deep well, a glimmer and then a beacon of light washed over me. As my recovery continued, I thought of my mother and how her last years had been so compromised by the de-mons she battled. I wished she'd had the opportunity to experience the relief medication and therapy granted me.

As my energy level and self-confidence increased, I began thinking about leaving the Lyndon Town School. I'd learned a great deal as an associate principal, but I wanted my own school. And too, a sense of community—something vitally important to me—remained an elusive goal due to the sheer size of the school's population of 750+ students and close to 100 teachers and support staff. Sue and I spent many weekends mulling over possibilities, and we settled on two criteria: I would look for a principal's position in a small school, within an hour's commute from Lyndon.

In May, I interviewed for an opening that met my parameters. The village of Walden, Vermont, was looking for a principal for its 100 K-8 students. The interview, held in one of the town's four still operating one-room schoolhouses, went well and a job offer followed. I asked for a few days to decide. I wanted to be certain the little town of Wal-den would be a good fit for me. I did some research.

In the mid-'90s Walden was remote even by Northeast Kingdom standards. Although close to Lyndon, ninety percent of the roads within its borders remained unpaved and snowfall amounts were legendary. There was no post office, zip code, gas station, or centralized village. Local food purchases were limited to one dank general store whose shelves held only the most basic supplies.

Less than twenty percent of adults in Walden had attained a college degree. Close to fifty percent earned a living by farming, logging, hunt-ing and fishing, or in the construction trades. The population was overwhelmingly white and household median income well below the state average. In the local paper, Walden was often portrayed as backward and broken. On the surface, it looked like a hard place to work.

However, I knew the departing principal, Eileen, and her partner, Polly. I admired Eileen. Not only had she acknowledged her sexual orientation at a much younger age than I, but she and Polly had a son, birthed by Eileen. I couldn't imagine having had those options twenty years before.

Now, Eileen and Polly had added to their family of three by adopting a mixed-race baby boy. After two years as Walden's principal, Eileen wanted to be a stay-at-home mom. She and I were traveling in different directions.

I called Eileen, told her I'd been offered the Walden position, and asked if we could get together. I wanted to find out as much as possible about the school and the town before making my final decision. We met for dinner at a nearby pub.

After placing our orders, Eileen asked me why I wanted to leave Lyndon. I explained I wanted my own principalship in a much smaller school.

"And it's more than that," I admitted. "I just want to be me. I haven't hidden my sexual orientation in Lyndon, and I am guessing it won't be an issue in Walden either."

Eileen nodded. "I was excited when I heard you'd applied. I haven't run into any problems in Walden. Everyone pretty much minds their own business."

My spirits soared when I heard these words. "So, tell me what you've learned during your two years in Walden."

"Linda, this could be an amazing opportunity for you. I really believe things are on the brink of change here. Given the experience you've had in Lyndon, I think you'd be a great fit."

I knew Eileen was referring to the situation I'd faced in Lyndon when I'd begun my administrative career. There I'd seen how Lyndon's consolidated school had brought children together under one roof and improved opportunities for students. Currently Walden's K-8 pupils were woefully underserved in four one-room buildings scattered throughout the town's thirty-nine square miles. But recently, after six failed attempts, Walden voters had finally approved funding for a single centralized school. New possibilities loomed in Walden, though on a much smaller scale.

"What about the staff and the superintendent?" I asked. I wanted to get a sense of all the players. In such a small setting, personalities could be critical.

"The staff in Walden is dedicated and talented. They work long hours in decrepit buildings and they really care about the kids. The superintendent is completing his second year. He's extremely supportive and forward thinking."

By now we'd finished eating and drained our beers. Not yet 8:00 p.m., most of the customers had left. Evenings in the Northeast Kingdom ended early. But I had one more question.

"And the school board? The Lyndon board has five members. But Walden only has three. What are they like? Do they understand their role as a board?"

Eileen smiled. She knew what I meant. "I'm really impressed with the board chair. She's not a local but has lived in the town for several years. She's knowledgeable about public school education and under her leadership the board has worked hard to improve the educational environment." I nodded. "But the board members understand their role. They don't micromanage. They leave the day-to-day operation of the school to the principal. And..." Eileen hesitated for a moment, before continuing, "the board chairwoman shares our sexual orientation."

Walden sounded better and better. "Now that a new building is promised, what do you see as the major problems I'd be faced with in the interim?"

Eileen paused. "Behavior is a huge issue, especially among some of the older boys. Admittedly, overcrowding contributes to the problem. In some buildings just getting up to sharpen a pencil means asking everyone around you to stand up so you can get by."

"I've dealt with plenty of behavior as both a classroom teacher and an administrator," I replied. "But the space issue sounds extreme. When I interviewed with the board, they were hopeful construction would be completed by next spring and occupation could take place over the April vacation. Do you think that's possible?"

Eileen frowned. "Maybe. I sure hope so." Then her face brightened. "Linda, everyone at that interview was impressed with you and your ideas. They've got their fingers crossed you will take the job. I'd love handing the reins over to you."

I left the restaurant in high spirits. I couldn't stop grinning. I'd spent over twenty-five years as a public school educator. I was fifty-five. Retirement was in sight, maybe five or six years away. I yearned to take the leadership skills I'd developed and implement them where they could really make a difference. But taking the job meant a $12,000 pay cut.

Sue was waiting for me when I arrived home. I burst in and thrust one fist in the air. "I guess I don't have to ask you how your meeting with Eileen went," she said with a smile. "Have you come to a decision?"

We hugged. "Yeah, I want to take the job." I began to babble, filling her in on all Eileen and I had talked about—both the pros and the cons. Sue listened patiently. I concluded with my salary concern.

"Linda, listen. We'll be OK financially. Focus on the opportunity. You have a chance to bring about real change. I know that's important to you."

Sue's comment sent sparks surging through me. It felt wonderful to have her support and understanding. And change didn't scare me, even though there'd been times in my life when coping with change had been hard, so very hard. Right then, change seemed exciting. My sons were all doing well, living independent lives. I was in a healthy relationship. My mental health was improving. Everything in life looked hopeful.

Fortunately, during happy moments, we are never given foreknowledge of the struggles we will face down the road.

TWENTY-EIGHT

Unexpected Challenges, 1994

I licked my lips and grinned broadly on the July morning when I pulled out of the driveway just after 7:00 a.m. and began the thirty-minute trek from our house in Lyndon to my first official day as principal of the K-8 Walden Elementary School. Adrenaline surged through me. I brimmed with confidence.

When I pulled up at the Noyesville School, where several weeks earlier I'd had my interview with the school board, Gloria, the chairwoman, was waiting for me. She'd agreed to give me a tour of the other three one-room schoolhouses—named Walden Heights, South Walden, and Star. I got into her car and we set off.

As we headed down the dirt road, Gloria provided more details. She explained how each school had been built decades before as clusters of families settled in various locations in town. The buildings were designed to hold twelve to fourteen students ranging in age from six to thirteen, and originally, they lacked running water or central heating.

But by the early 1970s, when the town started dividing kids by grades, these buildings stopped being neighborhood schools. Walden's lone school bus made a contorted loop through town picking up kids and dropping them off at their respective classrooms—two grades in each building.

The schoolhouses we stepped into all looked similar. Wooden floors had long lost their luster and cracks and chips marred the slate blackboards. Dropped ceilings all sported water stains. The town employed four cooks who prepared daily hot lunches in each school's tiny kitchen. Gloria admitted the buildings were poorly insulated and the plumbing precarious. They weren't fit for children to be in all day, every day. Walden had been out of compliance with state standards for years.

I found it hard to understand why it had taken seven votes to pass financing for a new school, but old traditions die hard. The multiple bond votes had resulted in a highly divided town. I recalled the many stories I'd read in the local paper about the civil war that had consumed Walden over the course of each vote. Families had split down the middle and life-long friends had stopped talking to each other. As we exited the last schoolhouse I sighed and shook my head.

"Wow! I had no idea!"

Gloria nodded. "Yup. That's why construction of the walls and roof trusses for the new school has already begun off-site, even while work on the foundation continues." She echoed Eileen's comment. Hopefully the new school would be ready by April. The timeline sounded unrealistic to me.

Tour completed, Gloria wished me luck and drove off trailing a cloud of road dust. I stood alone, the morning silence broken only by the lowing of a small dairy herd that grazed in the adjacent pasture. My chest tightened slightly, and a chill passed through me. I squinted at the sun's rays cutting through the distant maple trees. "What have I gotten myself into?" I asked the cows.

As the opening of school neared, student enrollment grew to over 100, far more than the existing buildings could accommodate. Across the dirt road from the Noyesville School stood the Walden United Methodist Church. The church elders (who had heard stories about the behavior of "those big kids") reluctantly agreed to let the district rent their large basement room and convert it into a middle school classroom for forty sixth-, seventh-, and eighth-graders and their two teachers. With Sue's help, I used a couple of sheetrock panels to partially close in a corner of the Noyesville school and created a "principal's office." Mornings, kindergarten claimed the remaining space, followed by an afternoon preschool group. A primary class and two intermediate classes shoehorned into the remaining three schoolhouses.

Soon after school began, a few male students started challenging the two experienced middle school educators. The boys' behavior included inappropriate language, bullying, fist fights with each other, and destruction of school and individual property. Daily interruptions made it difficult to provide a program conducive to learning.

One day I answered a call to help the teachers manage an unruly student—the acknowledged ringleader. He outstripped me by several inches and weighed over 200 pounds. In a fit of rage, the boy had overturned several tables and chairs. As I entered the church basement, he saw me and bellowed "Fuck you!" I called his mother to pick up her son and take him home. But as I well knew, this student, regardless of his oppositional behavioral disorder, was entitled to be educated with his peers in the least restrictive environment possible. I needed to come up with an accommodation to make that happen.

I recommended the school bus driver, a woman named Cathy, be hired as a temporary middle school classroom behavioral aide and Dr. Hull, my superintendent, supported me. Cathy, a well-known Walden local, lived with her partner on a nearby farm where the two women raised llamas. A no-nonsense individual, she had the respect of both adults and kids who saw her as "one of us." With this additional supervision and zero tolerance for misbehavior, things began to improve. An already tight budget took a serious blow with the extra hire, but I'd survived my first crisis.

The challenge of turning around a dysfunctional school quickly began to take its toll on me personally. The system lacked the basic cornerstones of a well-organized program: a defined and coordinated curriculum, procedures to measure student progress, a teacher and administrator evaluation process, written policies regarding school governance, job descriptions for non-teaching personnel, a guidance program, instruction in the arts—the list went on and on.

Twelve-hour workdays became my new normal. A myriad of meetings—construction, school board, staff—all took place after the students' day ended. The bus broke down. School cooks and teachers needed substitutes. The wells that supplied water in two of the schools became contaminated. Wherever I looked I saw more to do. So, I pushed myself harder and harder. Often, I ate in my car as I drove from classroom to classroom. Sleep became elusive, I couldn't shut off my brain. I wanted to fix everything. Instantly.

At times frustration overwhelmed me. My inability to affect change left me feeling inert and reminded me of Steve and those long ago days in Port Jefferson. Old feelings of helplessness flooded in. Transforming sick systems was so hard—even when I had the power and experience to do so. I knew I needed to keep pushing for change in Walden. These children deserved to be able to learn without dodging leaks in the roof or enduring a long ride to school (when the bus worked, that is). Like Steve, they deserved access to an educational system that would maximize their potential.

Steve arrived to spend Thanksgiving with Sue and me, and wasted no time making an announcement. "Jim and Denise have a baby! I so excited!"

Jim confirmed Steve's news, adding the baby was due in early spring. Sue and I agreed once the baby arrived, Steve needed to move on. We began working with Robert Vaillancourt to find another caregiver. Now I had an additional problem needing my attention. I had to shift some of my focus from Walden to my son.

But Sue and I weren't certain anymore that Steve, now twenty-eight, should remain in the Hanover area. We rarely traveled there other than to pick up Steve and bring him to Lyndon for a visit. Meanwhile, Mike and his partner Pamela had both graduated Macalester College and now lived in Burlington, Vermont. Firmly established as a couple, they said they'd love to have Steve live nearby. Additionally, Sue and I had several close friends in Burlington and during the winter months we often made the drive there to follow the University of Vermont's women's basketball team. Perhaps Burlington would be a better alternative for Steve and for us.

Such a move meant crossing state lines and we had no idea what relocation entailed in terms of services or funding, other than Steve couldn't continue to be supported by United Developmental Services if he left New Hampshire. When you are dependent on such support, moving becomes complicated.

In January Sue and I met with Robert in his office and broached our idea of moving Steve to Burlington. He called the Howard Center, the agency covering the Burlington area, and discovered Steve would need to live in Vermont for a year before becoming eligible for services.

I groaned. "Damn it! Why is there always an unending series of roadblocks?"

But Robert remained undaunted. "Give me some time to research this, Linda. Steve's disability shouldn't restrict your desire to have him move to Burlington. I actually live in Vermont. I'm familiar with the Howard Center. They run an outstanding program and match up well with what we offer here."

"Can we pull this off by summer?" I asked Robert, thinking back to Hanover and when I'd failed Steve in 1989.

He nodded. "Yes, I really feel we can. What you wanted for Steve years ago is seen as best practice now. We don't have to invent something or convince anyone of what works for Steve. New Hampshire and Vermont have a history of collaboration. I know the key players in both states. Give me a couple of months. I'll keep you posted. You're working hard enough in Walden. Let me do my job."

Robert was right. I needed to let go of some of the control I'd always wrapped so tightly around Steve and his life, both for Steve's sake and for mine. Besides, the undertaking I'd so eagerly begun in Walden had recently turned into something I could never have anticipated.

TWENTY-NINE

Taking Flight, 1994-95

Soon after Gloria and I had toured the one-room schoolhouses, she'd resigned her position on the school board. Her intent all along had been to leave once funding for a new school had been secured. I couldn't spend time mourning her departure. Each day it seemed there was one more ball to juggle. Only one individual expressed an interest in filling the opening created by Gloria's departure and the remaining two board members reluctantly approved his appointment. Initially I didn't understand their objections to Logan "Hutch" Hutchinson but listened as they tried to reassure themselves the appointment was temporary. Hopefully another town member would step up and file for election at the town meeting several months away.

Town Meeting Day is a Vermont institution, dating back to the mid-1700s. Held annually on the first Tuesday in March, residents in each town gather to discuss business and vote for public officials. As Town Meeting Day 1995 approached, only Mr. Hutchinson had filed for the open school board position. He ran unopposed, his election a foregone conclusion. So much for temporary.

Over the months I'd become familiar with Hutch. I knew he wasn't my friend. A third-generation Walden native with a pugnacious demeanor, he and his wife had seven children, the oldest an eighth grader. Hutch's staunch conservative beliefs included a well-known disapproval of same-sex relationships. Soon after his election, the board met to reorganize. Hutch indicated his enthusiasm in becoming board chair. The other two members acquiesced, and the nature of board changed profoundly. My base of support began to erode.

By early April I was really struggling. One evening as I pulled into our driveway at midnight, I realized I'd just put in a seventeen-hour day. Six hours later, when my alarm jarred me awake, I stumbled out of bed. No one could maintain that pace and stay sane. Once again depression began to overtake me.

On a Saturday morning a trivial incident occurred at home. I sat at the computer composing the weekly Walden parent newsletter. Suddenly I heard breaking glass followed by "Oh shit" from Sue. Concerned she'd injured herself, I dashed into the kitchen to find her sweeping up the last shards of a wine goblet from the previous night's dinner. Without any foresight or reason, I snapped.

"How can you be so clumsy?" I snarled. Storm clouds swirled within me. In a haze of adrenaline, I grabbed the broom from Sue and began brandishing it wildly. "Look at this mess! Everything in my life is a mess right now." I didn't intend to harm her. I didn't intend anything. But pent-up fear and frustration clamored for airtime and self-control eluded me.

I stepped away from Sue, still flailing the broomstick. Sue backed away too. "Linda, Linda…," she said quietly, trying to calm me. She knew I wasn't fully aware of my actions. "It's OK, Linda. It's just a wineglass."

I noticed the broom in my hand and turned away, flinging it to the floor. It skittered along the linoleum and came to rest under a table. "I can't stand my life," I sobbed. I collapsed onto the kitchen floor, oblivious to the broken glass, and curled into a ball. My body racked with tremors. Black spots floated behind closed eyelids. I moaned. Tears puddled under my face. I felt as helpless as a newborn. Sue retrieved the broom and cleared the glass away as best she could. When my crying dissipated, she urged me to take a shower. She made me a cup of tea.

This time my primary care physician referred me to a psychiatrist. In her office, we discussed the broom incident. I surprised myself by stating I'd never intended to harm Sue, that I'd actually wanted to hurt myself. The doctor increased my dosage of Zoloft and advised me to resume seeing my therapist. I followed her directions but despite these interventions, I continued to spiral deeper and deeper into depression. Once again feelings of isolation and unworthiness took over where hope and determination used to live. Sue's alarm for my well-being increased weekly, but I pushed her away over and over. I found a distorted comfort as a victim.

At work I repeated the pattern I'd established in Lyndon and convinced myself no one noticed my desperation. Working with Logan Hutchinson became more and more difficult. He inserted himself into the daily operation of the school on a regular basis. He stated he saw me as the board's "agent," and questioned many of my decisions. I started wondering if I could continue at Walden.

But when the board asked me to return for a second year and offered me a small raise, I decided to hang on. In my eyes, resigning would constitute failure, and I'd never been a quitter. Once again, I ignored the same perfectionist determination that kept me in my marriage to Roger too long and pushed me to fulfill the traditional roles assigned to young women. An inner voice urged me to stay in Walden—convinced me I could overcome Hutch's need for control. The same voice persuaded me success meant more than doing what was right for me. I wanted to conquer something. Prove something.

I could make good choices for others, but not for myself. Sure enough, the tension between Hutch and me escalated.

In early summer a certificate of occupancy meant the July school board meeting was held in the sparkling conference room of the new Walden School. Seated at a rectangular table, I gazed around at the freshly painted walls and the gleaming waxed floor. But I was too tired to appreciate how much had been accomplished.

The first item on the agenda concerned the newly created middle school para-educator's position. Student behavior in this age group had improved since I'd hired Cathy and the board had decided to make the position a permanent one. By law, this meant the opening needed to be advertised. My job over the past weeks had been to review applications, check references, interview several candidates, and provide the board with two finalists. I nominated Cathy, who had already demonstrated her ability to work with these students. As the second finalist, I selected a young man fresh out of college who'd done his student teaching in a neighboring high school. Hutch asked me to review the qualifications of each candidate for the board.

I offered my observations and told the board why I believed Cathy to be the best fit for the job, stressing the importance of continuity. But Hutch surprised me by refusing to accept my recommendation. He wanted to wait until Superintendent Hull arrived. I sat stunned. This hire was my responsibility, not Dr. Hull's.

I remembered several weeks earlier when a friend told me about a comment he'd overheard Hutch make at a party they'd both attended.

Hutch had stated he was determined to "...rid my school of lesbians."
I'd tried to dismiss the comment as gossip. But now, knowing Hutch
was well aware of Cathy's sexual orientation as well as mine, a cold
lump settled in my stomach. I could feel the jurisdiction which came
with my position eroding like the banks of a swollen river.

When Dr. Hull finally arrived at the meeting, Hutch tilted back in
his chair and raised the faded visor of his ever-present cap.

"Linda has nominated two finalists to the board. And although she
prefers Cathy," Hutch scratched the stubble on his chin, "I think we
need more men in the school. I propose we hire the young guy."

My shoulders slumped with resignation. I knew his decision had
nothing to do with the best interests of the students or teachers. Dr.
Hull nodded his agreement. How could this be happening? Again?

The meeting ended around midnight, and the minute I was home I
fell into bed empty and numb. Once again, I'd been rendered powerless, my voice silenced by the patriarchy. This tape was a familiar one:
a doctor calling my son a mongoloid idiot; a husband keeping information from me; a school official deciding how Steve's needs could
best be met. Now a superintendent and a school board chair telling me
whom to hire.

The next morning, several upset teachers crowded into my office.
Word had gotten out regarding the board's decision. They couldn't
understand why I hadn't supported Cathy. I explained I had recommended her, but the final decision rested with the board. I knew my
creditability as a leader had just taken a major hit. I had let the teachers down, to say nothing of Cathy.

The following day Sue and I boarded a plane for Seattle. We'd
booked an all-women's kayaking excursion in an area known as the San
Juan Islands. For the next two weeks, I gave myself over to the natural
beauty surrounding us and tried to let it soothe my wounded soul. We
relaxed into our limited responsibilities: set up our tent each evening at
a new campsite, take it down the following morning, get into a two-
person sea kayak and paddle away. All meals were planned and cooked
for us. Our experienced guides determined each day's travel based on
tides, currents, and wind direction. The steady rhythm of paddling and
the gentle company of women soothed me. Once again, I was Outward
Bound. Sightings of wildlife—eagles, sea lions, and whales spouting in
the distance—enthralled me, and perfect weather blessed us. On our last
day, I didn't want to get out of the kayak.

"I could do this forever," I told Sue. "I don't want to go back home." But we both knew that wasn't a choice.

I headed into work the first day after our return to Vermont and discovered Hutch's candidate had turned down the para-educator's position. Hutch wanted to advertise the opening again. He didn't want me involved. He formed a committee consisting of the teachers who'd be working with the middle school students. He directed the committee to handle screening and interviews of applicants and to bring two candidates to the board. Whatever! I was happy to step out of what had become an emotionally-charged process. I did my best to bury my apprehension about Hutch's obvious homophobia and the growing isolation surrounding me. Maybe everything would work out.

When Cathy's name appeared as a finalist a second time, Hutch again spurned the recommendation. He added two community members to the committee. The enhanced committee still picked Cathy as their top choice.

I felt vindicated, but Hutch refused to give up. The opening of the school year was two days away when he walked into my office. Hutch had convened an unscheduled board meeting the previous night, where board had decided not to accept the committee's decision. "We're going to re-interview every applicant ourselves," he told me. "Please let the teachers know."

I gulped. Indignation filled every fiber of my body. This marked the third time Hutch had opposed Cathy's nomination. His behavior was outrageous. It was sexist, disrespectful, and wrong. A shiver shook me. I'd reached my limit.

I rose out of my office chair and exclaimed, "I can't continue to work like this. What you've done is illegal. You held a board meeting without notification. You can't operate unilaterally like that." I gathered steam. "This is not your private school to run as you see fit. I'm not delivering your message to the teachers. Do it yourself." I took a deep breath before adding, "I can't work with you, Hutch. Maybe I should just quit."

Hutch's beefy face reddened, and he stomped out. The room spun. My ears roared. Everything I'd worked for during the past fourteen months dissolved behind tear-clouded eyes. I grabbed my purse and car keys and walked out of the building. Just as I'd done so many times before when faced with adversity, I fled.

THIRTY

Psych Ward, 1995

"Linda! Linda!" Footsteps pounded…closer and closer! Panic roared through me. My head bent down. My arms pumped even harder. I had to get away. I couldn't let them catch me.

"Linda?" The soft sound of someone calling my name and a shaft of blinding sunlight sucked me from unconsciousness and out of danger. I rolled over and opened my eyes. A woman I didn't recognize stood over me holding a tiny paper cup with several pills of various sizes and colors. I looked around the small room: cream colored walls, linoleum floor, one window. "Tuesday, 9/20/95" was inscribed in blue ink on the small whiteboard screwed to the wall opposite the twin bed where I lay. Momentarily I wondered…*Where the hell am I?* Then I noticed the identification band on my right wrist and the bandage on my left hand. *Shit.* I turned away, drew my knees up to my core and wrapped my arms around my shoulders. My chest hurt. Waves of nausea rose in my throat. A low moan escaped my lips. This was no nightmare. I was really here. "Here" was the locked psychiatric ward of Dartmouth-Hitchcock Hospital in Hanover, New Hampshire, where Sue had taken me the previous afternoon.

During the three weeks since I'd had my confrontation with Hutch, my life had unraveled. On the day I'd fled the school, Superintendent Hull called me at home. "What's happening?" he asked. "Logan Hutchinson just left my office. He said something about you quitting."

I told him about the message Hutch asked me to deliver to the teachers and my refusal to do so. "This process of hiring a para-educator began a month and a half ago. Hutch clearly doesn't want

Cathy in this position. He keeps resetting the rules, and when he doesn't get the desired results, he changes the rules again. I can't work with him and his homophobia."

What I didn't say was how threatened I felt by Hutch. Not only did he not want Cathy working in the school, but was he trying to get rid of me too? I knew things had gotten way out of line. Why couldn't Dr. Hull see this?

But my supervisor said he didn't want to discuss things over the phone. Couldn't I just put this aside for now and focus on the opening of the school year?

"No," I responded. "I can't put this aside! Hutch wants me to act as his puppet and there's no way I'm going to do that!" But I agreed to meet Dr. Hull at school the following morning.

I'd fallen asleep by the time Sue got home but awoke as she got into bed. I told her what had happened earlier and about Dr. Hull's call. We talked, and I cried, long into the night. Sue shook her head in disbelief as I recounted my interaction with Hutch and my phone conversation with Dr. Hull. As a superintendent herself, she knew Dr. Hull and had attended many regional meetings with him. She also knew how tense things had become between me and Hutch, and my concern about what I felt was eroding support from Dr. Hull.

"I can understand why you are so upset," she said. "But do you really want to resign? You've worked awfully hard to get to the point where you are now."

I'd worked hard for sure. I'd thrown all of myself into this job, as I had done with everything in my life. I'd supported the Walden students and staff as if I were advocating for my own children. "I don't know what I want to do!" I wailed.

I wasn't fully conscious of what was happening under the surface. I thought the stress I felt was because of the power struggle between Hutch and me—trying to do what was right for the kids and the community while feeling his resistance to me personally and my role as a leader. I wouldn't fully grasp until much later that the way Hutch stripped me of power triggered all the other times in my life when men had used their voices to silence mine. My energy for pushing for what I believed to be right was depleted. I couldn't explain all this to Sue because I lacked the insight to put it together.

Sue didn't try to tell me what to do. Some part of me wished she would. The last thing I remembered before I drifted off to sleep was her telling me to take care of myself. She would stand by whatever I decided.

I awoke the next morning certain of my course. Every human has a basic need to be seen and understood. I wasn't willing to put my needs aside any longer. Hadn't I done just that for too much of my life? When Dr. Hull and I met at the school, his tone hadn't changed.

"Just focus on getting school opened, Linda. We can deal with your concerns about this conflict with Mr. Hutchinson at another time."

I reached into my purse, pulled out my letter of resignation, and handed it to him. Within hours all hell broke loose.

My departure made the front page of the local newspaper. Dr. Hull was quoted as saying, while all boards micromanaged to some degree, he viewed my reaction as extreme. I felt mortified by the public scrutiny.

At home the phone rang incessantly. The opening of school was pushed back three days. Teachers were confused, then angry. At me. For abandoning them. Rumors flew. Many parents blamed the school board. I didn't handle the fallout well. I suffered several panic attacks. I couldn't sleep or eat. I dug at the skin on my left hand until it bled. Sue didn't know what to do other than to try and reassure me I wasn't a bad person. She took time off from work. She drove me to the psychiatrist's office several times for emergency interventions. I sank deeper and deeper. Finally, my psychiatrist decided I needed intensive treatment and offered two alternatives: sign myself voluntarily into the psychiatric ward or she'd commit me herself.

Don't ever let anyone tell you that voluntarily signing yourself in for a psychiatric evaluation isn't a big deal. It's huge. You are in a locked ward. You can't leave without an escort. You are never certain when one of your fellow inmates might explode. You are watched carefully when taking medications. You may be asked to open your mouth to make sure you aren't hiding the pills under your tongue. The morning when the nurse woke me, shame bound me like a straitjacket. My soul had been hijacked.

During the first few days, I barely spoke and made little eye contact. Medication kept me groggy. Initially my overwhelming emotion was relief. I had no responsibilities. Nothing I needed to do. No place I needed to be. No decisions I needed to make. I discovered art therapy provided some release. I let my hands create without thinking. But every time I tried to make some sense of what had happened, how I'd ended up in such a state, my world caved in on me again. What had I done? Why had I resigned? I became certain I'd ruined a thirty-year career as a public school educator. The only other role I'd defined my-self by, except that of mother, was gone. What did I have left?

Skilled therapists worked with me in both individual and group sessions. They urged me to be gentle with myself, to appreciate all I'd accomplished throughout my long career. Between the rest and the medication, my mental state began to slowly improve. I understood many things had factored into my breakdown. I couldn't hold myself solely responsible for a systemic failure. With perspective, the depression lifted a little.

Mike and Josh phoned our home several times. Sue kept track of calls from educational colleagues, friends, parents. Even a grandparent of a current Walden student phoned and delivered her gratitude for changes I'd made during my year as principal. I began to realize I'd been caught in a perfect storm. I had much to live for and be thankful for. Eventually I was able to string several hours together without crying.

On the weekend of my seven-day stay at the hospital, little happened in the way of treatment. The reality of being in a locked ward closed in. I wanted out from what felt like a jail. I resolved to meet the requirements for release.

After a week, I knew I'd made progress. I'd become an active participant in group meetings. I'd started offering my own ideas in individual counseling. Nurses trusted me to take my medications without supervision. One huge hurdle remained, however. As part of my treatment plan I'd been asked to identify those with whom I most needed to make amends. I knew the answer: the staff at the school. I agreed to allow hospital personnel to set up a reconciliation meeting between myself and the Walden teachers. These were the folks I'd worked most closely with for the past fourteen months. Before my hospitalization, I'd been told by Dr. Hull not to communicate with the staff. That directive was, and continued to be, hurtful—an impenetrable block to my recovery. I wanted and needed to talk with these individuals face to face.

But the concept of meeting with the Walden staff in a locked psychiatric hospital ward both terrified and embarrassed me. What had they been told about me? What did they think about me? I envisioned them conjuring up a scene from *One Flew Over the Cuckoo's Nest*. Did they view their former principal as an insane crazy person? Did I see myself that way? Or could I hold on to the understanding I'd been in the double bind of having responsibilities without the power to execute them—not for just this last year, but for decades?

The therapist assigned to my case assured me these meetings happened often. I wouldn't be alone. She would be present. The format would be tightly regulated. "I" statements only. No blaming. She'd help me prepare ahead of time.

When I entered the conference room, five teachers were already seated. I looked for Cathy, who I knew had finally been hired as the middle school para-educator, but she wasn't among them. Everyone looked grim. No one, including myself, felt particularly comfortable. We were all wounded.

After explaining the ground rules, the therapist facilitated the hourlong meeting. I'd received a lot of coaching and unlike three weeks earlier—unlike much of my life before Sue—I felt supported and cared for. I'd prepared an opening written statement, but as I looked around, I pushed my notes aside and spoke from my heart.

"I'm so sorry for the pain I caused you. Please know that was never my intention. I have nothing but respect for each and every one of you." My eyes began to fill, and I struggled to keep my composure. "I got caught up in a power struggle that lasted far too long." Then I straightened my shoulders and looked around the room. "But I have certain core values that I've always held dear. These include fairness, integrity, and justice. I couldn't continue without compromising those values." As I said this, I knew I'd spoken my truth. The monstrous dissonance between my beliefs and my ability to live by them had gobbled me up and spit me out.

The tension which clogged the room lifted a bit. One by one everyone spoke. Lips quivered and tears dribbled down faces. The teachers told me they felt "blindsided" and "abandoned" by my resignation. Hard words for me to hear. I didn't feel any forgiveness coming from the staff. Any understanding of the pressures I'd been under. They couldn't know I wasn't someone who abandoned others. That I was a woman who'd made a lifelong commitment to my grown child, a commitment I'd never put aside. They were still mourning their own losses. They couldn't see me in a nuanced way. Even so, difficult truths were bravely spoken. This courageous action on the part of everyone cleansed me.

The following morning, Sue attended my hospital discharge meeting. I was advised to rest and keep things simple. I agreed to return over the course of several weeks for ten sessions of outpatient treatment. When I walked out on Tuesday afternoon, September 26, I took a deep breath. I couldn't believe how good the fresh air tasted.

On our way out of Hanover, Sue drove past the stately Dartmouth College buildings surrounding the five-acre quadrangle known as The Green. I blinked back tears and remembered the summer day eighteen years earlier when our family first rode by the same spot, after a long drive from Long Island. Back then my heart had swelled with hope and promise. Promise for a break in the relentless obstruction I'd been facing in Steve's education. I felt a connection between this moment of freedom from the psych ward to that moment of freedom from the dark days of Long Island.

Sue and I pulled into the driveway of our home. I stepped out of the car and gazed at the freshly mown lawn and the blazing leaves on my favorite maple tree.

"How are you doing?" asked Sue as she reached for my hand and we walked toward the house.

"It feels good to be here," I replied, "but I'm scared too. I can't believe I've only been gone a week. It feels like much longer." As we stepped inside, I spotted the bouquet of fresh flowers on the dining table. "Oh!" My hands closed over my heart and I reached for the attached card. It read: "Love you forever, Mom. Steve, Mike, and Josh."

I began to cry. Sue wrapped me in her arms, and as I relaxed into her embrace, she whispered into my ear, "It's OK, sweetie. Everything is going to be OK."

THIRTY-ONE

Slow Recovery, 1995-96

And just where was Steve as I fought my demons inside and out? Thriving in Burlington. True to his word, Robert had worked a deal between United Developmental Services and the Howard Center in Burlington. Until Steve established residency in Vermont, UDS would continue to fund the support services carried out by the Howard Center. Robert had even found someone to live with Steve, a second-year student enrolled in the University of Vermont's masters of social work program. *And* Robert had arranged for Steve to be transferred from the Hanover Grand Union grocery to one in Burlington. Although Steve said he was a "teeny bit sad" to be leaving Jim, he also admitted "babies pee and poop and cry—*a lot*." By the time I left the hospital he'd been happily living in Burlington for more than a year.

In early January, an eager crowd of basketball fans pressed forward as the doors to the University of Vermont's Patrick Gymnasium swung open. I grabbed the shoulder of Steve's heavy winter jacket.

"Stay close, Steve," I said. "We don't want to lose you!"

As we approached the ticket counter, I began rooting around in my purse for my wallet and glasses.

"Shit," I cried out. "I've got my wallet, but my glasses are missing. Maybe they fell out as we were coming in." Although my mental state had improved since being discharged from the hospital four months earlier, any stress could still trigger me.

Sue agreed to stand in line while I backtracked my steps. Minutes later I found my prescription lenses lying on the lobby floor—crushed. Tears filled my eyes as I made my way back to Sue and Steve.

"Find 'em?" asked Sue.

"Yeah, but they're wrecked." I reached up to wipe my eyes. Mentally I ordered myself to calm down, but I could feel my face begin to flush. I teetered on the edge of panic.

Steve's small hand closed over mine. His eyes searched my face. "Remember your job, Mom? Keep your feet on the ground."

"What?" I replied.

"Same thing with your glasses. Keep your feet on the ground." Steve's voice was earnest; concern flooded his face.

I looked down and drank in my son's wise soul. Until this moment I'd no clue how much he understood about my breakdown. I'd never spoken to Steve about any of my struggles, but somehow, he knew. Had he talked with his brothers? With Sue? It didn't matter. Here he stood, offering me sage advice. Sometimes his emotional intelligence surprised me, and on this afternoon Steve's sensitivity felt comforting.

Throughout the fall and early winter, I'd been an unhinged weather vane, sometimes pointing true, but also swinging wildly without direction. There were days when questions rattled at me as if shot from a machine gun. Why hadn't I held on at Walden? Was my career as an educator over? How long could Sue and I survive financially on one paycheck?

My therapist, my psychiatrist, and the staff of the hospital outpatient program all urged me to step back, take time to heal, and consider some different pursuits. I signed up for weekly watercolor classes taught by a gentle, kind, encouraging woman. Some days I painted passionately for hours, losing myself to the process.

I was asked to join the Dorothy Canfield Fisher Book Award Committee, responsible for running Vermont's Children's Choice program for readers in grades 4-8. Members read and reviewed several hundred recently-published juvenile fiction and nonfiction books to determine the thirty titles for the annual master list. In late spring kids voted for their favorite and the author of the winning book was invited to Vermont to speak to students and teachers from throughout the state. I loved the work and the people on the committee.

In early December I attended a two-day training for ski instructors, earned a Level I certificate, and joined the ski school staff at nearby Burke Mountain. On weekends I taught in the children's program, but some of my most satisfying lessons occurred during the week when I introduced "never-ever" adults to the sport I loved.

These activities kept me active and positively engaged. Slowly my brain gained a bit of space. My obsessive thinking about what happened in Walden lessened. Confidence began to seep in. Days felt a bit lighter.

But I turned the corner on my path to recovery when I received a call from the director of special education at Lyndon Institute, the local high school. We knew each other from my days as associate principal of the Lyndon Town School. She wondered if I'd be interested in tutoring a unique group of students, who for various reasons had stopped attending classes but were still eligible for services.

We met in her office and she reviewed their records. Jason had significant metal health issues. Tom had set fire to a trash can he'd stuffed with paper towels in the boys' bathroom. Tyler came from a dysfunctional family and struggled with depression.

This prospect felt like a good fit. These were the kinds of kids to whom I'd always been drawn. And now, more than ever, I had some understanding of the demons related to each boy's behavior. I asked about the pay.

"We pay our tutors $15 an hour," answered the director.

I cleared my throat and ignored my sweaty palms along with the butterflies in my stomach. I knew her offer was well above Vermont's minimum wage of $5, but within me a voice whispered: *Linda, you are worth more.* "Oh" I replied. "I am interested in working with these students, but my hourly rate is $20."

"I think I can make that happen," she responded. "These guys need someone like you."

My eyes widened. My inner voice cheered: *Good for you, Linda!*

The director's willingness to pay what I'd ask meant she respected my skills and what I could offer these troubled students. My self-esteem ratcheted up another notch.

Once Steve had established residency in Vermont, the Howard Center took over from UDS as my son's official service provider—a relationship which would continue for the next nineteen years. I felt Steve, now almost thirty years old, was truly settled.

He loved his life in Burlington. He relished the hustle and bustle of the city's vibrant downtown core, known as Church Street Marketplace. Restaurants and shops lined both sides of the pedestrian-only thoroughfare that stretched for four blocks. Steve could wander from store to store without worrying about vehicle traffic. Saturdays meant a stop at Dunkin' Donuts for a chocolate-glazed treat, "my favorite." Before long the counter people greeted Steve by name when he entered. During the warmer months the varied entertainment provided daily by buskers left Steve enthralled. Occasionally he was spontaneously included in their show.

His job proved a different story. Although Steve had been awarded a transfer to the Grand Union in South Burlington, this store was three times larger than Hanover's Grand Union. The size and faster pace was a poor fit for Steve. He complained, "This too hard."

Sue and I met with Steve's team and we all agreed he needed a different placement. Howard's job developer promised to find something less taxing. Several months passed and eventually Steve began working at a much smaller health food market. The sparkle returned to his eyes.

During his second summer in Burlington, Steve also gained a sister-in-law. The previous summer I'd taken a phone call from Steve. He was so excited he could barely speak.

"M-M-Mom, y-y-you not b-b-believe this. M-M-Mikey-Boy and P-P-Pamela get m-m-married!"

"What, Steve?" I knew Mike and Pamela were vacationing in Maine and planned to stop in Lyndon on their way back to Burlington. Had they eloped? "Slow down, Steve. What are you talking about?"

"Mikey-Boy c-c-call me! I so excited! Pam b-b-be my sister-in-law!"

Eventually I was able to establish Mike and Pamela had gotten engaged. Sue and I decided on a unique way to let them know Steve had shared their exciting news. Sue lettered a message on an old white bedsheet with a red marker: "Congratulations! Now Pamela will have not one, not two, but THREE mothers-in-law!" Roger and Polly had married, thus the bounty of mothers-in-laws. When the two lovebirds pulled into our driveway, the sheet hung on the side of our house.

The destination wedding in June of 1996 was held at a rustic lakeside resort in northern Minnesota near Pamela's hometown. Pamela wore her mother's wedding gown and Mike looked handsome in my father's tux. The ceremony took place outdoors in front of the resort's chapel built in the late nineteenth century. Besides family and friends, invited guests included Domino, the bride and groom's dog, tended to by Josh. Sue and I handed out bubble containers and iridescent orbs floated through the air as Pamela and Mike intoned the original vows they'd composed for each other. My body tingled with happiness as the two exchanged rings. They had been partners for a long time and I was old-fashioned enough to rejoice at their decision to formalize their love for each other.

During the reception dinner Steve offered a wedding toast. After stating how happy he was to have a sister-in-law, he added, "I no get married. I no like sex." My cheeks burned crimson with embarrassment. *Where did that come from?* But Mike and Josh burst into laughter along with the other guests.

The two days and nights at the Hanging Horn Lake Resort were magical. Sue and I spent much of that time with Roger and Polly. It was easy being around them. I held no animosity toward Roger and warmed up quickly to Polly.

One afternoon Roger and I ended up alone on the lake shore. I used the opportunity to ask a burning question. "Are you happy?"

"Yes. Very," he answered softly.

"I'm glad," I responded. "I never wanted to hurt you." Gratefully I released my burden of guilt to the breeze that fluttered the leaves of the birch trees nearby and watched it drift away.

But on the flight back to Vermont, a sadness wiggled its way into my thoughts. Sue and I'd been a couple for almost eight years. Together we owned our house. We'd stopped using separate checking accounts. With the help of an investment counselor we'd created a joint portfolio. But unlike Roger and Polly, and now Mike and Pamela, we had no legal status. Would we ever be able to marry? I couldn't imagine a future where that might be possible.

Throughout the fall I continued to make tiny steps toward a full recovery. I saw my therapist regularly, and the psychiatrist every six to eight weeks. I continued to paint. I picked up more tutoring clients. I signed up for a second season of ski instructing.

One December morning I dashed out of the house, running late for a tutoring appointment. I entered our oversized two-car garage, climbed into my van, and turned on the ignition. I shifted into reverse and stepped on the gas. CRASH! I'd neglected one small detail—to open and raise the door behind the car. Whoops!

Standing in the driveway I surveyed the damage. The lower two panels of the wooden door were pushed out and splintered. I felt familiar rage beginning to churn inside me. *Shit! Look what you've just done! How could you be so stupid?!* But then, instead of tears, something tickled my stomach. The sensation increased. A hint of a smile turned the corners of my mouth. Followed by a giggle. Replaced by full-bellied laughter. What a surprise! I bent over and hugged my ribs. Then straightened up and tipped my face to the sky, arms raised in a victory *V.* I stood facing the absurdity of what I'd just done. But I wasn't crying! I wasn't angry! I knew I'd achieved a monumental milestone. Minutes passed. I stood in the cold air as a few snowflakes drifted around me and declared myself cured of depression.

I felt whole and strong.

THIRTY-TWO

Different Hospital, 1997

I needed every ounce of strength when the phone rang at 3:00 a.m. on the morning of March 17, 1997. Steve's caregiver explained she was in the hospital with him. She'd come home from an evening out and heard Steve calling her from his bedroom. He was on the floor, unable to get up. An ambulance had transported him to the emergency room.

"I didn't call you sooner because I didn't know what was going on," she explained. "But I've just talked with a doctor. Preliminary tests indicate Steve has a mass on his brain." My body froze. "The doctor said I should call and let you know."

"Sue and I will leave immediately," I choked out. "Please stay with Steve until we arrive."

During the hour-and-a-half drive through the pitch-black night, the same tape kept playing in my head—back to the time, thirteen years earlier, when Steve had awoken hemorrhaging from his nose. A mass on his brain sounded at least as serious. Desperate, terrifying thoughts cycled through me, as they always did whenever a medical issue developed with Steve. I always went to the worst place and saw him teetering on the edge between life and death. Is this a tumor? A burst blood vessel? Will my son still be alive by the time Sue and I arrive?

Sue brought the car to a halt in front of the emergency entrance and I tore through the door, prepared to elbow anyone in my way to the side. Fortunately, the waiting room was empty, and I approached the woman behind the counter.

"My son, Steve Cohen, was admitted here earlier this evening," My heart pounded. My mouth was dry. I was frantic with worry. "I'm his mother, Linda Morrow. I need to see him immediately."

Steve, thirty-one, lay in a curtained cubicle surrounded by medical personnel in blue scrubs. Multiple IV lines ran from his body and a heart monitor beeped a continuous rhythm. His eyes fluttered with recognition, but he didn't speak. I bent over, my face inches from his. I saw the little baby I'd held in my arms so long ago, and the childhood I'd fought so hard to give him. "I'm here, Steve. Try to relax. Everything is going to be OK."

"Hi, Mom," he replied weakly.

"What's going on?" I asked the assembled crowd.

The lead physician stepped forward. "We have a few more tests to run before we can know for certain."

"Is this connected in any way to Steve's Down syndrome?" I asked.

"No," sighed the doctor. "No, not as far as we can determine." He placed a hand on my shoulder. "Just rotten luck."

I looked for a pay phone and called Roger.

Steve spent the next seventeen days in Fletcher Allen Hospital recovering from a brain aneurysm. Determining a treatment plan proved complicated and eventually surgery was ruled out because of Steve's congenital heart issues. Instead, medication was used to shrink the abscess. Surgeons installed a PICC, a peripherally inserted central catheter, to administer industrial strength doses of antibiotics four times daily. It would be mid-May before the PICC line came out.

But while the antibiotics slowly reduced the aneurism, Steve struggled with the toxic medicine's side effects. Stomach cramps reduced him to tears. Even small sips of water often led to violent vomiting. Lightheadedness made walking nearly impossible.

Sue stayed with me in Burlington during the first few days of Steve's hospitalization. But as a new work week approached, she reluctantly returned to Lyndon. I clenched my fists in anguish as I watched her walk out of Steve's room and down the hallway. I knew she couldn't be absent from her job any longer. I hoped I'd have the strength to advocate for Steve by myself.

Mike and Pamela visited frequently. Roger called at least once a day from Milwaukee, as did Josh from Bozeman, Montana. Sue returned to Burlington on the weekends. I appreciated their support, but mostly I soldiered on alone.

One afternoon I watched as a nurse helped Steve get out of bed and into a standing position. Without warning, his eyes rolled back in his head and he lost control of his bladder.

"Steve!" I shouted. "What's happening?"

Steve stood there stunned. Then he looked down at the stain spreading in the crotch of his pajamas. Embarrassed tears filled his eyes. "I sorry. I pee on myself."

Wild-eyed, I turned to the nurse. "Did you see that? With his eyes? What just happened?"

She told me he'd had a seizure. I helped her replace Steve's sodden pants with fresh ones. "You're OK, Steve. We're getting you cleaned up. This wasn't your fault." Despair flooded me. Dilantin, an anti-seizure drug, was added to his medical cocktail.

The two and half weeks Steve was hospitalized rendered me exhausted and numb, sometimes almost catatonic. Each night after Steve fell asleep, I'd grab a few hours of rest at his apartment, returning to the hospital before he awakened in the morning. Logically my behavior made no sense. I knew my physical presence wouldn't speed his recovery. But all mothers feel that need when their child is hurting. Mothers are supposed to protect their children. Always. I couldn't stand being apart from Steve. Heal, I pleaded with each breath I took. Heal.

When Steve was deemed recovered enough for discharge, he didn't want to leave the hospital. I understood. Despite the frequent needles and other procedures, Steve felt safe there.

"I no go home. It too scary," he cried, tears streaming down his cheeks.

My jaw clenched and I turned away from him for a few seconds. I shared my son's fears. But I couldn't let him know that.

A compassionate nurse arranged for a two-hour pass and I drove Steve home so he could reconnect with his own space. "This is just a test," I assured him. "I promise we'll go back to the hospital. But it will be good for you to see your apartment."

Steve nodded and his lips trembled. "I not see my room for a long time."

Back at the hospital, Steve began taking down the many drawings he'd made and gave them to his favorite staff people. Thursday, April 4, Sue arrived in time to join Steve, Mike, and me for the family discharge meeting. By mid-afternoon Steve was happily settled in front of the TV in his apartment's living room. Mike insisted that Sue and I take ourselves out for dinner while he stayed with Steve for some brother time.

As we began the five-minute walk from Steve's apartment to Church Street in search of a restaurant, I flexed my shoulders and quietly exhaled. I could almost see the tension floating from my body. *I did this*, I whispered under my breath. I'd tapped into my inner reserves and handled a difficult situation mostly on my own. A year earlier, I probably wouldn't have been able to deal with the overwhelming stress. But for seventeen days I'd shown up for Steve and I'd done it well. I knew I was healthy enough to move forward in my own life. Maybe I could resume my career as an educator and erase the cloud of failure which still hung over me.

THIRTY-THREE

On Stage, 1997-98

On a mid-summer morning, Steve stood on the sidewalk in front of his apartment looking anxiously down the one-way street.

"I see it! I see it!" Steve's mouth stretched into an excited grin. His eyes lit up.

A white Lincoln stretch limo pulled up to the curb. A uniformed driver, resplendent in a starched dress shirt, black tie, black jacket, and trousers stepped out and walked toward Steve. He doffed his hat and clicked the heels of his gleaming dress shoes before speaking.

"Mr. Cohen, I presume? I am Jack, your chauffeur for today's trip."

"Cool," exclaimed Steve. "I ready. I look inside?"

The limo, which would deliver Steve to his new residence a few miles away, was a special treat arranged and paid for by his dad.

The trip taking place this day was the result of a significant change I'd requested of the Howard Center regarding Steve's overall care. The IV therapy of massive antibiotics had successfully eliminated the aneurysm, but at a great cost to Steve's general health. Although the two years of apartment sharing with graduate students had gone well, now I wanted more supervision. Steve's case manager at the Howard Center searched recent applications for potential caregivers and found a promising one. When I met and interviewed Brenda and Wayne Lawton, a couple in their mid-fifties, my intuition told me they and Steve would be a great match. They signed a contract to become Steve's new caregivers. Today he was moving into their house.

Jack held open the passenger door as Steve stepped in and sat down on the luxurious black leather couch. His eyes scanned the elongated and elegant accommodations with enough room for perhaps a dozen people before settling on the extravagant wet bar.

"Would you care for a beverage, Mr. Cohen, before we embark on our journey?"

Bewildered, Steve didn't reply to Jack's question.

"He is asking you if you would like a drink, Steve," I translated.

"Yes, please, I do. Root beer my favorite. You have that?"

Jack did. A glass was filled and off they went. I'd asked Jack to spend thirty minutes taking a roundabout route so Steve could fully enjoy his unique mode of transportation while I headed directly to the Lawtons' with Steve's possessions. Brenda and Wayne were outside waiting when the limousine arrived and Steve stepped out.

Brenda, her wavy auburn hair cut short, held a bouquet of multi-colored balloons indicative of the bundle of energy contained in her short frame. Wayne, a lean and lanky guy whose silvered strands sat behind a receding hairline, rushed forward and wrapped his arms around Steve. His mischievous eyes twinkled though frameless glasses. Like Brenda, he'd moved to Burlington as a youngster, and graduated from Burlington High School.

The Lawtons welcomed Steve into their home, provided nutritious home-cooked meals, and embraced him with warmth and kindness. Parents of adult children, they introduced him to their vast network of family and friends and included Steve in many gatherings. To meet Howard's square footage requirements for dedicated client space, Brenda and Wayne had moved their bedroom to the first floor guest room and turned the second floor—a master bedroom, sitting room, and full bath—over to Steve. It didn't take long for me to know I'd struck gold.

Steve also had ten hours of community access services per week provided by a semi-retired guy who'd spent his career supporting adults with developmental disabilities, mostly in the Adirondack regions of New York state. Dave took Steve to routine medical appointments, workouts at the YMCA, and to the barber for his monthly buzz cuts. Not my preferred style, but certainly Steve's! They also hung out at the coffee shops on Church Street and attended movies. A deep and lasing friendship formed between Dave and Steve.

In late August, Sue, Steve, and I spent several amazing days exploring Toronto. Although we checked out many of the city's sights and amusements, the featured event was the Canadian production of *Phantom of the Opera* staged at the 2,200-seat Pantages Theatre. Steve startled with surprise, along with the rest of the audience, when the chandelier crashed to the stage floor at the end of the first act. He sat enthralled at the play's conclusion as the boat carrying the Phantom and Christine sailed through a cloud of dry ice. Steve's love affair with the theater had begun when he was quite young, but he'd never seen a production the likes of *Phantom*.

The curtain fell and the last notes of Andrew Lloyd Webber's "Finale" sounded. Steve turned to me.

"I wish I do that," he said. "I wish I be in play like that."

Hmmm, I thought. I'd never seen a performance of any kind include individuals with cognitive or physical disabilities. I wondered. Why couldn't a cowgirl in a wheelchair be part of the cast of *Oklahoma*? Why couldn't someone like Steve join the chorus of a similar show? I added the thought to my always-expanding mental list of things I wanted Steve to be able to do someday.

The following spring, while visiting Steve in Burlington, my eyes lit up when I read a brief article in the *Free Press,* the city's local paper. The Lyric Theatre Company, one of the community's largest groups, would be preforming *The Wizard of Oz* for their spring musical. The story included audition dates.

"Perfect," I murmured. "This is the perfect show for Steve." After all, he'd watched the original movie starring Judy Garland numerous times on TV.

I called the number listed in the article and spoke to the director.

"My adult son, Steve Cohen, has Down syndrome, but he loves the theater. Would you be open to having someone like him in the upcoming show?" I held my breath waiting for his response.

"Well," he replied. "Steve would need to audition like anyone else."

"Of course, I wouldn't want it any other way." I kept my voice calm and neutral. I knew the director couldn't see the grin which spread across my face or feel the warmth filling my body.

Steve responded with an enthusiastic "*Yes!*" when I asked if he was interested in this venture. Later Brenda told me Steve spent the next several days singing "Follow the Yellow Brick Road" and "We're Off to See the Wizard" over and over. She rented the VHS of the movie for Steve to watch before the tryouts. He auditioned for the Munchkin chorus and was selected, joining a total of sixty actors and actresses in the cast.

As the date for the first performance neared, Steve called me and said, "I might have small stage fright." But I knew he was ready. He'd attended every required rehearsal thanks to Brenda and Wayne's wholehearted willingness to provide transportation and other forms of support. Another adult member of the Munchkin gang had taken Steve under her wing and helped him learn all the dance moves.

On opening night, April 24, 1998, Jane, who traveled from Boston, joined me for Steve's debut. We settled into our seats and turned the pages of the playbill. Quickly we found what we were looking for: Steve's photo and brief bio, along with other members of the Munchkin chorus. Jane and I turned toward each other, eyes glistening. Soon the lights dimmed and the curtain rose. Every one of the Flynn Theater's 1,411 seats was filled. Each time Steve appeared on stage, my eyes saw only him. I swelled with pride and gratitude. My face glowed. *Steve's "village" made this possible*, I thought. My advocacy had paid off.

Over the course of twelve performances, many more of Steve's supporters saw him onstage, including Brenda, Wayne, and Dave. Jane's daughter, Heather—now the mother of two young girls—made the two-hour drive from her home in western Massachusetts.

At the closing performance, in addition to Sue and me, the audience included Roger, Josh, Mike, and Pamela. Collectively they'd traveled hundreds of miles to celebrate Steve's triumph.

After the final curtain, we crowded around Steve in the auditorium as, still in his stage makeup, he autographed each of our programs.

"You see me?" he asked over and over. "You see me? I a star!"

Yes, I nodded, *always and forever*.

THIRTY-FOUR

Deserved Recognition, 1998-2001

One afternoon in mid-May, shortly after Steve had concluded his run as a Munchkin on the big stage, I sat alone on our deck drinking in the deepening spring surrounding me. A recent warm spell had caused the Northeast Kingdom to pop. Leaf buds appeared on branches that just days before lay bare. Stray dandelions decorated a lawn that would soon need mowing.

The beep coming from the driveway announced Sue's arrival from work. Her face broke into a wide grin when she spotted me on the deck. She plopped down in the matching forest-green Adirondack chair next to me and ran her fingers through her graying hair.

"Hey, you're home early," I said reaching for Sue's hand. "How was your day?"

"Great! Only twenty-three more to go."

Sue looked forward to her upcoming retirement. For the past eight years she'd worked tirelessly as superintendent of a thirteen-school supervisory district which sprawled for miles along the Vermont-Canada border. Initially Sue had shared leadership responsibilities with two male colleagues in an innovative model which played to her strengths as a collaborative leader. But one by one, both men left for positions where they could be totally in charge. During her final years, Sue had handled on her own what had been a three-person job. Now fifty-five, with thirty-three years in education under her belt, she qualified for a full pension. Why keep working?

"Speaking of which," I replied, "I've been thinking about your retirement gathering. What do you think about inviting Steve? You know he's always up for a party."

Sue laughed. "Of course, he should come! Let me change my clothes and I'll give him a call."

But a couple weeks later, when Steve arrived at our house on the day prior to the celebration, he expressed his confusion.

"Why you have party?" he asked Sue. "It not your birthday."

"No," agreed Sue. "It's not my birthday. I'm retiring."

"What that?"

Sue responded with her typical humor. "That means from now on I won't take any job that requires a resume."

Sue's response didn't help Steve's understanding at all. But once she assured him that the party included dessert, hopefully cheesecake, he was all in.

The following evening Steve stood in our kitchen eagerly waiting for Sue to appear from our bedroom where she was getting dressed. Earlier that day he'd come to me with an idea—something special he wanted to do for her. Now he couldn't wait to give his "best friend in Lyndon" his surprise.

Sue emerged clad in a flowing mid-calf black skirt and silk turquoise blouse that accented her tanned skin. Steve stepped forward, hands behind his back.

"I have surprise for you," he said with a grin. Then he handed her the corsage we'd picked up that afternoon.

Sue gave her buddy a hug and helped Steve attach his gift to her blouse. Then the three of us embarked on the half-hour drive north and Sue's big night.

The Eastside Restaurant, located in the same town as Sue's soon-to-be former office, stood on the shores of Lake Memphremagog, the thirty-one-mile-long glacial body of water which spans the international border between Vermont and Quebec. Inside the restaurant's large event room, picture windows framed the sparkling, dancing ripples backed by distant mountains.

Steve, looking sharp in an open-collared dress shirt and khaki pants, gazed around the room filled with Sue's colleagues and friends. When he spotted an empty seat at a front row table, he headed for it, but I stood contentedly in the back and let the spotlight shine on Sue. I swelled with pride and gratitude as I listened to the testimonials offered by several speakers. Yes, they knew the professional Sue, but I knew my longtime partner on a much more intimate level. A woman with deep reservoirs of kindness and patience. Someone who'd seen me at my worst, but never wavered in her support or belief in me. Someone who had embraced my sons as her own.

Nevertheless, as happy as I was for Sue, I could feel Walden still tugging at the edges of my consciousness. Sue was going out on a high note. I longed to do the same. Driving home, I let Steve call "shot gun" and sat in the back lost in thought. Steve seemed fully recovered from his aneurysm and settled in a home with excellent support. I'd never intended to drop out of the work force permanently, but I'd needed almost two years to recover from my own crisis. Now, I knew I was ready. I felt strong. I wanted to return to a full-time job in education.

In early August a chance for personal redemption came in the form of a phone call from a friend and educational colleague. Sheila was the principal of the tiny K-12 school in Orford, New Hampshire, fifty miles due south of Lyndon—a straight shot on Interstate 91. She'd been one of the first people to reach out to me and show me compassion after the debacle in Walden. We'd kept in touch.

On the phone, Sheila cut straight to the chase. "Linda, our librarian just resigned, and I immediately thought of you. Do you think you'd be interested?"

School librarian? I'd never thought of that! "Yes," I responded. Her offer sounded intriguing. But I didn't have the proper certification, and at fifty-eight I had zero interest in taking classes to gain the necessary credentials.

Sheila understood. "Look, you know kids and you know books. Right now, the New Hampshire Department of Education identifies school librarian as an 'area of need.' That means I can hire you on a waiver and you can apply for alternative certification by demonstrating competency based on your experience."

Exhilarated by Sheila's appreciation of what I had to offer, hopefulness fluttered within my belly. "Let me run this by Sue," I answered. "Thanks so much for thinking of me."

When I broached the topic of my returning to full-time work, just as she'd begun her retirement, Sue didn't hesitate. "Call Sheila back right away and tell her yes!" My heart soared with gratitude. Sue understood how important reclaiming my career was to me.

Two weeks later, I'd jumped through all the necessary hoops, been approved by the Orford school board, and had signed a contract. School began just after Labor Day.

Thus it happened on a late afternoon in early October that Sue and I, along with Fuzzy, found ourselves floating silently in an azure sky while gazing down at a brilliant pallet of crimson, amber, and gold— the quintessential colors of a New England fall.

Floating? Fuzzy?

Sue's retirement gift from her colleagues was a hot-air balloon ride for two. And Fuzzy, a stuffed teddy bear, belonged to a first grade class at Orford. Each Friday, Fuzzy left the classroom clutched in the hands of one of the students to spend the weekend at the home of the chosen little girl or boy. The following Monday, the hostess or host reported on Fuzzy's visit. After reading a story to these first graders and telling them of my upcoming adventure, Fuzzy's owners entrusted me with their precious buddy—but only after I promised them photos and copious details of the balloon ride.

On that October afternoon, the seemingly different paths Sue and I were traveling merged for three glorious hours. Over the next four years, while Sue perfected her golf game and other retirement skills, I reveled in my role as school librarian. When I too retired in June 2002, I did so feeling fulfilled.

Early Saturday evening on January 6, 2001, snowflakes swirled in the tunnel of light created by the headlamps of our car. Sue and I bounced along the dirt road on our way to the house belonging to our friends Jean and Meg. Several years earlier, Jean had earned a master's in divinity from the Episcopal Divinity School in Cambridge, Massachusetts. In 1998 she'd been ordained an Episcopalian priest. The phone conversation I'd had with Jean less than an hour before went something like this:

Linda: Hey Jean, Sue and I were wondering if you could do a civil union for us.

Jean: Sure, I'd love that. Do you have a date in mind?

Linda: How about in an hour or so?

Jean: You mean, like tonight? Meg and I have plans to go out to dinner.

Linda: Great! We have dinner plans too. How about we meet you at your house in a half hour? The certificate is filled out. We just need your official signature.

Poor Jean! I wasn't going to take no for an answer! We had an aching need for this to happen. In December, Sue's dentist informed her that she needed extensive and expensive work done on her teeth. Due to her retirement, she no longer had dental insurance. But I still worked as the school librarian in Orford. The passage of Vermont's

Civil Union law in 2000 meant Sue could be covered under my plan, as my legal spouse.

Like many same-sex Vermont couples, we viewed the state's answer to marriage equality as a step in the right direction, but not quite there. Yes, civil union was better than domestic partners (which sounded a bit like a relationship with your pet) but "getting civil unioned" tripped awkwardly off the tongue and what did that mean anyway? The end of some conflict between two previously warring individuals? But money was money and Sue's dental appointment was just weeks away.

Our two cars met at the bottom of Jean and Meg's driveway. I hopped out of the passenger side into the thickening snow, clutching the precious document and a pen. Jean rolled down her window.

"You guys are too much! What's the big rush?"

My explanation sent both her and Meg into gales of laughter. But unlike Lyndon's assistant town clerk, who'd given us a bit of a stink-eye when we'd asked for "Vermont's License and Certificate of Civil Union," Jean smiled broadly as she signed in the box marked "officiant."

"By the powers invested in me, I pronounce you civil unioned," she exclaimed, handing me the document. "Hope you enjoy the dentist, Sue!" And off they sped leaving a blizzard of twirling flakes trailing behind them.

Sue and I left our own snow cloud trail as we headed to our dinner date with two friends.

"Are we going to tell Michelle and Frank what we've just done?" I asked.

"Of course," giggled Sue. "Won't they be surprised to discover they're attending a civil union celebration dinner?"

We continued in silence. While at some level we both mocked the action we'd just taken, our eleven-year relationship had finally gained legal status. That affirmation felt powerful.

THIRTY-FIVE

A Forever Home, 2001-02

In the summer of 2001, Steve began his fifth year with Brenda and Wayne. The bond between the three ran deep.

As Steve's official caregiver, Brenda produced monthly narrative reports detailing his various activities and general health status. These summaries weren't required by Howard, but I appreciated her extra effort. I knew Steve was safe under her watch.

Wayne's laid-back personality reminded me of Sue. And his sense of humor matched Steve's. Over the years they'd developed some standard comedy routines.

Some evenings Steve would wander into the kitchen while Wayne was doing the dishes and ask, "What you doing, Wayne?"

"Sweeping the floor!" he'd reply.

At this Steve would twirl one index finger close to his ear and shout, "You crazy!"

Steve loved visiting Wayne's workshop where the two worked on simple projects. Summers they cheered on the Lake Monsters, Burlington's class A minor league baseball team. Steve especially liked watching Champ, the team mascot.

"You see that?!" he'd exclaim whenever Champ danced on the dugout roof or did something else especially silly.

In Wayne, Steve had a male peer, something he needed and relished.

But Brenda and Wayne were my age, which meant in 2001 they were in their early sixties. So, I shouldn't have been surprised when one September day Brenda called to tell me some big news. Her voice rang with excitement.

"You know how Wayne and I spend two weeks in Ocala, Florida, each winter? Well, we've bought a house there!" Brenda went on to say that they would be spending several months in Ocala that winter and put their Vermont house on the market the following spring. "We will still spend summers in Burlington, but we are going to live in a trailer park near Lake Champlain with other snowbirds."

Denial followed by anxiety claimed me as Brenda shared her news. My brain said, *What? No way!* My gut hurt and I wanted to reel back our conversation. I knew I should feel happy for Brenda and Wayne, but I dreaded the task of finding both live-in support and a new place for Steve to live.

Over dinner Sue and I discussed Steve's future. As always, she did her best to soothe my jangled nerves. Immediately I traveled to the most radical solution. Should we sell our house in Lyndon and buy one in Burlington? Have Steve live with us?

"No," counseled Sue. "That's an extreme reaction and one that wouldn't be good for you or for Steve."

"Yeah, I know," I answered. "But I just hate having to deal with this. Finding a place for Steve to live and someone to live with him always lands in my lap. Not his father's." My lips pressed together. Tightness gripped my chest like a vise. Sometimes life felt so unfair.

But I couldn't hold myself entirely blameless for this situation. I was the one who'd left Roger and asked for a divorce. He lived almost a thousand miles away in Milwaukee with Polly. Realistically I couldn't expect him to participate in this task.

Sue reached across the table for my hand. "Think about it. In a way Brenda and Wayne have given us a gift."

I raised my eyebrows and added, "I don't get your point." I couldn't imagine what she meant.

"Essentially they've provided us with more than a year's notice. And Brenda told you that, like past years, we can have a family member stay with Steve while they're gone."

"Yeah, I know. And usually Roger has done that. But several months is a lot different than two weeks. He's not going to agree to be gone from Polly for that long."

"But remember, I'm retired!" Sue replied. "During the coming winter I can live with Steve at the Lawtons' house. On weekends you can come to Burlington, or Steve and I will drive to Lyndon. We're going to have plenty of time to figure this out."

I let out a sigh of relief. My hand tightened on Sue's. Of course! I wasn't alone in this! When it came to Steve, Sue and I were a team, a powerful one. Together we could solve anything!

We continued to talk throughout the summer and eventually a vision began to develop—one that could change Steve's life in a significant way, and mine.

After learning of the Lawtons' retirement plans, Sue and I began to consider various options. Because of his disability, Steve was eligible for a federal program called Supplemental Security Income. SSI supported adults with impairments, including those with a cognitive or physical challenge. Qualified individuals gained access to other federal programs including Medicaid/Medicare, food stamps, and something called the Housing Choice Voucher program, also known as Section 8.

One August evening Sue and I sat on our back deck watching the sun lower toward the distant ridgeline. The sky darkened, the bird songs quieted, and the first fireflies flickered by.

"You know, Sue, if Steve owned his own house, that would eliminate half of the housing shuffle each time caregivers changed." I'd recently discovered that in Vermont, unlike some other states, Section 8 vouchers were available not only for rentals but for home ownership.

"Wouldn't that mean he'd lose his SSI and medical benefits?" Sue knew that SSI came with strict financial resource limitations. Steve's liquid assets ceiling was $2,000 cash or anything that could be converted into cash.

"No," I answered. "I'm pretty sure the one thing that doesn't count as a resource is a residence. I think the housing voucher is something to explore. Owning a place will give Steve stability." Since leaving our family home in Hanover at age twenty-two, Steve had lived in five different locations with five different caregivers over the past fourteen years.

Sue's head turned and her eyes peered at me through her glasses. "If I'm going to be spending a lot of time in Burlington this winter while Brenda and Wayne are in Florida, I could take the lead on this." She grinned. "Figuring out how to make home ownership happen for Steve would be a great project for me."

My eyes locked on Sue's, drinking in this moment with gratitude. As always Sue had my back.

The next day I called Roger who kept up with the laws and guidelines related to Steve's situation. He confirmed that Steve could indeed own residential property and keep his SSI. Moreover, he shared and supported my vision for what this could mean for Steve.

"This is just another example of your ability to think outside the box," he commented. "And another way for Steve to be a pioneer. Go for it and I'll help in any way I can."

Roger's response didn't surprise me. Although we'd been divorced for more than nine years, the constant tension I'd felt during our marriage had, for the most part, dissipated. What remained was a commitment to work as a team when it came to our children.

Starting in January 2002, Sue began working in earnest to make our vision a reality. The Lawtons' willingness to let Sue live in their house for several months with Steve while they stayed in Florida was a statement of how much they cared about Steve's well-being. Being in Burlington made it easier for Sue to coordinate discussions between several agencies.

Sue began by contacting the Burlington Housing Authority, or BHA, the agency responsible for issuing the home ownership vouchers and providing mortgage assistance. There she met Emily, a single mother raising two young children. In her late twenties and passionate about her work, Emily took a personal interest in Steve and our hopes for him. While Steve easily met BHA's income eligibility and other requirements, in 2002 not many people with a disability of any kind owned their homes. In Steve, Emily saw an opportunity to open up BHA benefits to a population that was currently underserved.

In early February Sue and I met with Emily in her office at the BHA. She spread out some paperwork in front of us and laid out the steps we needed to follow.

"First, Steve will have to attend a full day homeownership workshop," she said. "Once he completes that, I'll recommend some potential lending institutions we've worked with before so Steve can be preapproved for a mortgage. Then you can begin shopping for a house in your price range."

Inwardly I groaned. *A full day workshop?* Steve hated meetings and handled his boredom by checking out and falling asleep in his chair.

"That sounds pretty straightforward," replied Sue. "Then what?"

A smile lit Emily's round face. "When you find something you like, you'll need to get the place inspected, and make certain you meet our financing requirements. After Steve closes on his place the BHA will make a monthly subsidy payment to his bank account to help cover the mortgage costs."

"Sounds great," I responded, feeling heartened by this unexpected financial windfall. "But does Steve really need to sit through an all-day workshop? I can't imagine he'll get anything out of it. Can one of us attend in his place?"

"I'm afraid not," replied Emily. "Of course, you are welcome to join Steve, but he needs to be present."

"OK," I sighed.

Once we left Emily's office, I vented my frustrations to Sue. "How am I going to get Steve through seven and a half hours of information he won't understand?"

Sue looked down at the workshop schedule Emily had given us. "The day includes an hour for a pizza lunch. Steve will love that." Then she added, "Do you think Roger would be willing to help out with this? If so, we could each take a turn with Steve."

I liked Sue's idea and when I called Roger, he didn't hesitate. "Sure, I'll come. I'm due for a visit with Steve anyway." Unlike the loneliness I'd experienced as a young mother, now I had help. I just needed to remember to ask for support.

On the day of the workshop, I took the first shift. Before long I understood why Emily insisted on Steve's participation. The program director welcomed the fifty or so participants and then asked each individual to stand, introduce themselves, and state why they wanted to become a homeowner. Steve shifted in his seat. I could tell he was getting ready. Another chance to be in the spotlight.

"I Steve Cohen," he announced when his turn came. "I want house. I no like moving. I stay in my house forever."

My face glowed with pride as the audience applauded. Once again, I had underestimated my son. With his simple heartfelt statement Steve gave a face to a new kind of homeowner.

Workshop completed, Emily told us since Steve would need a caregiver living with him, she'd approved a three-bedroom voucher. The local credit union set his mortgage limit at $129,000. Sue engaged the services of a realtor and together they began combing through a variety of condominium listings located on bus lines and close to Burlington's downtown core.

The search yielded almost immediate results. We knew we'd found the right place the first time we toured the condo located in the Burlington neighborhood known as the Old North End.

The property, listed at $130,000, dated back to the late 1880s and had originally housed a successful merchant and his family. In 1979 developers had constructed seventeen townhouse-style dwellings in what had once been a spacious backyard and converted the original two-story brick building into two units.

As Sue and I walked through the good-sized living room and into the combination kitchen-dining area, the sound of our footsteps on the wooden floor bounced off the walls of the empty rooms.

"The kitchen's kind of tired looking," I commented. The counter-tops were cracked, and the dark-stained wooden cabinets made the galley-style area feel closed in.

Sue shrugged and then peeked through the opened door between the counter and refrigerator.

"Hey, look at this."

I walked into a long narrow room, which obviously had once been a back porch as evidenced by the brick wall which formed one side of the space and large window on the other side. "Actually, this is kind of cool," I smiled. "Funky. But if we added a closet unit at one end, it could be a bedroom, especially given the three-quarter bath off the kitchen."

We moved back through the living room and up the stairs. The second floor held three rooms off a central hallway, all carpeted, and a full bath. The 1,570-square-foot property also included a basement with a partial dirt floor—valuable storage space despite the many spider webs.

Back outside, I could barely contain my excitement as we got into our car. "What do you think?" I asked Sue.

"The setup has great possibilities," she replied. "If Steve used the back room off the kitchen as his bedroom, a caregiver could have the entire upstairs."

"Exactly what I was thinking!"

Without hesitating we wrote an earnest money check to indicate our interest and arranged for Steve to see the condo.

Steve was understandably anxious as we pulled up in front of 83B North Champlain Street. Change in his routine unsettled him. Although I'd gone through the reasons for Brenda and Wayne's retirement with him many times, and despite his rousing speech at the housing workshop, he didn't truly understand that he would need to move again.

"I live here?" he asked as we walked up the shoveled, snow-free steps to the door where the realtor stood waiting.

"Maybe," I responded. "Right now, you are just going to look inside and check it out."

Steve loved the place. After we'd gone through both floors, he announced, "I like it! I show you my bedroom?"

"Do you have one already picked out?" responded Sue.

Steve nodded and led us to the narrow room behind the kitchen. "This one," he stated firmly. "I like this one."

Sue and I exchanged relieved glances. We both assured him he'd made an excellent choice.

In April Sue and I joined Steve around a crowded conference table at the Burlington Housing Authority for the closing on the condo. Emily beamed as the attorney we'd hired for the closing handed Steve one document after another for his signature. Steve's face bent close to the paper as he printed his name on the indicated line.

"You next," muttered Steve each time he passed another page to me for my co-signature.

I glanced at Sue. "This wouldn't be happening without all your work," I murmured. Sue smiled. Her fingers tightened around mine.

Eventually the attorney handed Steve the final document. "Congratulations Steve, that's it."

"Thank God!" Steve looked up. "Now I move?" Steve wondered.

"No," I explained to Steve. "Things don't happen that fast when you buy a house."

"Rats," he replied.

Swallowing hard, I stood in a corner snapping photos to record this auspicious moment. I'd never imagined this for him—his own forever home, a place where he'd always be safe and happy. This milestone had gone so smoothly, facilitated by dedicated professionals who saw Steve as an individual and kept his needs and best interests at heart. So unlike the struggles I'd continually faced during Steve's childhood.

Of course, the purchase of Steve's condo called for a celebration. Steve's Open House was held in June and for three hours he proudly showed off "my house" to all who entered. Guests included Roger and my dad, along with Steve's brothers. That evening, back in Lyndon, Sue and I lay in bed together talking about the day's events.

"Wow and whew," said Sue.

"Yeah," I answered. "That was amazing."

"What amazed you?"

I rolled over and looked into Sue's brown eyes. Her lined face broke into a soft grin. "I was just thinking," I said, "about all of us sitting together in the living room this evening once the guests left...you know, when Steve said he was so happy?"

"Yeah." She nodded. "That was pretty special."

"And what was even more special for me was looking around and realizing how important family was in making this happen...Roger, you, me." My eyes began to fill. "Our family now looks a lot different than what I imagined when Roger and I got married. But it works. We were all there for Steve."

Sue ran one hand softly over my cheek. "Yes, our family does work, and Steve is the heart that keeps this family together."

THIRTY-SIX

Hospital—Again, 2004-05

Sue and I sat out on our back deck sipping cold beers after a day of golf. Inside the phone rang.

"I'll get it," said Sue. Seconds later. "Linda, you need to take this. Someone is calling from the Howard Center."

I glanced at the watch on my left wrist: 5:15 p.m. My stomach heaved. *Shit*! An after-hours call from the agency which oversaw Steve's care couldn't be good.

A voice informed me that Brian, Steve's current caregiver, had just phoned. Steve had fallen and there was something wrong with his arm. They were on their way to the hospital. Brian would call me from there.

I stayed calm as I relayed the information to Sue. Perhaps Steve, now just a month short of his thirty-eighth birthday, had broken his arm. I remained by the phone. Fifteen long minutes went by before it rang again. When I answered, I recognized Brian's voice, heavy with concern.

"Linda, we're at the hospital now. Steve's having trouble talking and can't move his right hand or arm. The doctors are doing tests. They think he may have had a stroke."

"Sue and I will leave right away. Please let Steve know we are coming." I threw some clothes in an overnight bag. Sue did the same and together we headed for our car. Our beers languished on the arms of the Adirondack chairs on the deck, forgotten.

Once again, silent minutes crawled by on the drive from Lyndon to Fletcher Allen Hospital in Burlington.

Once again, my entire body ached as I replayed the familiar tape in my head. *Will Steve still be alive when we arrive?*

Once again, while Sue parked, I dashed through the emergency room entrance, following a nurse to the cubicle where my son lay surrounded by medical personnel.

Steve's terrified eyes met mine. His chin trembled. He struggled to speak, to make himself understood, his words slurred and garbled. "T-T-T-This n-n-n-not f-f-f-fun. I c-c-c-can n-n-n-not t-t-t-talk." He turned his head toward his right arm. He strained with a futile effort to lift it. "M-M-M-My arm n-n-n-not w-w-w-work." Blazing overhead lights caused Steve's tears to glimmer as they tracked down his face. Morbid thoughts churned through me. How much more trauma can he endure and still maintain his quality of life? He looked so small, so vulnerable. But I couldn't let Steve see my desperation. So, I smiled for him and bent close to his ear softly singing our comfort song. "I love you, a bushel and a peck…"

For the next three hours Steve's anxiety and agitation ratcheted higher and higher as nurses and doctors circled around him. Sue moved in close to Steve every time I stepped out of the emergency room cubicle to confer with physicians. One, a neurologist, drove me nuts with his alarmist comments.

"This is a serious situation."

No shit! Rage boiled inside me. *Do you really think I don't get that?*

Finally, after the last test, an MRI, Steve was admitted and taken to a private room—something Sue negotiated with the emergency room charge nurse. Sue stayed with him while I called Roger, Josh, and Mike. Roger, who'd had several strokes over the past few years, attempted to talk me down from my mounting panic. He tried to tell me there was hope. Recovery was possible. While I gave free range to my emotions with Roger, I forced my voice to remain calm when I spoke with Steve's brothers.

It was well after midnight by the time I completed my calls. Sue headed to Steve's condo for the night, while I crawled into the narrow cot the staff brought into Steve's room. Finally, Steve's regular breathing told me he'd fallen asleep.

At dawn, Steve barely stirred when a nurse took his morning vitals. Outside his room, still dressed in yesterday's rumpled clothes, I met with the neurologist on duty who confirmed the initial diagnosis of a stroke, with continuing paralysis affecting Steve's right arm and hand along with partial paralysis in certain facial muscles. The physician was unwilling to speculate on the prognosis for full recovery but assured me Steve's life wasn't in danger.

OK. But what will that life look like? Like windshield wipers in a driving rain, questions whiplashed through me. Would people be able to understand his speech? Would he be able to continue to live in his condo? Would he regain enough function to return to work? And finally... how would this latest health crisis change *my* life? I brushed those questions aside as Steve's voice rang out.

"Mom? Mom! Where are you?"

I returned to his bedside. Right now, my job was to explain to him just what had happened. The concept of a stroke was completely beyond him. "I'm right here, Steve. Ready to start the day?" I raised his bed to a sitting position and sat on the edge of the mattress.

"My arm not work," he said as tears filled his eyes. "I not know why."

"So, Steve, do you understand why you are in the hospital?"

He shook his head.

"Right now, your brain is having trouble talking to your arm. It keeps telling your arm to move, but your arm isn't getting the message."

"I scared."

"I would be scared if this happened to me," I responded.

Suddenly I realized something had changed from last evening. My heart leapt. Steve wasn't slurring his words! "Hey, do you want to hear some good news?"

"I do. I need good news."

"Do you remember last night how you had trouble making your voice work?" Steve nodded gravely. "But are you having trouble with your voice this morning?"

"No! My voice work now!" A crooked grin creased his face.

I reassured him that this was a positive sign, and now folks in the hospital would help him get his arm and hand working. I knew if Steve believed me, he'd spare no effort during the rehabilitation phase.

In the afternoon I watched as a physical therapist walked him down the hallway. Over and over she placed Steve's right hand on the wall railing as they moved step by slow step, trailing an IV pole beside them. But each time Steve's hand slid off and his arm dangled numb and useless by his side. Watching, I could feel my own right arm tense and jerk as I tried willing my son's arm to start functioning. By the third day Steve's hand had regained some feeling and he was able to hold onto the railing.

"It work," exclaimed Steve. "My hand work! I better!"

I offered my thanks to the Goddess. I knew recovering function soon after a stroke was vital.

After five long days, Steve was transferred to a rehab center and Sue returned to our home in Lyndon. Steve and I settled into a new routine. I spent nights sleeping in a fully reclining chair next to Steve's bed. Mornings I dashed to Steve's condo for a shower and change of clothing before returning to the rehab center.

The rehab staff treated Steve's whole person. While the hospital focused only on his medical diagnosis, here they seemed to recognize how keeping his mood elevated and his hope engaged was essential to his healing. Steve couldn't articulate this difference, but I knew he sensed the change. He looked forward to "playing games" during his physical therapy sessions in the center's gym and loved ordering each meal from the daily menu. "This like a restaurant."

The first evening at the rehab center, as the sky darkened, Steve insisted that I take him outside to the parking lot. There he sat in the center's required wheelchair and gazed reverently at the waxing moon as it neared fullness. A thin ribbon of saliva leaked out the right corner of his mouth and I bent close to gently wipe his face clean. I noted the random flecks of gray in his hair, his dry, chapped lips.

"Give me power, moon. Make my arm work." His voice was solemn and ripe with belief. I did my best to relax, to ignore the signs of aging that seemed to have appeared overnight. I strained to be present in just that moment and let some of Steve's peacefulness flow into me. We returned to seek strength from the moon each evening until Steve's release.

The rehab center encouraged visitors and Steve had many. Brenda and Wayne Lawton, in Burlington for the summer, stopped by several times. Heather, Jane's daughter, visited from her home in western Massachusetts. Steve became especially excited whenever one of his co-workers from the Healthy Living Food Market, where he'd been employed for the past six years, stopped by.

One afternoon, the market's founder and owner, Katy, walked into the day room where Steve and I sat working on a jigsaw puzzle. I watched as Steve ran to Katy and wrapped his arms around her.

"Katy! I miss you!"

My eyes filled, along with Katy's. "I miss you too, Steve. Everybody misses you. You need to get better fast."

"I will. You have welcome back party for me?"

Katy's eyes crinkled in a smile. "You better believe it." Then she handed Steve a card filled with staff signatures. Steve barely had time to look at it before his favorite nurse entered to take him for a physical therapy session.

Katy walked over to me and we exchanged hugs. "Thanks so much for coming, Katy. Seeing you means everything to Steve."

Katy's hands grabbed onto my shoulders and her brown eyes held mine. "Linda, I just want you to know, when Steve is ready, we want him back." She paused before continuing. "Regardless of his capacity, we will make whatever adjustments necessary. I can't imagine Healthy Living without Steve."

My stoic façade crumbled, and I sank back into my chair as my knees trembled. Tears of gratitude poured out. Work provided structure to Steve's days, and contributed to his self-worth. Like most adults, Steve's job gave him a sense of purpose. Surrendering that would crush him. The weight of my fear that Steve might lose his job lifted from my chest. Long after Katy left, I remained seated staring at the unfinished puzzle. I let my mind drift back to the days when my dreams for Steve's ability to hold a meaningful job seemed so impossible, so distant.

"Mom! Mom! I back." Steve's voice cut through my reverie, as I blinked and looked around the rehab center's day room. "Why you not answer me?" he wondered. "Why you not finish puzzle?"

"Sorry, Steve. I guess I was daydreaming."

"You silly. Dreams for night, not day!"

"You're right, Steve. How did you do at PT?"

"I do good. I almost better. I go home soon."

A few days later Steve was discharged and returned to his condo, almost two weeks since Brian had called me from the hospital. I'd been in Burlington for the entire time, thankful for my recent retirement. Steve's program manager arranged for additional coverage while Brian was at work, and I returned to Lyndon and Sue.

But the effects of the stroke lingered. Steve never regained full function in his right hand. Holding a pencil or pen proved so difficult he stopped trying and switched to his left hand. His initial efforts at writing his name produced shaky, barely legible results and left Steve distraught.

"That look awful."

But he persisted and with effort his handwriting improved and eventually he gained enough confidence to return to drawing, something he'd always loved. Steve's complex and detailed drawings, rendered in his unique style, had always been prized by family and friends. He produced three pictures of Harry Potter characters which were so good I had them framed as a triptych. Steve hung his creation in his living room. So much for what IQ tests can predict.

Of greater concern to me than his writing and drawing was that some muscles on the right side of Steve's face remained paralyzed. He couldn't feel the drool escaping from his mouth. I wondered how this might affect people's interactions with Steve. Would Katy still want him back at Healthy Living?

Three months passed. In late November, Brian left for a new job in Portland, Oregon. He had lived with Steve for three years and he and Steve had become especially close. "I sad Brian leave, but I get to stay here right?"

Josh moved from Bozeman, Montana, to become his brother's caregiver. Both guys were delighted. I relaxed knowing Josh would always have his brother's best interest at heart. But I worried too. I'd never wanted either Josh or Mike to put their adult lives on hold and feel responsible for Steve. Josh insisted Burlington was where he wanted to be and during the time he lived with Steve, Josh enrolled in a nursing program and earned his degree as a licensed practical nurse. After several years with Steve, he returned to Bozeman where his LPN skills made him a valued member of the ski patrol at Bridger Bowl.

Early in 2005, Steve resumed his part-time job at Healthy Living supported, for the first time, by a job coach. I briefly mourned this sign of Steve's diminished independence. But not Steve. All he cared about was the promised welcome back party, which Katy soon organized.

Steve called to tell me about the gathering. He filled me in on all the details of the celebration including the flavors of both the cake and ice cream. I listened as he chattered excitedly. I recalled Katy's words when she visited the rehab center six months before: "We want Steve back whatever his capacity." Waves of understanding crashed over me. *People.* It had always been about people. The right people dropping into Steve's life at just the right time. Individuals, not systems, had moved Steve forward in his life.

"Mom? You hear me? You not say anything."

"Oh, sorry, Steve. What did you just say?"

"I call Dad now. Tell him about party."

I hoped Steve didn't hear the catch in my voice as I congratulated him on his achievement before hanging up. Beginning with the Hanover Food Co-op in 1987, his career in the food industry had now spanned almost twenty years.

Phone call over, I grabbed my parka, hat, and mittens and walked into the living room where Sue sat watching TV. She hit the pause button and looked up.

"I just got off the phone with Steve. He told me all about his welcome back party at Healthy Living."

"How did he sound?" asked Sue.

"Deliriously happy," I replied. "His condo and his job are the most important things in his life," I added.

Sue nodded. "Where are you heading now?"

"I'm just going to step outside for a few minutes. I need to breathe deeply and collect my thoughts." Sue understood my need for nature's healing peace. "And while I'm doing that, I just might bring a few pieces from the woodpile to top off the log holder on the back porch. The forecast calls for temperatures in the single digits over the next several days."

Outside, snow crunched under my feet as I gazed up at a deep, dark sky untarnished by any light pollution—one of my favorite things about our rural location. A sliver crescent moon (banana moon in Steve speak) and the Big Dipper hung in sharp contrast to the blurred path of the Milky Way. "I don't begin to understand this universe," I whispered. "But tonight, right now, I offer up my gratitude for Steve's life and for all those angels who have helped him along the path he's traveled over the last thirty-nine and a half years." I felt every muscle release and my body lighten as the final tendrils of the tension I'd held since Steve's stroke soared skyward. Once again, he'd beaten the odds. Although the physical changes wrought by the stroke would always be a part of Steve's appearance, his grit, determination, and personality continued to move him forward.

After several more moments of quiet meditation I turned and headed up the shoveled trail to the woodpile.

THIRTY-SEVEN

Dad in Vermont, 2006

During the winter of 2006, Dad's long-time companion passed away at age ninety-one after breaking her hip. He'd often told me, "If I outlive Helen, I want to come to Vermont and stay with you and Sue. There won't be anyone left for me in North Carolina and I don't want to be alone."

I'd assured him we would make that happen, and so Sue and I got ready to accommodate my father. We converted the first-floor study into a bedroom for Dad and replaced the tub in the adjacent bathroom with a walk-in shower. In April we drove south, attended Helen's memorial service and several days later headed north with my father, towing his few processions in a small U-Haul cargo trailer.

Sue and Dad quickly bonded over their mutual love of breakfast. At least twice a week the two set out for one of their favorite restaurants followed by a leisurely drive along the Northeast Kingdom's scenic dirt roads in search of wildlife. One day they spotted a mama moose and her calf feeding in a muddy marsh less than a mile from our house. When they returned my father breathlessly detailed this milestone—one animal he'd been longing to spot.

During the summer I relished the lazy afternoons Dad and I spent in the Adirondack chairs on our back porch, sipping coffee. Sometimes we were content to just sit quietly watching Dad's favorite "hummers" flit back and forth between the nearby flower beds. Other days we reminisced—stories from his childhood or mine. One afternoon, Dad brought up my relationship with Sue.

"You and Sue seem really happy," he observed. "I'll admit I didn't understand when you first told your mother and me that you were a lesbian, but now? You two are just like any other couple who love each other."

I smiled, basking in the glow of Dad's acknowledgement. "Yeah, except we still can't get legally married, but that day is coming."

"I just wish I knew why your revelation upset your mother so much."

I looked at my father. Should I share the thought I'd been holding for the past several years? "I think I might have an explanation," I replied. "Stay here while I go get something I discovered when I was helping you clean out your house back in 2002 before you sold it and moved in with Helen."

I returned to the porch holding a book. "Here," I said handing Dad the tome. Without a dust jacket, the dark green cover looked nondescript. "I found this tucked away in a corner of the top shelf of the bookcase in your family room."

Dad turned the book over in his hands, the spine faded after many years of exposure to natural light. He opened the cover. "Pete's name is here." He pointed to my mother's ink-inscribed signature: Petra M. Morrow. "Obviously she got this sometime after we were married in 1937. But I don't remember her ever showing it to me." Aloud he read from the title page: "*The Well of Loneliness* by Radclyffe Hall." He looked at me. Dad read the copyright date. "1928. Wow! This is old." He paused. "I've never heard of the book. Have you?"

I nodded. "Yeah, I read it soon after I came out." I explained the furor that occurred when Hall's work was published and how it gained underground fame as an early lesbian novel. "It's a pretty sad story, about shame and unacceptance."

"Oh." Dad's Adam's apple bobbed and the wrinkles on his neck rippled as he swallowed several times. His cloudy blue eyes peered at me behind his glasses. He touched a wispy gray strand of his thinning hair. "Oh," he repeated.

I held one of Dad's blue-veined hands and waited. He seemed far away and lost in thought. Eventually he began to speak. "When I asked Pete to marry me, she said: 'Are you sure? I'm not normal, you know.'"

My stomach muscles tightened. "Really?" I exclaimed. Had my father just confirmed what I'd suspected after discovering my mother's copy of *The Well of Loneliness*? Mom and Dad had moved many times. Yet she'd always kept this book. Had Mom struggled with her own sexuality? Had she been even more miserable, more alone, than I'd imagined? Was that the reason she'd reacted so strongly to my coming out?

"Wow. What do you think she meant by that comment, Dad? Did you ask her?"

"I don't know, that was so long ago," answered Dad. His eyes blinked rapidly, and he gave his head a slight shake. "I don't think I ever asked Pete what she meant. I just wanted to hear her say 'yes' to my proposal."

"And she did," I smiled. I wondered if I'd crossed a line and caused my father pain. "You were married for over fifty years."

Dad sat in silence. Through the screen door I could hear Sue getting dinner ready in the kitchen. "We had a good marriage," he commented. "At least I feel we did." Was he trying to reassure himself of the truth of his statement?

I nodded in agreement. "Yes, you did. Remember the T-shirts I gave you both on your fiftieth wedding anniversary with the words, 'We've come a long way together' on the front?"

Dad smiled briefly and returned to his burdened mind. "You know, ninety-nine percent of the time, when we had sex...," he paused, "I was the one who initiated it."

I nodded. This was not a conversation I wanted to have. But my heart ached—for both of my parents.

"Was it that way for you when you and Roger were married?"

My face flushed. Was it his age that gave Dad permission to talk about sex with me, his sixty-five-year-old daughter? Or was he seeking some guidance to toggle this new information into place? I looked down at my bare feet on the wooden porch floor.

"Yeah," I acknowledged. "But I think that is true in a lot of heterosexual relationships. It doesn't have to mean anything about Mom's sexuality."

Internally however, my mother's extreme reaction to my coming out, combined with my discovery of the book and now Dad's comments left me feeling my mother *had* struggled with her sexual orientation. We continued to talk until Sue stepped out to let us know dinner was ready. Dad and I left our thoughts out on the porch to drift away in the summer air. Neither of us ever brought up the subject again.

Living with Sue and me in Vermont meant Dad was less than two hours away from Steve and Josh. He delighted in his proximity to both grandsons in Burlington. Having his grandfather nearby was good for Steve. He'd recovered as much as he would from his stroke. While he continued to work at Healthy Living, his personality was more subdued, and it was harder to get him engaged in activities outside his predictable routine. But he lit up in his Pa's company and offered a hand to steady his grandfather without prompting. For me, it was refreshing to see Steve in the role of caregiver.

Steve viewed his fortieth birthday celebration in September 2006 as a very big deal. "I teeny bit nervous. I never be forty before."

Sue, Dad, and I drove over from Lyndon to Steve's condo. Josh planned the celebration and arranged for a friend to give his brother a ride on his motorcycle—a gift that both excited and terrified Steve. After the "scary ride" Steve opened his other presents. The baseball cap sent to him by Mike and Pamela especially delighted him—a navy blue hat with white lettering spelling out "Old Fart."

"That me! I old fart now!"

How true. Each time I saw Steve his hair contained more gray. A fungal infection in his toes required regular trips to a podiatrist who carefully trimmed his yellowed nails. He wore his "stupid stockings" (compression socks) daily to reduce swelling in his legs due to venous blood pooling. Not only had the brain aneurysm and stroke taken their toll, but I knew that folks with Down syndrome aged more rapidly than the typical population. I tried to reassure myself, remembering advances in health care had extended the average life expectancy of people with Down syndrome from twenty-five in 1983 to close to sixty years in 2006.

Dad's health also weighed heavily on my mind. He'd long had a Do Not Resuscitate order and for years had stated, "I just want to die in my sleep." While cognitively he remained sharp, physically he'd become increasingly frail. His nitroglycerin pills were seldom far from his side.

As the trees lost their leaves and the first hard freeze hit, Dad became more and more concerned about the approaching winter. How would he stay warm? He consulted both Josh and Mike to get their advice on what brand of long underwear he should purchase. One day the UPS driver delivered an order Dad had placed using a catalog. He opened the cardboard box and pulled out a pair of women's fleece-lined slippers in a red and white snowflake pattern, and a navy-blue cotton balaclava—stylish, but not practical for northern Vermont winters. Dad called us into his bedroom to view him as he modeled his purchases. Both Sue and I smiled broadly and refrained from making a comment about his choices.

On November 8, Sue, Dad, and I sat at the dining table eating dinner. The topic of conversation turned to the 2008 presidential election—

two years away. Both Hillary Clinton and Barack Obama had begun floating early trial balloons as potential Democratic candidates. Dad was energized by both possibilities, but he looked so worn and frail in the light of the overhead hanging lamp that a thought flitted through me: *I wonder if he's hoping he won't live long enough to cast a vote in the primary elections.*

Around 8:30 p.m. Dad asked me to help him shower before bed, a request he'd never made. Of course, I said yes. He no longer showered daily—too exhausting. A deep sense of privilege coursed through me as I followed him into the bathroom and helped him remove his clothing. Naked, his wrinkled skin sagged and hung from his thin arms and legs. I tenderly took Dad by one elbow and he stepped into the cascading shower. Gently, I used a soap-laden washcloth on his back and between his legs—places he could no longer reach on his own. As I toweled him off and began to pull his flannel nightshirt over his head, a series of groans escaped from between his cracked lips.

"Dad, what's the matter? Am I hurting you?"

"I need my nitro pills," he mumbled. He moved slowly as I gripped his elbow and helped him to his room. "How many do you want?" I asked.

"Two," he gasped and swallowed them before I could fill a glass with water.

As he lay down, I pulled the covers up under his chin and kissed him softly on a pale cheek. "Good night, Dad. I love you. I hope you feel better tomorrow."

He nodded, removed his glasses, and placed them on the nightstand. "Love you too," he murmured. I turned off the overhead light and left the room, closing his door behind me.

The call came the following noon at the tiny school where one day a week I served as the school librarian, post-retirement. A student handed me the portable phone from the secretary's office and Sue's voice answered.

"Linda, it's your dad. I'm sitting next to him on his bed. I can't get him to respond; I think he's dead."

I made the twelve-mile drive home in record time, tears pouring down my face. I found Sue keeping watch over my father, our two cats curled around his still body. At ninety-five and a half, Dad had gotten his wish. He'd died in his sleep.

Ironically, as Sue and I held each other and sobbed, Mike and Pamela were on a plane flying east from Seattle to Burlington, Vermont. They were due to land early in the evening. Mike hadn't seen his grandfather in over a year. When I called Josh to tell him that his Pa had died, he said he'd tell Steve and then his brother and sister-in-law when they landed. They would all drive to Lyndon the following morning.

Two days later, November 11, we headed to the funeral home. Dad had stated his desire to be cremated many times, but I wanted his grandsons and Pamela to see him first. I wondered about Steve. How would he handle this? He understood Pa had died, but I knew he'd never seen a body before. I didn't know if Mike or Josh had either. Over breakfast I tried to prepare Steve for what he would see.

"I teeny bit nervous," Steve said in a quivering voice. "I scared and I sad."

"That's OK, Steve," I replied. "We will all be with you. Pa will just look like he is asleep."

"He wear his PJs?"

At the funeral home the director led us into a viewing room. A weak November sun peeked through a bay window where Dad lay on a raised platform draped with a rich forest-green velvet cloth. I reached for Steve's hand. Uncertainly we all made our way across the room and lined up in front of the body. Dad wore his navy velour jogging suit. White cotton socks peeked out from his new slippers. His folded hands held his Red Sox baseball cap. I smiled as I noticed his glasses perched above his nose.

Steve wriggled his way out of my grasp and approached his grandfather. His small hand reached up and his clubbed fingers rested on Dad's arm. "Bye, Pa," he said softly. "I sad you die. I miss you." Then he stepped back. Once again Steve's ability to speak so simply, with such honesty, resonated with me. *Goodbye, Dad. I am sad you will no longer be with me. I will miss you.*

One by one each of us stepped forward—Mike and Pamela, Josh, Sue, me. Except for Sue, we remained dry-eyed, but tears coursed down her cheeks as she bid her breakfast buddy farewell. Steve moved to Sue and put his arms around her. We all filed out, but not before I gently removed the Red Sox cap from Dad's hands.

Outside the sun warmed the day and the six of us stood around, wondering what to do. Steve spoke up.

"I want a toast for Pa."

Josh knew exactly what Steve meant. "Do you want to go to McDonald's for milkshakes? Like you and Pa used to do?"

Steve nodded. "You got that right, Shrimpo."

At the restaurant, Steve headed to the counter. The uniformed young woman asked for his order and he replied with confidence. "I Steve. My grandfather pass away. I want to make a toast. Two shakes, please. One strawberry and one chocolate." Then he paused, turned around, and looked at us. "I pay." He reached for his wallet.

Drinks in hand, Steve led us to an empty booth, and we all crowded in. "This one mine," he said holding the strawberry shake. "That one Pa's." He nodded to the chocolate one.

"Who is going to have Pa's shake?" asked Josh.

"You all share," Steve said and grinned wickedly. "I not share my mine."

Steve raised his cup. "To Pa, my best grandfather. Amen."

"To Pa," we chorused. As Steve began attacking his strawberry shake, Josh took a sip of the chocolate one and handed it to Mike.

Here's to you, Dad, I said silently as the shake passed to me. *And to Mom and to my sister. May all the Morrows find peace.*

THIRTY-EIGHT

Deliberated Decisions, 2009-12

Just as I'd predicted to my father, the day did come when Sue and I were able to legally marry. In the spring of 2009, the Vermont legislature passed the Marriage Equity Act, becoming the fourth state to legalize marriage between same-sex couples. Both Mike and Josh called to offer their congratulations, but when the law took effect on September 1, 2009, we did not rush to any altar. We knew who we were to each other.

Several of our straight friends asked, "When is the wedding?"

"Who knows?" we answered.

Our ambivalence continued for many months. We attended several same-sex weddings, some lavish, others much less so. Eventually Sue and I agreed on a modest celebration. No family, just our close friends, Frank and Michelle Green, who'd been urging us to hold our ceremony at their home.

On the afternoon of September 10, 2010, we took our marriage license to be signed by a justice of the peace and then drove to the Greens' home where they stood waiting in their gravel driveway. Sue and I smiled warmly as we took in their attire. Frank, casually elegant, was outfitted in white shirt, blue tie, and black slacks. A black bowler sat at a jaunty angle atop his thinning hair. Wearing a blouse and floral-print ankle-length skirt, Michelle handed each of us a bouquet of sunflowers cut from her exquisite flower gardens. They directed us to the bridge which arched over a small stream in their backyard, while they stood on the freshly mown lawn facing Sue and me. Frank spoke a few words and then it was our turn.

On the way to the Green's, I'd asked Sue, "Have you written any-thing down? Do you know what you are going to say?"

"Nope," she answered, "what about you?"

"I haven't written anything, but I *do* know what I want to say!"

"In that case," said Sue with a grin, "you go first."

Now we faced each other, two senior citizens, ages seventy and sixty-six, wearing classic blouses over capri slacks, to which Sue add-ed a black watch cap atop her silver hair. I thought back to the time so long ago when naming myself a lesbian had left me feeling "less than" and uncomfortable. No longer.

Neither of us remembers what we said that afternoon, except for this: we told Michelle and Frank, "After twenty-plus years together, we are smart enough not to promise anything to anyone!"

An equally modest wedding dinner, prepared by Michelle, consist-ed of hot dogs and baked beans followed by a specially ordered decadent wedding cake. Then we left for a week on Cape Cod. I re-member telling Sue as we headed south, "I don't feel any different, but I'm sure glad you are my wife." Little did I know how much I would lean on Sue as Steve made the turn into middle age.

Throughout his thirties and forties, Steve was a walking contradiction in ways most adults are not. He claimed to still believe in Santa Claus. Whenever he was with me in a large box store, like Walmart, he gravitated to the toy aisles. But he also was completely responsible for doing his own laundry, making simple meals, remembering to take his daily medications, and taking out recycling on the appointed day. He was a true man-child, with feet firmly planted in both worlds. A man I sometimes felt I didn't really know.

On the surface, Steve moved through his world as a mostly con-tented, mellow, and trusting individual. I was certain he experienced occasional alienation or loneliness, and I longed to know the inner workings of his mind. But either he didn't have the words to express those thoughts, or I lacked the skills to help him access his feelings. His emotional radar, however, remained finely tuned. He could tell when someone didn't "get" him or acted in a condescending fashion toward him. In those situations, he simply ignored the perpetrator and retreated into his own bubble.

Meanwhile, aging continued to lay a heavy hand on Steve. He ex-perienced painful episodes of gout, something familiar to both his father and brother, Mike. But difficulty articulating his symptoms meant treatment was often delayed. Many of the other issues he faced were somewhat typical for adults with Down syndrome, but information on this segment of the population remained limited as the medical profession played catch-up.

Steve's energy level decreased, and his cardiologist urged me to have a sleep study done, which resulted in a diagnosis of obstructive sleep apnea. We struggled to convince Steve to use his prescribed CPAP machine at night. Eventually he learned to tolerate six and a half hours of continuous use and his energy rebounded somewhat. But Steve disliked wearing the device and my heart broke every time he told me, "I hate stupid mask."

He started complaining about food getting "stuck" at mealtimes. Despite Josh's directives that he "take small bites and chew before you swallow," Steve often left the table, dashed to the bathroom, and vomited into the toilet. Mealtimes became stressful, especially at restaurants, and Steve loved going out to eat. His primary care physician ordered a barium swallow test which revealed a benign stricture of his esophagus. She scheduled a same-day hospital operation for dilation. I drove to Burlington to be with Steve. When Josh volunteered to go with him into the procedure room I happily agreed. I'd watched Steve struggle too many times in hospitals. The dilation brought relief. But four years later, the procedure would be needed again.

I always accompanied Steve on his annual cardiac visit. Over the years, these appointments had become routine: a couple of tests, including an EKG, then a meeting with his cardiologist, who reviewed the test results, listened to Steve's heart, and proclaimed him stable. Over time I let my guard down and stopped stressing about these yearly visits.

In 2012 I sat in the bland examining room when the door opened and the doctor breezed in. He took note of Steve, now forty-six, who had fallen asleep on the exam table—his usual response whenever he got bored.

After greeting me he asked how I thought Steve was doing.

"OK," I responded. "Obviously he is aging, but overall the quality of his life is good."

The doctor nodded. "Steve's heart has been working overtime for a long while now," he commented. My stomach fluttered. "Do you think his shortness of breath has increased over, say…the past four years?"

"Yes." I paused before adding, "Definitely. Especially if he has to walk up an incline. Steve calls those 'heavy hills.'"

The cardiologist continued. "I can prescribe a medication, called Tracleer, which appears to increase exercise capacity for patients with Eisenmenger's syndrome. Might even extend his life expectancy some, since it seems to reduce the strain on the heart. But I have to tell you, Steve is not going to live to be an old man," he cautioned. Then he added, "Besides, by the time they reach fifty, most adults with Down syndrome develop Alzheimer's."

My face flushed. This no longer felt like a routine checkup. The doctor hadn't told me anything I didn't already know. Recent research showed by age forty, the brains of people with Down syndrome are clogged with beta-amyloid plaques and other protein deposits called tau tangles. These accumulations increase the risk of developing Alzheimer's. But the option—to increase Steve's longevity only to see him develop Alzheimer's—filled me with dread. I didn't want the horrible disease to rob Steve of his main strength—his vibrant personality.

Of course, I wanted Steve to be comfortable. I hated seeing him struggle to catch his breath. But… "I'll have to think about it," I muttered.

One weekend, while visiting with Steve in Burlington, he and I headed for a mall and some shopping. Inside a DVD store, I remained by the checkout counter while Steve cruised the aisles trying to decide which movie he wanted to purchase. He approached me with a stricken look.

"Sorry, Mom, I have accident."

The stain spreading down his pants told me he'd lost control of his bowels. I hurried him to the women's restroom and searched his knapsack for the spare clothing he usually carried.

Nothing. I cleaned Steve up as best I could, while he repeated his apology over and over. My voice stayed low and calm, but internally I ached. Steve was mortified.

"Steve, we have to throw out these pants. You're going to need to stay here while I buy you a new pair."

"OK, I do it." His voice was so low I could barely hear him.

I stepped out of the stall and told Steve to lock the door. Ten minutes later I returned to the restroom and headed for the cubicle where Steve waited, a pair of black sweatpants in hand. We headed back to his condo without a new DVD.

A month after this incident, I met with Steve's primary care physician who'd cared for Steve since his aneurysm in 1997. Seated in her office, I told her about Steve's last cardiac visit and how conflicted I felt. Dr. Berger looked at me with compassion. "Yes, I read the doctor's notes following that appointment." Her voice was gentle. "What is your greatest fear?"

"That something terrible will happen to Steve...like another stroke...something...." I paused to gather myself. This was such a hard conversation. "Steve is such a social being. His personality has always been one of his greatest assets. I'd hate for him to lose that. The thought of Steve lingering in the fog of Alzheimer's terrifies me. Or if he did have another stroke, I don't want him kept alive but in a vegetative state." Then I added, "I'm considering having a Do Not Resuscitate order on file for him."

"I think a DNR is an excellent idea," she responded.

My eyes filled. "I just don't know if I have the right to make such a determination for Steve; I mean I have a DRN for myself but making that choice for Steve..." My voice trailed off.

Dr. Berger gently reminded me of the many decisions I'd made on Steve's behalf during his life. She added I wouldn't be the first person to consider a DNR for a loved one. She reached behind her into a file and handed me a brochure written on just such a perspective.

"Is there anything else you're concerned about?"

"Yes. Steve's having more frequent toileting accidents and one of his staffers has suggested using adult diapers." I paused before adding, "I'm just not ready to take that step yet. Steve's so embarrassed when he does have an accident but putting him in diapers would be equally humiliating."

Dr. Berger suggested some dietary changes and assured me I didn't need to decide on anything that day. I left her office clutching a DNR form and feeling more confused than ever.

When I returned to Lyndon and stepped into our home, Sue needed only to look at my face before asking, "What's wrong? What happened at Dr. Berger's?" She wrapped me in her arms as my tears spilled over. "Come on," she said, "Go sit down while I get us a drink."

As always Sue's calmness steadied me. She reminded me I didn't have to decide about a DNR today, or even in a month. "Just sit with your feelings for a while; over time you'll know what to do."

Steve's bowel control improved with a change in diet, but I continued to worry about a debilitating and lingering illness without recovery. Several months later I added a DNR order to both Steve's medical and Howard Center files. Steve never took the medication suggested by his cardiologist.

THIRTY-NINE

Sailing to Heaven, 2013

On January 3, 2013, Josh phoned from Bozeman, where he'd returned to live after several years as Steve's caregiver. He'd just ended a call with Roger's wife, Polly. Roger had had a massive stroke and was in the hospital on life support. Both he and Mike were heading to Milwaukee. The following day the brothers and Polly said goodbye and Roger, seventy-four, died fifteen minutes after the removal of the breathing tube.

January 26 dawned crisp but achingly clear as Steve and I stood in the nearly empty sanctuary of the Unitarian Universalist Church in Milwaukee, Wisconsin. Steve looked good, dressed in black slacks with a sharp crease and a rust-colored crew neck sweater. His father's memorial service wouldn't begin for another half an hour, but I wanted him to see the room where it would be held.

"I still sad, Mom. I miss my dad."

"I know, Steve." I put my arm around his shoulder, pulling him close. "I'm sad too."

Three sections of aluminum-framed chairs with black upholstered backs and seats formed a semi-circle in front of a low platform containing a wooden lectern. A silver chalice and a simple arrangement of white roses occupied the narrow cloth-draped table located to one side of the lectern. We made our way down the aisle, and Steve stopped to introduce himself to the piano player, arranging sheet music above the keyboard.

"Hi, I Steve Cohen. My dad pass away." Steve reached out his hand in greeting.

"Pleased to meet you, Steve. My name is John. I'm sorry about your dad. I hope you'll like the music I'm going to play for him today." Steve smiled and reached out playfully toward the keyboard.

"Come on, Steve. John needs to practice. Let's look around some more." The two of us made our way toward the lectern. I knew Steve was curious about the service and how things would unfold. "See this? This is where the minister will stand. And you and your brothers will stand here too when you take turns talking about Dad."

"I be a teeny bit nervous."

"I know, but you still want to tell your story about Dad, right?"

Steve nodded a strong affirmative yes. Suddenly Steve stopped in his tracks and stood frozen, looking from side to side. "Where the coffin?"

I'd been waiting for this. I knew he would ask this question. There was *no* way I wanted to attempt explaining cremation to Steve. I cleared my throat. "Well, some people, when they die, want to be in a coffin and buried in the ground. And some people...uh, they just want to be free and have their spirit move through the air. That's what your dad wanted."

"I have a dream after Dad pass away. He in heaven now. How he get there?"

"Ummm..." My eyes traveled down to the program in my hand. "Look, Steve. See this drawing of a sailboat? Remember how much Dad liked to sail? This is the boat that took Dad and sailed him to heaven."

Steve smiled. "Dad have fun sailing to heaven!"

My eyes glistened and I gave Steve another hug.

"People are beginning to find their seats. Do you know where you want to sit?"

"I tell Polly I sit next to her. She be sad."

"That's so sweet, Steve. I know you will take good care of Polly. Why don't you go find her?" Then I bent down close and added, "Don't forget to use the restroom."

"I know that."

During the service Steve sat in the front row between Josh and Polly, along with Mike and Pamela. Their daughter Piper joined Sue in a side aisle. I took a seat behind the brothers and glanced down at a photo I'd brought with me from Vermont—a five-by-seven color photo of Roger and me—and began sobbing quietly. On that day so long ago we stood on a sandy beach in Maine clad in jeans and sweatshirts. I stared directly into the camera while Roger, head turned to one side, had his arm around my shoulder pulling me close. I smiled through my tears. We looked so young—our tanned faces were unlined, no gray strands poked through our brown hair.

The reverend opened the service by lighting the chalice and recognizing the family members in attendance. I startled when, after identifying me as Roger's former wife, she spoke Sue's name, before adding "Linda's spouse." I knew Polly had provided this information and my body warmed with gratitude. I watched through my tears with pride as Mike eulogized his father. His voice sounded strong and sure, but I knew he'd wept while writing the words he now uttered. Josh followed Mike. Over the years he'd filled out and the sport coat he found in Roger's closet looked good on him. Tears poured down his face. He croaked, "My father was the smartest man I've ever known." That was all he could manage.

Steve's turn came next. He gripped the microphone and faced the audience that filled the room. Mike, Josh, and I all knew he was about to share a Steve Cohen classic.

"I have a story about my dad. One time he take me to the hospital for blood test. The nurse say which arm? I point to my dad's arm and tell her, 'That one!'" Steve grinned broadly as the congregation burst into laughter. "My dad was a great guy. He call me every Saturday. Amen."

Later as Steve and I left the church he looked up at me and asked, "I do good, Mom?"

"You did great, Steve. I'm really proud of you, and so is your dad."

FORTY

Unpredictable Future, 2013-14

On our flight back to Vermont, I glanced over at a sleeping Steve. Once again, I'd been worried about how he'd handle an unfamiliar experience. And once again he'd shown me how capable he was. But little did I know that in nine months' time I'd be faced with a decision which would further challenge my acceptance of Steve's independence and capabilities.

In 2011 Sue and I had purchased a condo in Bellingham with the idea that someday.... We'd fallen in love with the Pacific Northwest on our kayaking trip in 1996 and after Mike and Pamela settled in Bellingham in 1999, had visited them many times. Compared to our rural Vermont setting, Bellingham, with its population of 85,000, seemed like a big city to us. But a permanent move there remained in the distant future. I couldn't wrap my head around the concept of putting 3,000 miles between Steve and myself. But then Sue's health took an unexpected turn.

In early summer 2013, she entered Dartmouth-Hitchcock hospital in Hanover for a total replacement of her left hip—her sixth major surgery in seven years. The operation went smoothly and after four days I brought her back to Lyndon to continue her recuperation. Two weeks later, as Sue picked at her food during dinner, I could tell by the look on her face she was in pain.

"You look like you are hurting," I said.

"No."

"Really?"

"Well, maybe. A little. I'm just tired." She left the table and headed to bed.

The following morning at breakfast Sue looked worse, her face pale under her dark tan, her lips pressed together. I insisted she take her temperature—the thermometer read 102.2.

"Let me look at your incision." Angry red lines streaked the site. "I think you've developed an infection. I'm taking you back to the hospital."

We arrived an hour later, Sue's pain so intense she could barely speak. A culture showed bacteria in her blood stream. I waited alone while doctors reopened the incision site, flushed out the infected area, and admitted her to the hospital.

The next morning Sue and I listened as her surgeon and an infectious disease physician stood by her bed arguing. The surgeon remained certain the infection was superficial. His colleague feared the bacteria may have gone deeper. He recommended removing the prosthetic joint and waiting six weeks to make certain the infection had cleared before inserting a new one. Sue would be bedridden during that time. Our heads spun as the two discussed various options. My mind tumbled back to the days when Steve was young and the many decisions I'd had to make for him without having all the information I needed. The surgeon won the argument and the artificial joint stayed.

Over the next two days, Sue's white blood count decreased, a good sign, but the incision site continued to drain. She was given a blood transfusion along with an order for a complex compression bandage to be placed over the oozing wound. But the dressing, which required the combined efforts of two nurses each time it needed replacing, did nothing to staunch the bleeding. Nevertheless, on the fourth day a nurse walked in and announced Sue was no longer "sick enough" to be in the hospital. She could go home.

"What about changing her dressing?" I asked.

"You can do that. Twice a day."

I burst into tears. The 120-mile round-trip drive I'd been making each day from Lyndon to Hanover had me exhausted. "You've got to be kidding me," I wailed. "It takes two trained nurses to change the dressing and you want me to do this on my own? No! I can't take on that responsibility."

The surgeon agreed with me and revoked the discharge order.

When it became obvious the compression bandage had failed, Sue was attached to a bulky machine called a wound VAC, along with a PICC line to deliver a six-week course of antibiotics. On July 17, after being in the hospital for ten days, an ambulance transferred Sue to our small local regional facility, just a few miles from our home.

Josh called and offered to fly from Bozeman to Vermont to help us. Initially I refused his gracious offer. Fortunately, he didn't listen to me and arrived within the week. He cooked meals, recognized my exhaustion, and provided a sounding board for my escalating fears. He also joined me when I met with doctors and, with his LPN training, helped translate their medical jargon. It felt good to have a nurse in the family. I realized how much I needed Josh's support. I could no longer do everything—not alone. By the time Sue came home on August 17 she'd spent a total of forty-two nights hospitalized. We were both rubbed raw. We had to face a truth. Our lives had changed. Dramatically.

Sue's many surgeries, along with the lengthy antibiotic regime, had slowed her cognitive processing and left her very weak. Would the surgeries keep coming for her? What would happen if my health started to fail? So far, I'd been able to care for Sue, but if I couldn't, who would support us? In Burlington, Steve had a well-established and loving network. But in Lyndon, Sue and I had only each other.

Unless...I thought of the Bellingham condo and I heard myself say to Sue, "I think we need to sell this house and move to our place in Bellingham. Soon. The condo is all on one floor. It's close to a good hospital. The milder winters will make it easier for both of us. I need more support. Being closer to Mike and Pamela, as well as Josh, will make things easier."

The words I spoke meant I'd decided to prioritize my needs and Sue's over Steve's. Guilt's familiar agitation coursed through me, and I turned to the most important member of Steve's team for support.

Jamie McEnroe, a veteran employee with the Howard Center, had been Steve's program manager for fifteen years. Not only did she coordinate Steve's care and serve as the leader of Steve's support team, she also supervised his live-in caregiver. Sue and I had an amazing working relationship with Jamie. She was sharp, articulate, and decisive. She cared deeply about Steve and his welfare. We trusted her without reservation. I drove to Burlington to meet with Jamie.

"You've had quite the summer," she said as I entered her office. "How are you doing? How is Sue?"

"We're both pretty wiped out," I admitted. "And we're thinking about a monumental change."

Jamie listened intently as I reviewed our discussion about moving to Bellingham and the reasoning behind it. "But I'm really concerned about Steve and how this decision will affect him," I added. "I'm going to ask if he wants to move with us, but I'm pretty sure I know what his response will be."

Jamie tucked a strand of her shoulder-length light blond hair behind one ear and nodded as a grin creased her face. "Linda, I empathize with you, I really do. But if Steve wants to remain in Burlington you know he will be fine. He's well established here. He has so many people behind him. You need to do what's right for you and Sue." Jamie paused and leaned toward me. "You know, we have many clients in Steve's age bracket who have outlived their parents, or don't have family members nearby. You've always been a valued member of Steve's team. I have so much respect for you. Regardless of where you live, I know you will continue to support Steve. But I promise you, I will be here for him. My eyes will be on him."

I believed Jamie, but I still wanted Steve to have a choice. That afternoon I told Steve about our plans and asked if he would like to leave Burlington and move to Bellingham with us.

"No way," he answered without hesitation. "I no leave my house. I no leave my job. I no leave my friends." Steve's answer didn't surprise me. He'd lived in Burlington since 1995 and in his condo since 2002. This was his community. But then he looked at me and added, "I sad you and Sue move far away." My shoulders slumped and my eyes filled.

Over the next months I worked to convince myself that for Steve's entire life I'd done all I could to keep him safe and moving forward. I needed to trust Jamie and the other folks at the Howard Center. *You are just a plane ride away*, I told myself. *You can Skype as much as you want to. You need to let go. Again.* Even so the dissonance between caring for Steve and living my own life tore through me—just like it had on the morning in 1989 when I drove down the driveway of our Hanover home with Steve heading for the group home in Albany, New York.

Sue and I officially became "Bellinghamsters" in early October 2013. Guilt rode with me on the evening flight from Boston to Seattle. As the Jet Blue plane hurtled through the night and the miles between us and Steve increased, my internal pain grew. Even though we'd already made plans to return to Vermont for Christmas, leaving Steve in Burlington was the hardest thing I'd ever done. Harder than experiencing the death of my twenty-one-year-old sister. Harder than leaving my marriage. Harder than coming out to my parents. Harder than leaving Steve at the group home.

At the time Sue and I moved, Steve's current caregiver had been living with him for over a year. Initially, Paul seemed perfect: mid-fifties, retired, with no plans of leaving the Burlington area in the near future. Both Sue and I had vetted him with the hope he'd be with Steve for many years. But over time, we'd begun to question our choice.

We'd always had a no-smoking policy inside the condo or in any car transporting Steve. When Jamie made a home visit and thought she smelled a cigarette odor, Paul assured her he only smoked outside. Then a new name began cropping up in conversations with Steve. When I questioned him about this person, he responded, "That Paul's son, he sleep here."

I asked Jamie to check this out. "He's just visiting, and Steve loves him," Paul told her. But over time it became clear his son had moved in. Desperate to make this work, Jamie, Sue, and I met with Paul. He was new to caregiving, we told ourselves. Paul promised us honesty and spoke of his commitment to Steve. We believed him. We allowed the son to stay but asked he help cover utilities.

As Sue and I settled into our new urban lifestyle in Bellingham we discovered Paul had replaced the cleaning service we'd retained and hired his son instead. Then we received notice Steve's respite funding had run out. Paul had been paying his son to provide respite care even though he was living in the condo. In December, when Sue and I returned to Vermont to spend Christmas with Steve, concerns about Paul had escalated. His passive-aggressive behavior toward Jamie and other team members had created a rift in the chemistry of the people who supported Steve—many of whom had been with Steve for years. Paul clearly didn't understand how to be a team player. Sue and I had never faced a situation like this before, but team cohesiveness was vitally important with us living so far away. Reluctantly we concluded Paul needed to be terminated and Dave, Steve's community access person and friend, moved in with him on an interim basis.

Soon after our return to Bellingham, the unthinkable happened. Jamie received a well-deserved promotion to service director. She would no longer be Steve's program manager. Jamie was replaced by a new hire who found a caregiver for Steve to replace Paul, but my gut told me something wasn't right about this one either. So, in March 2014, I flew back to Vermont to check in on Steve.

The temperature lingered in the mid-twenties on the late afternoon I arrived at Steve's condo. I found my son in front of his TV shivering. The window next to him was open. I asked him about the window. "Priscilla do it," he answered. "She say it stink in here."

Steve was right. A strange unpleasant odor permeated the first floor. I closed the window and walked into the kitchen. Unwashed dishes filled the sink and counters. Something indescribable simmered in a saucepan. An emaciated dog lay sleeping in a corner. I opened the refrigerator door and rotting food spilled out. Priscilla was nowhere to be found. I called the Howard Center and asked to speak to Steve's program manager.

Priscilla was given forty-eight hours to vacate the premises and I took Steve to a Burlington hotel for a "surprise" vacation. Two days later when I checked with the Howard Center to make certain Priscilla was gone, Steve's program manager told me based on a recent phone call she thought so, it sounded as though Priscilla was packing up her car. But she couldn't be certain since Priscilla had hung up on her.

When Steve and I walked into his condo, Priscilla was still there. She grabbed Steve's mobile phone, stormed outside, and called the police to report that I was stalking her. Two officers arrived within minutes. Steve became distraught.

"Mom, I scared! Police here! You go to jail?"

The officers quickly assessed the situation for what it was. Insane. The male officer spoke to Priscilla while his female partner did her best to reassure both Steve and me. Steve's phone was returned, and Priscilla drove off. Only later did I discover she'd also reported *me* to the state of Vermont for elder abuse of my son.

During the next two weeks Dave and others on Steve's team pitched in while I cleaned up the mess Priscilla had left behind. The support these loyal folks extended to both me and my son slowly calmed me. As equilibrium returned to his life, Steve began to share stories about the trauma he'd endured. He spoke of times when Paul yelled at him and slammed his fists against a wall. "That scary. He say it not my business if he smoke." About Priscilla he reported, "Her dog pee and poop on the floor and I clean it. I not like that." Guilt roared in.

Fortunately, one of Steve's longtime team members stepped forward and recommended a young couple she felt would be perfect for Steve. When I met with Mattie and Sean, my gut told me they were the right people. Both were graduate students and forthright about their interest in living with Steve and becoming his caregivers. Their stipend would allow them to quit their part-time jobs and focus on their studies. They were willing to make a two-year commitment, beginning in June and lasting until June of 2016. Once again Dave agreed to move in with Steve as his interim caregiver.

By the time I returned to Bellingham with Mattie and Sean lined up as Steve's new caregivers, I felt order had been restored and Steve was safe again. But I was shaken by what I'd experienced. Steve's new program manager was slow to set up the required training for Mattie and Sean, missed several home visits with them, and took a long time responding to my emails. I tried to be patient and give her time to grow into her position. But eventually I asked she be removed as Steve's program manager.

In September of 2014 I stood in the Bellingham airport waiting to welcome Steve to our new hometown. Sue had traveled east for a college reunion and offered to bring Steve back with her to celebrate his forty-eighth birthday. When I spotted him among the crowd of arrivals, I could barely keep myself from leaving the designated waiting area and running toward him. I waved my arm, but Steve ignored me. In fact, he walked right by me! But I knew he was teasing me and let him have his fun.

He tapped me on the shoulder. "I fool you," he said and laughed before flinging his arms around my waist. Then he added, "I see your new house? You give me tour?" I explained first Sue, he, and I were stopping at Mike and Pamela's place.

I'd planned a surprise for Steve. He didn't know Josh had flown in from Bozeman the day before. When we arrived, Mike led him into the kitchen where Josh stood holding out a Bud Lite for Steve. Steve broke into tears before he recovered.

"Shrimpo! What you doing here?"

A week later I accompanied Steve on the flight back to Burlington. "Look out, Burlington," he exclaimed as the plane taxied to the gate. "Steve is back!" Mattie and Sean greeted us enthusiastically as we entered the condo. The place was spotless and a wholesome meal simmered on the stove. I returned to Bellingham without one ounce of guilt.

FORTY-ONE

Family Meeting, 2015

One by one we arrived and entered the waiting room of the local dispute resolution center in Bellingham. After a few moments of polite small talk, a gray-haired woman and balding man appeared. "Good morning, folks! Would you follow us, please?"

OK, here we go! My fingers curled into fists and I inhaled deeply in a futile attempt to soothe my frayed nerves. Led by the facilitators, I moved down a hallway accompanied by other members of my family. We entered a conference room flooded by August sunshine. With me were Sue, Mike and Pamela, and Josh.

In May, Mike, Josh, and Steve had traveled to Las Vegas together on a "just brothers" trip. Years earlier Sue had taken Steve to Vegas and he'd talked of a return trip to see the "hubba-hubba girls" ever since. On the first full day of their adventure my phone sounded, and I opened a photo sent by Mike of Steve staring at a balloon representation of an enormous penis, just one of many shots that proved "What happens in Vegas should stay in Vegas." But despite their fun and crazy antics, Mike and Josh returned from Sin City worried about Steve. They felt he'd aged a lot since he'd visited Bellingham seven months before. Each day's activities exhausted him, they told me. They urged Sue and me to consider moving Steve to Bellingham, closer to family. Pamela supported their idea.

Their proposal left me very unsettled. Bringing Steve to Bellingham would impact all our lives in profound ways. We'd need to develop a network from scratch as we investigated and set up resources to support Steve. And Steve's anxiety would ratchet up to an intolerable level once he became aware of this monumental change.

Even though my sons accused me of overstating my concerns, I'd insisted on using the mediation center to facilitate our family discussion. So much was riding on this decision. I wanted a structured format to ensure everyone's voices were heard.

One of the mediators explained the meeting would begin with opening statements from everyone. Then added, "Linda, let's hear from you first." My palms were sweaty and my throat tightened as I began.

"Sue and I share your concerns about Steve's premature aging. Right now, Mattie and Sean are doing a fantastic job caregiving. However, they'll be leaving in a year. So, I'll need to begin looking for new caregivers very soon." Stating this reality out loud caused my stomach to curl with tension. The caregiving debacle I'd endured just a year earlier had left me very tender. My eyes filled and I struggled for composure.

One of the mediators prodded gently. "What else are you concerned about?"

"Everything. Everyone," I said.

I took a deep breath and directed my next comments to my sons and Pamela. "I'm not sure any of you can truly understand how moving Steve to Bellingham will impact all of our lives. Sue and I have been orchestrating Steve's care for a long time. I'm seventy-five. Sue is seventy-one. I don't know if either of us have the energy or emotional resources to start over again." Sue reached for my hand and I continued.

"I don't know what to do," I admitted. "Over the years I've always felt so certain of what path to take, how to support not only Steve, but…," I paused and looked at Mike and Josh, "…both of you too. But now? I'm so unsure. Besides, we all know Steve won't want to move. Burlington is his community. What is his role in this decision? Does he get to have a say?"

Mike jumped in. "That's why we want Steve here, where we can help you. You don't have to do this alone anymore, Mom."

"I appreciate your willingness to help," I said, looking at Mike. Both he and Pamela worked in human services. In addition to their concern for Steve, both were well aware of the funding challenges in Washington State. I referred to some notes I'd compiled.

"The Howard Center's most recent annual budget for Steve exceeds $67,000. Of that, close to seventy-five percent is earmarked for direct support in the areas of community-based employment, community access, and home caregivers—the key components of Steve's life in

Burlington. We all know that level of funding isn't possible here. And you can't place a price on a network that has taken years to assemble: Steve's medical care providers, the Howard staffers who know Steve so well, his friends, and social activities." I wanted my sons to understand what Steve had in Burlington had been a massive labor to create. I rubbed the back of my neck as my agitation increased. The room heated up as bright sun poured through west-facing windows. How could anyone really know the value of the work it'd taken to establish Steve's community? Least of all my boys who were children themselves when I'd started advocating for Steve. "Also, we will need to find a place for Steve to live and Mike, you've said your research shows the local adult family care homes aren't a good option."

"No," said Mike, his lips pressed together. "I don't want Steve living in one of those. At least not the ones I'm aware of."

I took a deep breath.

A mediator interrupted and reminded me this was a time to get all concerns and options on the table.

Over the three-hour session various positions emerged. Sue thought Steve should remain in Burlington until his health deteriorated to such a point where his location wouldn't matter—to him. Mike and Pamela wanted Steve moved to Bellingham before he got to that place. Josh stated he simply needed to see Steve more frequently.

As I listened, my confusion escalated and my mind raced. This was my family. The people I cared about deeply. I wanted everyone to be happy, but I could feel a crushing weight settling on my shoulders.

Josh's voice cut through my fog. "Would anyone object if I moved to Bellingham and lived with Steve? I've lived with him before; I can do it again."

Everyone, except me, eagerly agreed to his offer. I knew he'd been seeing someone in Bozeman for a while now, and recently she'd wanted them to make a lifelong commitment to each other. How could Josh hold onto their relationship while caring for Steve at the same time? Especially if he moved to Bellingham? If anyone knew how managing Steve's complexities could affect a couple, I did.

I sat in silence as the conversation rattled around me. Sue and I had been choreographing Steve's care for a long time and when things went well, our life was easy. But when the network stumbled, like it had the previous year, relationships suffered. Sue and I had experienced stress over Steve's care, and I didn't want to pass that stress on to my sons or their partners. I knew I needed the support my kids were offering me. But I also knew I couldn't control what the support would look like. I'd always been a mama bear when it came to Steve, strong-arming limited resources to bend to our needs and overseeing everything. Could I let go? At least a bit? But what might happen if I let Mike and Josh take the lead and things didn't go well? What would that do to our family? As I stewed about what could go wrong, I remembered the advice Steve gave me soon after my breakdown. "Keep your feet on the ground, Mom." *OK, I can do that*, I thought.

I asked for some time to let my mind settle.

After a second mediation session, we signed off on an agreement. As initial proof of my willingness to let others share in Steve's oversight, I canceled my planned trip to Vermont in September to celebrate Steve's forty-ninth birthday. Except for Skype, I hadn't seen him since the mess I'd found in Burlington seven months earlier. But everyone felt I needed to demonstrate my willingness to give up some control. This would be my test.

Sue had scheduled an east coast trip in September for a reunion with friends and offered to extend her visit. Josh jumped in and agreed to meet her in Burlington. Together they'd help Steve celebrate his big day and explain to him how much we all wanted him near us. Mike and Pamela agreed to use their extensive networks to help access services for Steve in Bellingham. I proposed to begin looking for a place for Steve to live, something like what Steve had in Burlington, with separate space for a caregiver. Then, with all the pieces in place, Josh would move to Bellingham and live with Steve for a few months while he settled in and a more permanent caregiver could be found. We congratulated ourselves on a successful mediation. Steve wouldn't need to move until Mattie and Sean left in June 2016. We had plenty of time to make this plan work.

When Sue and Josh met with Steve in September, he reluctantly agreed to the move. "I want my own house and I no want live by myself," he stated. They assured him his two requirements would be met.

I began the search for the right house. I told myself I needed to do this because the current housing market was tight, and competition for housing in our price range fierce. But in reality, I needed to act. I needed to convince myself our decision to move Steve was in everyone's best interests. I told myself finding a house would be a sign we were doing right by Steve. Sue and I agreed if I found a place that met our needs and Steve's, we'd move forward with a purchase, then list the house as a short-term rental until June.

In late October my realtor showed me a house that was being sold to settle an estate. As I toured the empty rooms, I had no trouble imagining Steve living there. The one-story rambler had two good-sized bedrooms and a full bath along with a living room and eat-in kitchen. The original garage had been converted into a master bedroom with its own bath. It even had a separate entrance! An oversized garage behind the house would provide plenty of storage and I could envision family picnics taking place around the fire pit located in the spacious backyard. Best of all, the property was located in a safe neighborhood, on a bus line, close to Mike and Pamela's home, and within two blocks of the Bellingham hospital. After checking out my find, Sue, Pamela, and Mike gave their enthusiastic approval.

I wrote a check for earnest money and set the wheels in motion to complete the purchase. *Maybe we can even bring Steve out for Christmas. Knowing he has a place to live and actually seeing it will ease his mind. Along with mine.* I relaxed a bit.

FORTY-TWO

Embracing Steve, 2015

On Friday, November 6, 2015, incessant ringing cut through my fog of sleep. I rolled over, glanced at my cell phone, and saw the area code: 802. Vermont calling. My heart dropped as it always did when those digits appeared. Could this be a call about Steve? I answered without hesitation. When I heard the voice of Steve's current program manager, Elena, I asked her to hold on while I reached for my hearing aids.

"I'm calling from the emergency room," said Elena. "It's 11:30 here and this morning Steve was running some errands with his community access person when he began coughing up blood. They drove directly to the hospital." A freight train of fear roared through me. Elena continued, "The nurse I spoke to knows Steve. She feels this is pretty serious and told me this is the worst she's ever seen him. The plan is to sedate him, pass a camera down his throat, and try to locate the source of the bleed."

My lips moved a couple of times before I could force any sound through them. Steve's medical emergencies always sent me to darkness. "OK...OK." I was wide awake now, sitting on the edge of my bed, shivering. I asked Elena to tell me who was with Steve. He was new to her caseload and Elena was not yet a part of Steve's circle of longtime supporters. She reported that Mattie, his caregiver, was present.

"OK," I choked out. "Can you call Dave too? He'll want to know about Steve and be with him." Although recently retired from the Howard workforce, Dave and Steve remained close and spent time together every week. I knew Steve must be scared. If I couldn't be there beside him and comfort him, Dave was my next best option. I trusted him beyond any doubt.

"Yes, I'll call Dave," replied Elena.

I imagined Steve hooked up to tubes and machines. Blood pounded through my veins. There was something else I needed to tell Elena. What was it? I fought through my panic and remembered. "And Elena, this is important. I have a DNR on Steve."

"Yes, I know," she answered. "The medical staff is aware of this as well. Can you hold on?" I gripped my phone and heard Elena speaking to someone. "Linda, a nurse just told me they are about to start sedating Steve. I'll call you back as soon as I have more news."

I stood. My head spun. In this moment the 3,000 miles between me and my son was like 3 million. Or more. Another planet. Another solar system. Another galaxy. What should I do? I was alone. By this time Sue was already at her water aerobics class.

"Phone calls," I said to the bedroom walls. "Sue. Mike. Josh."

But each call went to voicemail. I left the same message on each phone. "Call me. Steve has been taken to the emergency room at Fletcher Allen. He's coughing up blood. Things sound serious." Waves of loneliness crashed over me.

I reached the main desk at the Aquatic Center, described my wife's appearance, and asked the attendant to go find her. "Have her call me right away."

Mike and Pamela and seven-year-old Piper were at a resort about twenty miles north. I knew Piper was an early riser. Maybe they were at the resort's indoor pool? The main desk transferred my call to the pool area.

"Please see if Mike Cohen is in the pool with his family. I need to speak with him. This is his mother. It's urgent." I held my phone. Waiting.

"Hey, Mom, what's up?"

"It's Steve. He's at the hospital, he's bleeding internally." I made no attempt to hide my panic.

"I'll leave right away and come straight to you. I should be there within an hour." Mike's voice was calm, steady.

Sue's call came through next. "It's Steve, he's in the hospital. I need you."

Again, the phone rang. Josh, from Bozeman. "Mom, what's happening?" His voice dripped with fear and concern. I told him the little I knew. "I'm going to get a flight and head to Burlington," he replied. I knew nothing I could say would stop him. "I'll call from the airport and let you know my flight plans."

Sue walked in and we held each other without speaking. When we pulled apart Sue asked, "Should I start looking for flights to Vermont?" I nodded. With no direct routes from Seattle to Burlington, the flight time was at least seven hours, probably more.

Soon my phone rang again. "Is this Linda, Steve's mother?" queried a female voice who identified herself as an emergency room nurse. "I'm part of the team working on your son. We sedated him and began the procedure to pass a camera down his throat. But as we started, his heart stopped."

My stomach seized. Every muscle in my body tightened. "Oh! His heart stopped?"

"Yes." Then silence.

"Is he dead?"

"Yes, I am so sorry."

I heard screaming. From me.

My heart ripped from my body. My fists pounded the surface of our granite kitchen counter. Eyes wide, Sue ran into the kitchen and stood staring at me. "I've been looking for a sign," I gasped, "but not this one."

"Is Steve…?"

"He's gone! His heart stopped." Our sobs filled the condo.

When Mike walked in the door and saw Sue and me, he knew. "Steve's gone," I told him. "His heart stopped. He didn't make it."

He embraced both of us. "I'm so sorry. What do you need me to do?"

"Call Josh," I answered. "I got him at the airport and told him Steve died. He's insisting on continuing to Burlington, but that's not what I want. I want him to fly to Seattle. I want us all together. I need us all together."

Josh rerouted to Seattle and by dinnertime our family, smaller by one, sat together at Mike and Pamela's house.

Later in bed I tossed and turned, my mind in overdrive, thinking about how to mark Steve's passing. I knew I wanted a celebration of life, not a funeral. The gathering wouldn't be in a church, but where? Who should officiate? Who should speak? What songs should be sung? How should the space be decorated? For every question, an immediate answer appeared and throughout the night I scribbled each thought into a bedside notebook.

Saturday morning Sue and I, Mike, and Josh flew to Burlington. Josh sat next to me on both legs of the trip. "I thought Steve would live forever," he told me through his tears. I spent much of the flight lost in thought. I recalled the stricken look on my parents' faces when my sister Carol died. So this is what it feels like to lose a child. Blunt-force grief. I thought of Roger and our journey together. I took out my notebook and began to scribble out the first draft of Steve's obituary. The words flowed onto the page. I knew exactly what to write. Who was leading me?

The next days whirled and tumbled around me. My control gene kicked in. I laid out what I wanted. Sue, Mike, and Josh followed my lead.

On Sunday, the four of us checked out an event space recommended by friends. The Saint John's Social Club stood on the shore of Lake Champlain and had a room big enough to accommodate 150 people. I'd already called my friend Jean to ask if she would lead Steve's memorial. When she "civil unioned" Sue and me at the end of her driveway in a snowstorm, I couldn't have known I'd be asking for her services a second time. The club manager told us the coming Friday was open, and I phoned Jean to confirm the date worked for her.

Before leaving, we all walked the beach below the club, and I picked up pieces of beach glass.

Josh found a heart stone and pressed it into my palm. Then he said, "Mom, I just realized this Friday is November 13th."

"Is that a problem?"

Josh's eyes brimmed and overflowed. "No." He looked out over the water. "Steve always celebrated every Friday the thirteenth."

Monday, I finalized Steve's obituary and sent it out to papers in Burlington, Hanover, and Lyndon. Sue and I met with the Howard folks at the center's headquarters. Seated around a table in a conference room where I'd been so many times over the years, I cried, I laughed, embraced by love. Next Sue and I picked up Josh and drove to a local crematorium to meet with the owner. In his office I barely heard his earnest condolences. I just wanted to sign the paperwork so Steve's body could be retrieved from the hospital morgue. I had to get him out of there. Since his death I'd envisioned him in a drawer, naked, an identification tag on one big toe. I looked at Sue and Josh, wondering if they saw the same image.

Tuesday, Ann Patterson picked me up from our rental house and over lunch we talked about Steve and Robbie. We'd remained close ever since we first met as mothers of five-year-old boys with Down syndrome on Long Island. Both Ann and Robbie now lived in Burlington—Ann with her male partner and Robbie in a caregiver's home supervised by the Howard Center. Ann looked across the table. "I probably shouldn't say this...."

"I know exactly what you are going to say," I interrupted. "I am sadder than I can tell you, but I also feel a tremendous sense of relief. My job with Steve is over. I don't have to worry about him anymore. And if the shoe was on the other foot and Rob had died, I'd feel somewhat envious of you."

Ann nodded. For a moment neither of us said anything. Then we reached for each other's hand. I knew she understood how the complex combination of relief and grief could live together like they now did in me.

In the evening Josh, Sue, and I had dinner with Mattie and Sean. Mattie, who'd been with Steve in the emergency room, reassured us by saying although Steve was scared, he hadn't been in any pain.

On Wednesday Sue, Josh, and I headed to Steve's condo to pick out various items we wanted to use at the celebration. We walked into Steve's bedroom past the sign on the door which proclaimed, "Steve's Office." Steve's bed was neatly made. Along one wall stood a vertical tower with seven cubbies—one for each day of the week. Each Sunday evening, after doing his laundry, Steve obsessively organized his wardrobe for the week and placed an outfit in each cubby. Tension zapped and sizzled between us like electricity when we took in the tower's empty sections. Only the "Saturday" and "Sunday" spaces held clothing. Next to the tower stood Steve's desk, its surface covered with five calendars, where every morning he religiously drew an X through the day's date. On each calendar the X's stopped after November 6. Steve's presence filled the room. We all felt him. Any second I expected to hear him enter the condo, see me and exclaim, "Mom! You here! I so happy." That evening Mike picked up Pamela and Piper at the airport.

Thursday morning, I awoke crying. A cold rain poured down. Sue and I shopped for clothes for the following day. I selected a bright pink scarf to top off my white blouse and black dress pants. When we arrived at the crematorium to pick up Steve's ashes, the director told me he had saved Steve's clothes. Did I want them? No. He handed me Steve's wallet and his watch, along with a cardboard box filled with Steve's remains. The box felt surprisingly heavy. I wondered if I'd be allowed to carry the ashes onto the plane. No way in hell would I let Steve ride alone in the cargo hold.

Thursday night our rental house began to fill. Sasha, Josh's partner, flew in from LA where she'd been on a business trip. Josh walked in gripping her hand. My body warmed with relief as Sasha and I wrapped our arms around each other. Josh had been adrift without her.

Jane and Kevin stopped by before checking into a motel. Kevin's eyes overflowed. I knew his tears were for me but sensed something more. We raised our wineglasses in a toast to Steve. Kevin looked at me.

"I had a brother named Billy. He was my mother's tenth child, just a few years older than me. He was born with Down syndrome."

My eyes widened. My mouth hung open. "Oh, Kevin!" I'd known Kevin since he and Jane began dating as seventh and eighth graders in 1952. He was a member of the crowd I'd hung out with all through high school and I'd met several of his many siblings. But I'd never heard about this brother. Who else, besides Jane, knew about Billy? Did Kevin ever tell Roger? The two were good friends. But I didn't ask. I simply took a deep breath and listened as Kevin continued speaking.

"My mother was told to put Billy in an institution soon after his birth. She used to take me monthly to see him. She cried each time we said goodbye."

"What happened to Billy?" I asked.

"He had a heart defect, probably like Steve's," answered Kevin. "He died in his early teens." I reached out for Kevin and embraced him. Maybe he'd never told me because he didn't want to scare me while Steve was growing up. Or maybe his own grief just didn't allow him to talk. But I now felt a new closeness between us.

Heather, Jane and Kevin's daughter, was flying in from Phoenix where she lived with her wife. A text informed me she'd landed in Boston. She planned to drive to Burlington in the morning and assured me she'd arrive well before the celebration's start time. Polly, Roger's widow, called. She'd missed her connection in New York City, but was booked on an early morning flight into Burlington. I told her Mike would pick her up.

On Friday morning, Sue, along with a friend from New Jersey and her two children, headed to the Saint John's Club to decorate and arrange the function room. Josh and Sasha also went to the club to put the final touches on a slide show—photos of Steve depicting his rich life. Together with Mike and Pamela, they'd downloaded songs from some of Steve's favorite recording artists: Prince, the Stones, the Beatles, and, of course, Michael Jackson. The technology they employed that would magically transport the photos from a computer to a large display screen was beyond me. I was grateful for their expertise.

I decided, despite the cold drizzle leaking from a low gray sky, to go for a walk. I needed exercise and solo time to loosen the vise of tension that gripped me. As I walked through the rain, I unexpectedly sensed Roger's presence. Somehow, I was certain Roger knew. *Steve's journey is over*, I whispered to him. *But don't be sad. He had a great life. You were such a good dad to him, and together we were the best parents we could be.*

Slowly my body loosened. I centered myself. I was tired, but in a fulfilling way. I took no note of the weather. In my head, one of the songs a female guitarist would sing today played over and over. "My Way" was a perfect reflection of Steve and how he'd lived his life.

He'd lived a full and rich life. He'd had to overcome so many barriers before he was able to walk the paths, roads, and highways he'd traveled on. And always, always he'd done it his way.

The lyrics of another verse summarized my feelings. Yes, looking back on his life, there were times I'd experienced regret, but not many. Occasionally people had said to me, "I don't know how you do it." I'd always thought, *I do what I have to do. Steve is my son.*

Today I will shed no tears, I promised myself. I knew the time for grieving would come. But today I would be fully present and celebrate Steve.

When I entered the club shortly after noon, Sue checked in with me. "Does this look OK?" she wondered.

My eyes scanned the room. Along the wall Sue had arranged a replication of "Steve's Office." On a long rectangular table draped with a pink cloth rested many items: his five calendars, several pieces of his art—the Harry Potter triptych, a series of superhero drawings that Mattie had collected and placed in a three-ring binder, a drawing of Obama standing at a lectern. There was a gold top hat, a relic of some past New Year's Eve when Steve watched the ball drop on TV. I spotted the plastic change sorter he used to organize and wrap his nickels, dimes, and quarters. A gold-sparkly poster board was covered with photos—Steve in the "I Believe" Santa Claus shirt he wore each Christmas, Steve and Belinda rocking dance moves, Steve at one of his birthday parties, Steve and Robbie walking along the shore of Lake Champlain. Sue had left space on the table for others to place objects they'd been invited to bring that reminded them of Steve. Later I found an action figure of Captain America left by one of Josh's high school classmates. Around the toy's neck hung a handmade shield she created. The words on the shield read: "Super Hero Steve—with the powers of Love. Generosity. Joy. Goodness."

Pink balloons decorated the table where refreshments would soon arrive, catered by Steve's cherished Healthy Living Food Market. On a round table sat two empty pink plastic buckets along with notepaper and pens. A sign proclaimed this to be where "Notes of Love" for Steve could be deposited. Throughout the afternoon, two or three people would stand at the table writing. Later, when we cleaned up, both buckets overflowed with messages to Steve.

For seating, Sue and her friend had set up several rows of chairs in the center of the room facing a podium. Above the dais was a large monitor where images of Steve floated by. Small tavern tables filled the rest of the space.

"Everything looks great. You've done a fantastic job." I wrapped my arms around my wife. "Thank you," I whispered into her ear. "Thank you. I love you." I stepped back. "How are you doing?"

"I'm good," replied Sue.

"Me too," I said and smiled.

People began arriving well before the 1:00 p.m. start time. Friends from our Hanover days made the two-hour drive—parents of our sons' classmates, skiing and hiking companions, Steve's former teachers. A much younger group of forty-somethings clustered together. I struggled to recognize these childhood buddies of Steve, Mike, and Josh. Bill Boyle's wife, Susan, lamented that Steve's all-time favorite doctor had a previous obligation. I didn't see Maggie when she first entered. She'd driven from Rochester, New York, where she now held the post of vice-provost of Rochester University's School of Nursing. Maggie and I hadn't seen each other in twenty-five-years, but she looked much the same—tall and striking with salt-and-pepper hair. We greeted each other with a hug before she moved off to find a seat. Other folks from many of Vermont's small towns walked in. These included neighbors from the Lyndon area and educators with whom both Sue and I had worked. Guests from Burlington comprised close to fifty percent of the crowd. Many worked for the Howard Center. Several of Steve's peers entered the room. All were clients of the Howard Center and came with a support person or friend who provided transportation. Ann Patterson and Robbie arrived together. When I spotted Brian, who now resided in Pennsylvania and hadn't lived with Steve since 2011, I rushed to embrace him. He was Steve's loyal caregiver through some of the hardest times, including Steve's stroke. A huge contingent represented the

Healthy Living store—the owner Katy and her two adult children, along with many of Steve's fellow workers. Missing in the crowd was Brenda Lawton. Her husband Wayne had died a few years before and she was in her winter Florida home. Many folks found a way to include pink in their dress—a scarf, a tie, a shirt or blouse. Not everyone knew each other, but they all knew Steve.

Jean, dressed in black slacks and a long-sleeved black blouse, found me in the crowd. Her white clerical color circled her neck. "It's getting close to one. Do you want to start on time?"

"Yes," I answered. My eyes roamed the room searching for Sue and my other family members. We took our seats and others followed suit. Soon every chair was filled. Folks stood shoulder to shoulder along the walls. The room began to quiet.

The rain had stopped but a stiff wind whipped the gray lake waters and waves crashed onto the beach. Then, without warning, a brilliant shaft of sunlight cut through a break in the clouds and streamed into the room through the bank of picture windows which framed the view across Lake Champlain to New York's distant Adirondack mountains. My heart caught in my throat.

Jean stepped to the podium and struck the triangle in her hand. She smiled and gestured toward the windows at the clearing sky. "I think it is time to begin."

The program, which Jean helped me plan, commenced with a moment of silence followed by a blessing and a prayer. An employment consultant from the Howard Center and one of Steve's dearest friends read from Ecclesiastes: "For everything there is a season...." Jean's wife Meg shared a children's picture book, *On Morning Wings*. Written by Vermont author Reeve Lindbergh, the story is an adaptation of Psalm 139. The illustrations follow four young friends as they spend a day together, riding bikes, playing at a beach and in the evening roasting marshmallows around a campfire. The message imparted by Lindbergh is that whenever we may feel lost or lonely, friends are never far away.

In Steve's honor, the guitarist sang "My Way," and as the last chords sounded, Heather approached the podium. She hated talking in front of large crowds, she'd told me earlier, but she'd consented because of her deep love for Steve. Her tight strawberry blond curls were cropped close, framing her head. She looked at me, smiled, and began. During her tribute she described her bond with Steve. "My connection to Steve is precious to me and I am sure shaped who I am today. I connected with Steve on a level of heart and soul. He was my *anam cara*—a Celtic term for soul friend. After finding that connection with Steve, I wanted to find it with others. I have worked with adults with developmental disabilities my entire life." She looked around the room before offering a piece of advice. "I find it easier to connect with hearts and souls when the intellect is disabled. I highly recommended you all attempt to disable your own intellect on occasion, as it can get in the way of some of the best things life has to offer."

The little girl who sang by Steve's crib when he was an infant had become a wise, insightful woman. I hugged her as she returned to her seat next to her parents.

Mike spoke for our family. Before the arrival of his wife and daughter, he'd spent most of his time sequestered alone. I knew he'd been scribbling notes in a composition book he'd asked me to buy soon after we arrived in Burlington, but he hadn't shared his thoughts with me. He presented a brotherly perspective as he explained the origin of one of Steve's most famous "Steve-isms."

"Steve was the only person who could get me to Disney World. I went with a bad attitude, a horrible fever, and unprepared for the Disney experience. This was when Steve was obsessed with Teenage Mutant Ninja Turtles and was determined to collect autographs from actors portraying each one. At some point, in pursuit of Leonardo or Donatello, I lost my patience and got grumpy. Steve looked me in the eye and said, 'Mikey-Boy, that isn't very Disney.'" After pausing for the laughter to subside, Mike continued. "Steve was a shining star, a powerful force around which we all orbited. Some may not like to be seemingly always in the shadow of another family member, but I know, for my family, it has always been a beautiful place to be."

I looked lovingly at Mike. His voice was strong with no hint of sadness. I had yet to see him shed a single tear. Weeks later his wife Pamela would tell me he sobbed most of the way on their return flight to Seattle.

Tributes completed, I silently mouthed the lyrics as the guitarist played Jim Croce's "Time in A Bottle." In many ways it seemed my days with Steve had lasted forever. Certainly, we'd had far more time together than the pediatrician had predicted so long ago. So many of my dreams for Steve had come true, treasures I could revisit. Steve had left a legacy that would last for eternity.

Jean closed with a final prayer, less than thirty minutes after she began. Folks rose and started to mingle. As the party, which Steve would have loved, gathered steam, I swore I heard Steve's voice say, "Short meeting. I like it."

ODE TO STEVE—2015

Imagine a life lived without filters
Where joy knows no boundaries
And each sorrow is fully embraced.

Where the masks people wear
Are transparent.
But your mask remains
Fully intact,
Because of the assumptions other make when they look at you.

Where life flows so slowly
That each detail is observed with great wisdom.

Where you are never too old
To play with toys.

Where each breath gained is noted and appreciated
Never taken for granted.

Where kindness, no matter how small
Is acknowledged with a "thank you,"
And each request is bracketed with a "please."

Where choices are not always available
And this reality is accepted with grace.

And where those who embrace your light
And can see into your soul,
Are enriched with an understanding
So pure
And a knowledge so deep
That you will remain with them forever.

I gazed out the window as the plane banked for its final approach to Seattle's Sea-Tac airport. Exactly two weeks after Steve's death, Sue and I were heading home to Bellingham. We'd spoken little during the long flight, both exhausted and lost in thought. For seven hours my hands had cradled the box resting on my lap holding Steve's ashes. My fears about being able to bring his remains on board had proven unfounded. No one had questioned the contents of the plain-looking cardboard container. No one could see the gaping wound that was my heart.

Sue and I had spent our last days in Burlington doing mundane but necessary tasks. I went to the bank to close out Steve's checking account and walked out with $77.23. On Church Street I handed out the money to several homeless people gathered there.

Together Sue and I spent hours at Steve's condo, sorting through his possessions. We bagged up clothes to be given away. We took his TV, PlayStation, and video games to a day program recreation center operated by Howard for their clients. Tags were affixed to furniture: "to be given to [person's name]," "for Goodwill," "donate to [organization's name]."

Hardest of all was deciding what to do with Steve's many pieces of original artwork. Sue and I decided which ones we wanted to keep. I wrapped the framed Harry Potter triptych in Steve's work apron from Healthy Living, his name tag still attached. We delivered several boxes to UPS for shipment to Bellingham.

We met with many of Steve's friends from Howard. Over brunch Dave choked out, "I never saw Steve waste a minute of his life. He always knew the next thing he was going to do."

His job coach supervisor told us, "When Steve was talking about the 'big 5-0' at his forty-ninth birthday, I had a feeling he wouldn't make it to fifty." We took Steve's amazing current caregivers, Sean and Mattie, to dinner. I was relieved when they accepted our offer to remain in the condo through May, when they'd planned to leave anyway. I was certain Steve's spirit would return to his beloved home. I didn't want him to see it empty or occupied by someone he didn't know. We'd put it up for sale after Sean and Mattie moved out.

Back in Bellingham I struggled to manage my grief, mostly without success. Thanksgiving, my favorite family holiday, felt hollow, and three days later, on November 29, we all did the best we could to celebrate Mike's birthday. The next day the boxes we'd shipped from Burlington arrived. I couldn't make myself open them.

I continued to obsess about how the DNR order might have affected Steve's death. Dr. Berger replied to an email I sent her. She explained that had Steve responded to CPR he would have been on a ventilator for a "very long time, given his respiratory issues." She also said X-rays taken in the emergency room showed a "mass on his lung and a blood clot in his airway." She assured me having the DNR was "a good thing."

Meanwhile the box containing Steve's ashes sat on my desk. Waiting.

During a run in mid-December I had a vision of Steve. Heart no longer beating, he lay on the gurney in the emergency room, suspended in time. Behind him in the darkness he could hear me calling to him to come back. Ahead, a pinpoint of light. He paused a moment. Then his face broke into a grin. He rose and began walking toward the light, his stride purposeful. By the time I'd finished my run and walked into our condo, I knew what to do with my son's ashes.

On December 21, the day of the winter solstice, Sue and I along with three close women friends boarded a ferry bound for Orcas Island and the three-bedroom cabin I'd rented at the North Beach Resort, correctly described on their website as "a step back in time." Sue began a fire in the woodstove, the cabin's sole source of heat, while the others busied themselves with dinner preparations. I made my way to the beach through the persistent drizzle of a typical Pacific Northwest winter day. I stood motionless listening to the waves massage the pebbled shore. A cold breeze blew off the gray ocean and stung my face. Then I began to build a fire pit.

A half hour later, in a deepening dusk, I stood back to assess my work. Large rocks surrounded the shallow depression I'd dug with my hands. I'd tugged and dragged the biggest driftwood log I could manage and positioned it to deflect the gusty winds. I'd jammed a washed-up piece of plywood between the rocks and log for additional protection.

"OK, Steve, this will have to do. If you can stop the rain, that would be great."

Back in the cabin, dinner—a hearty soup accompanied by crusty bread and wine—added to the cozy warmth being pumped out by the old but efficient woodstove. *Memories of Vermont*, I mused. But my mind was on the weather outside. Could I get and keep a fire going? Sue sensed my concern.

"Are you still planning on the campfire?"

"Yeah," I replied. "I found some pretty dry tinder around the edges of the cabin. I think that, along with the split logs by the stove here and the newspaper we brought, should do it. And I have a fallback plan, too." I looked around the table. "Do you all mind cleaning up here while I get started down at the beach?"

I made several trips from the cabin to the seashore with armloads of wood and stacked it next to the pit. In the pit's center I wadded the newsprint and tented tinder around and over it. Although the rain had stopped, the air hung heavy and moist.

Back inside the cabin, I thrust the wrought-iron spade next to the stove into the firebox and carried the shovelful of glowing embers through the darkness back to my prepared site. Before long I had a roaring blaze going. Once the flames died to a bed of coals it would be time. I headed back to the cabin once more to Sue and our friends.

I'd spent the previous days completing a new container for Steve's ashes. The balsa wood box I'd purchased was now a six-sided collage of family photos which I'd printed from our computer. Steve, Mike, and Josh clad in life jackets, along with Roger and me in our boat sailing in Port Jefferson harbor. Steve and Heather dancing at his graduation/twenty-first birthday celebration in Hanover. Steve resting his head on Sue's shoulder on the porch steps of our house in Lyndon. Steve in his early forties clad in his red T-shirt with a caricature of Santa and the words "I Believe." Steve and Dave in Steve's Burlington condo; Steve and Pa holding their McDonald's milkshakes. Strips of typed "Steve-isms" overlaid the photos. "I teeny bit nervous." "What am I, chopped liver?" "Shit happens." "Sorry I rude." "I get my power from the moon." "Mikey-Boy." "Shrimpo." "I happy-sad."

Now I brought the box into the cabin's living room and held it as I talked about my son and his life. I wanted our friends to know the person we were honoring tonight. Interspersed with my comments Sue played the three songs we'd recorded earlier: "My Way," "Somewhere Over the Rainbow," and "Time in a Bottle." Then we headed to the beach.

Arms linked, we five stood silently for several minutes. Waves lapped the pebbled beach. Wind rustled the branches of towering pines. A sleepy seagull squawked. Embers popped and floated skyward.

I cleared my throat. "It's time. You were a great son, Steve, and you lived an amazing life. I love you." I stepped forward and gently placed the box on the pulsing coals. We watched transfixed as one corner caught and began to burn. Images curled, peeled, and disappeared. The last one to burn was a photo of the three brothers taken in Vegas the previous May.

Sue looked at me and I nodded. She inverted the paper bag she'd been holding and the notes of love, written at Steve's Celebration, sprinkled down to join Steve's ashes. As Sue stepped back toward us, she gasped and pointed. We all turned. What had she seen? There behind the pine trees a full moon rose in the clearing sky.

During the summer of 2016 Sue and I established the Steve Cohen Fund under the administration of the Howard Center. Howard clients in need of financial help while entering the competitive work force are supported by the fund. Initial monies came from pledges made by folks when, as part of a four-person team, I ran the first leg of the Burlington marathon on a blistering hot June morning. When Steve's condo sold, the profits from the sale were added to the fund. Friends and family continue to make annual donations. All money earned by sales of my memoir will be directed to the Steve Cohen Fund. To donate to this fund, please visit https://54461.thankyou4caring.org/ and be sure to choose The Steve Cohen Fund under Donation Information in the Designation section.

This sketch is of the sterling silver pendant I place around my neck every morning. Custom-made by a Bozeman artist, the images on the front represent my lifelong connection to the oceans' beaches and waters which are now Steve's home. The clear resin backing seals a "finger-pinch" of Steve's ashes.

He is always with me.

ACKNOWLEDGMENTS

What a journey this has been! By the time my son Steve reached his late teens I knew that one day I would write a book about his life. But never could I have imagined the story of our odyssey would be published the same year I turned eighty. Or that the gestation period for this memoir would encompass eight years. Ignorance is truly bliss! But my relocation to Bellingham, Washington, from Vermont proved fortuitous in two significant ways.

In autumn of 2012 I enrolled in a "Memory to Memoir" course taught by Laura Kalpakian, a nationally-known novelist, who resides in Bellingham. From that beginning came my introduction to the amazing community of writers who call this small Pacific Northwest city home. I am grateful to my critique group, the mighty Talespinners: Victoria Doerper, Cheryl Stritzel McCarthy, Kate Miller, Joe Nolting, Nancy and Roy Taylor. Your encouragement and honest feedback sustained me. Special thanks to Pam Helberg, my always-willing-to-listen walking buddy, and to Marian Exall for hosting yearly writing retreats in the incomparable Methow Valley.

Bellingham also introduced me to craft coffee and her many coffee houses—in particular, Tony's Harris Street Coffee, Avellino, and the Firehouse Café. Over time, the baristas at these quirky comfortable spaces not only learned my name, but started making my order—"non-fat latte, extra hot with no foam"—when I walked in the door. Thanks for my "writing studios."

Every writer needs a first reader and Jane Stephens, my friend for over seventy-five years, weighed in early and often. I'm indebted to my developmental editor, Cami Ostman, CEO of The Narrative Project. Her patience and support became invaluable as she helped me wrestle an unwieldly manuscript into shape. Thanks to Beta readers Kristin Jarvis Adams, Lori Anderson, Lyn Parker Hass, Linda Lambert, and Jane Stephens for your time and thoughtful suggestions. Gratitude to Mary DeDannon from Catchword Studio, an amazing copyeditor and cheerleader. Her wordsmithing skills applied the final polish to my story. I also want to express my deep appreciation to

John Doerper for his drawing of the pendant which appears at the end of the epilogue.

Unrestrained applause goes to publisher Lisa Dailey of Sidekick Press. I admire Lisa's extensive artistic skills, as a writer and a tech wizardess. Her gentle kindness and unlimited patience supported me during a difficult time.

A huge shout out to Serge Samoylenko at spokendesigns.com for his cover design, which conveys a powerful message.

To Steve's loving brothers, Mike Cohen and Josh Cohen, who always had his back and mine, special thanks for your support. I hope you like what I've written. Remembrance to Roger Cohen. You were a great dad and, in many ways, ahead of your time.

To my wife Sue...not only did Steve award you the title of "best friend," you've been my rock for over thirty years. I shall always be grateful for your advocacy and unconditional love.

ABOUT THE AUTHOR

Photo by Lisa Dailey

A native of New England, Linda Morrow graduated from Syracuse University with a BA in sociology and later earned her MEd in Guidance and Counseling. In her younger life, she raised three sons and enjoyed a thirty-five-year career in public school education. In 2013 she and her wife relocated to Bellingham, Washington: "The City of Subdued Excitement." She deeply appreciates a supportive and talented community of writers, and has learned to value the coffee shops of Washington, not just for the lattes, but also as places for her daily writing practice. Linda roots for the Red Sox and the New England Patriots, walks along beach and woodland trails, treasures time with her grandchildren, and continues to add books to her "to-be-read" pile.

CPSIA information can be obtained
at www.ICGtesting.com
Printed in the USA
FSHW021956240820 .
274FS

9 781734 494501